CRIMINOLOGICAL PERSPECTIVES
RACE AND CRIME

Criminological Perspectives on Race and Crime, Third Edition is an ideal starting point for those interested in examining how well criminological theory contextualizes racial and ethnic disparities. A perfect addition to either crime theory or race and crime courses, this is the only text to look at the array of explanations for crime as they relate to racial and ethnic groups. Each chapter includes a historical review of each theoretical perspective and how its original formulation and more recent derivatives account for racial/ethnic differences, and a consideration of potential weaknesses or criticisms of each theory in Gabbidon's effort to determine the success of these criminological perspectives. This third edition has been updated throughout, with the major addition of race-centered perspectives in Chapter 9.

Shaun L. Gabbidon, Ph.D., is Distinguished Professor of Criminal Justice at Penn State Harrisburg. He has also served as a fellow at Harvard University's W.E.B. Du Bois Institute for Afro-American Research, and has taught at the Center for Africana Studies at the University of Pennsylvania. Professor Gabbidon is the author of more than 100 scholarly publications including more than 60 peer-reviewed articles and 11 books. Dr. Gabbidon can be contacted at slg13@psu.edu

Criminology and Justice Studies Series

Edited by **Shaun L. Gabbidon**, *Penn State Harrisburg*

Criminology and Justice Studies offers works that make both intellectual and stylistic innovations in the study of crime and criminal justice. The goal of the series is to publish works that model the best scholarship and thinking in the criminology and criminal justice field today, but in a style that connects that scholarship to a wider audience including advanced undergraduates, graduate students, and the general public. The works in this series help fill the gap between academic monographs and encyclopedic textbooks by making innovative scholarship accessible to a large audience without the superficiality of many texts.

Books in the Series

Published:

Biosocial Criminology: New Directions in Theory and Research edited by Anthony Walsh and Kevin M. Beaver

Community Policing in America by Jeremy M. Wilson

Criminal Justice Theory: Explaining the Nature and Behavior of Criminal Justice edited by David E. Duffee and Edward R. Maguire

Lifers: Seeking Redemption in Prison by John Irwin

Race, Law and American Society: 1607 to Present by Gloria J. Browne-Marshall

Today's White Collar Crime by Hank J. Brightman

The New Criminal Justice: American Communities and the Changing World of Crime Control by John Klofas, Natalie Hipple, and Edmund McGarrell

The Policing of Terrorism: Organizational and Global Perspectives by Mathieu Deflem

Corrections by Jeanne Stinchcomb

Community Policing by Michael Palmiotto

A Theory of African American Offending by James Unnever and Shaun Gabbidon

When Crime Appears: The Role of Emergence by Jean McGloin, Christopher Sullivan, and Leslie Kennedy

Voices from Criminal Justice edited by Heith Copes and Mark Pogrebin

Crime and the Life Course, 2/e by Michael Benson

Wrongful Convictions and Miscarriages of Justice edited by C. Ron Huff and Martin Killias

Human Trafficking: Interdisciplinary Perspectives edited by Mary C. Burke

Race, Law and American Society, 2/e: 1607 to Present by Gloria J. Browne-Marshall

Research Methods in Crime and Justice by Brian Withrow

Crime and Networks edited by Carlo Morselli

Wrongful Conviction and Criminal Justice Reform edited by Marvin Zalman and Julia Carrano

Questioning Capital Punishment: Law, Policy, and Practice by James R. Acker

Understanding White-Collar Crime: An Opportunity Perspective, Second Edition by Michael L. Benson and Sally S. Simpson

Criminological Perspectives on Race and Crime, Third Edition by Shaun Gabbidon

CRIMINOLOGICAL PERSPECTIVES ON RACE AND CRIME

THIRD EDITION

Shaun L. Gabbidon

Routledge
Taylor & Francis Group

NEW YORK AND LONDON

Third Edition published 2015
by Routledge
711 Third Avenue, New York, NY 10017

and by Routledge
2 Park Square, Milton Park, Abingdon, Oxon, OX14 4RN

Routledge is an imprint of the Taylor & Francis Group, an informa business

First edition published by Routledge 2007

Second edition published by Routledge 2010

Library of Congress Cataloging-in-Publication Data

Gabbidon, Shaun L., 1967–
    Criminological perspectives on race and crime / Shaun L. Gabbidon. —
Third edition.
        pages cm. — (Criminology and justice studies)
    Includes bibliographical references and index.
    1. Crime and race.   2. Criminology—Philosophy.   3. Discrimination
in criminal justice administration.   4. Ethnopsychology.   I. Title.
HV6191.G33 2015
364.3'4—dc23
2014032969

ISBN: 978-1-138-82661-8 (hbk)
ISBN: 978-1-138-82662-5 (pbk)
ISBN: 978-1-315-73916-8 (ebk)

Typeset in Adobe Caslon
by Apex CoVantage, LLC

Printed and bound in the United States of America by
Edwards Brothers Malloy on sustainably sourced paper

Additional Books by Shaun L. Gabbidon

African American Criminological Thought, co-authored with Helen Taylor Greene (SUNY Press, 2000)

African American Classics in Criminology and Criminal Justice, edited with Helen Taylor Greene and Vernetta D. Young (SAGE, 2002)

Race, Crime, and Justice: A Reader, edited with Helen Taylor Greene (Routledge, 2005)

Race and Juvenile Justice, edited with Helen Taylor Greene and Everette B. Penn (Carolina Academic Press, 2006)

W.E.B. Du Bois on Crime and Justice: Laying the Foundations of Sociological Criminology (Ashgate, 2007)

Race and Crime, 2nd edition, co-authored with Helen Taylor Greene (SAGE, 2009)

Race, Ethnicity, Crime, and Justice: An International Dilemma (SAGE, 2009)

Encyclopedia of Race and Crime, edited with Helen Taylor Greene (SAGE, 2009)

Race and Crime: A Text Reader, edited with Helen Taylor Greene (SAGE, 2011)

A Theory of African American Offending: Race, Racism, and Crime, co-authored with James D. Unnever (Routledge, 2011)

CONTENTS

PREFACE

As I noted in the first edition of this work, the idea for this book has its origins in Coramae Richey Mann's classic text, *Unequal Justice: A Question of Color* (1993). As a graduate student, I can recall reading Chapter 3, in which Mann reviewed theories that sought to explain offending and victimization trends among racial and ethnic minorities. After reading the chapter, I realized the importance of exploring the utility of criminological perspectives for contextualizing race, ethnicity, and crime. Thus, the first edition of this work represented the first attempt to provide book-length coverage of criminological theories that have been proffered to better understand race, ethnicity, and crime (for chapter-length discussions of theories used to explain race and crime, see Gabbidon and Taylor Greene 2013, Chapter 3; Leiber 2008). To say the least, the response to the first two editions was overwhelming! In addition to strong sales and scholarly reviews, I received emails and had personal conversations with countless colleagues from around the world who were appreciative of the work. Consequently, on the heels of this positive feedback, Routledge decided to publish this third edition.

This new edition has been updated with cuts in some places and additions in others. Even so, I cannot claim the work is fully comprehensive. The sheer number of works published each year precludes the inclusion of every study that tests the perspectives profiled in this book. Nonetheless, the work provides, as reviewers of the first edition noted (see Dawson-Edwards 2008; Henderson 2008; Knowles 2008), a starting point for those interested in examining how well criminological theory contextualizes racial and ethnic disparities.

The aims for the third edition remain the same as the first. First, this work is an attempt to produce a book that answers the question so many students and scholars ask—especially once they see data showing racial and ethnic disparities in crime and victimization (particularly as they relate to violence): "What explains such differences?" To answer this question, I have reexamined some of the "classic" theoretical works to determine whether they addressed the issue of racial and ethnic disparities. In addition, the third edition continues my efforts to explore criminological perspectives advanced by racial and ethnic minorities. Finally, I continue to be concerned with determining which, if any, criminological perspectives have been most successful in contextualizing racial and ethnic disparities.

To accomplish these aims, I have reviewed numerous articles and books that have directly or indirectly focused on this issue. The book is divided into 10 chapters. Many focus on traditional criminological theories; first I explain their basic tenets and then follow with a sampling of the scholarly literature devoted to exploring how well the perspective contextualizes crime among racial and ethnic minorities. Due to the nature of this book, the discussion of three well-known perspectives was excluded. Specifically, there are no chapters on learning theories, psychological perspectives, and rational choice theory. These perspectives were excluded because only a limited number of research studies have used these perspectives to contextualize racial disparities, although occasionally some studies integrated aspects of them. In such instances, the assorted theories included in the integrated perspectives are noted. Even with the absence of these staples, the book reviews an abundance of relevant studies on the remaining theoretical perspectives. Finally, in line with traditional theory books, each chapter notes some general weaknesses of each perspective.

The book begins with an introductory chapter that provides an overview of important concepts such as race, crime, and theory. In addition, the chapter closes by arguing that the earliest connections between race and crime can be found in religious doctrines. Chapter 2 examines biological perspectives on race and crime. Beginning with the well-known works of Lombroso, this chapter reviews the scholarly literature that has pointed to biology to explain racial disparities related to race and crime. Here, there is expanded coverage of the emerging biosocial approach. Chapter 3 is devoted to social disorganization and strain theories. Social disorganization theory has continued to be a staple among criminologists as well as among those who are seeking to better understand the plight of racial and ethnic minorities residing in disorganized communities. The multiple forms of strain theory are also reviewed in Chapter 3. Over time, its original formulation by Robert Merton has popularized the theory for race and crime theorists. In addition, Robert Agnew's general strain theory has significantly renewed interest in the perspective. This interest has spurred an increasing body of literature on the role of race discrimination as a stressor. This chapter reviews this emerging literature.

Chapter 4 covers subcultural perspectives on race and crime. Following an analysis of the early scholarly literature in this area, the chapter examines the well-known thesis on the subculture of violence and the increasingly popular "code of the street" perspective. For both perspectives, the chapter assesses the utility of such theories for understanding inner-city crime and violence. Labeling theory is the focus of Chapter 5. While over the last few decades the theory has lost its luster within the discipline of criminology, the chapter argues that the perspective remains important because of the renewed interest in the impact of stereotypes on racial and ethnic minorities.

Among the most widely used perspectives to contextualize race and crime, conflict theory, which is the focus of Chapter 6, has a long history of showing the relevance of one's class and position in society to understanding crime and justice. The chapter reveals that race also has historically been a central emphasis of scholarly literature examining the plight of racial and ethnic minorities in America. Chapter 7 focuses on social control perspectives on race and crime. Almost from the very beginning, theorists attached to this perspective have declared its "generality"; thus, they argue that the theory is race neutral and can contextualize crime among all racial and ethnic groups (here and abroad). By reviewing a sampling of past and current scholarship in the area, this claim is questioned. Chapter 8 examines the colonial model, which is arguably one of the most neglected and under-researched criminological perspectives. This chapter introduces the basic tenets of the perspective and also examines the limited scholarly literature devoted to the exposition of the theory.

Chapter 9 has been revamped. In the two prior editions, the chapter solely focused on feminist perspectives. In this edition, I have added race-centered perspectives as well. The section on gender-based perspectives examines the "two waves" of the feminist movement and the development of scholarly literature on gender, race, and crime. Centered primarily on the black female experience the section examines how the theory can be useful to race and crime scholars. Similar to the approach used in feminist perspectives, race-centered perspectives seek to explain the criminal behavior of one specific racial group paying close attention to their unique experience in America. This portion of the chapter is devoted to the race-centered perspective presented in Unnever and Gabbidon's (2011) book, *A Theory of African American Offending*.

Chapter 10 concludes the book by providing an overview of the numerous theoretical perspectives reviewed. No integrated race and crime perspective is presented because such an undertaking, as is evidenced by the contents of this book, would be futile. Racial and ethnic minorities are too diverse to have one theory. Even so, some theories are obviously more "generalizable" than others. The conclusion makes note of such perspectives.

ACKNOWLEDGMENTS

I thank Mike Bickerstaff, former senior editor at Routledge, for valuing and signing this project. Likewise, Steve Rutter, the current social science publisher at Routledge, is acknowledged for seeing the need for a third edition of the work. At Penn State, Dr. Steven A. Peterson, director of the School of Public Affairs, is acknowledged for his continuing support. SAGE Publications is thanked for allowing me to reprint portions of Chapter 3, "Theoretical Perspectives on Race and Crime" (pp. 70–102), from my earlier text, *Race and Crime* (2013, third edition), co-authored with Dr. Helen Taylor Greene. Finally, the anonymous reviewers are thanked for their positive comments and useful suggestions.

1

A Brief Introduction to Race, Crime, and Theory

The social sciences are filled with an abundance of excellent individual books on race, crime, and criminological theory. Thus, the primary goal of this chapter is to provide a brief overview of the areas that comprise the core elements of this work. The chapter begins with an overview of race and racism, which is followed by an overview of the concept of crime and a review of the rudimentary aspects of the nature and usefulness of theory. To begin the discourse on race, crime, and theory, the chapter concludes with an illustration of the early intermingling of race and crime in religious doctrines.

Origins of Race and Racism

While today the term "race" is primarily used to refer to the grouping of people (e.g. African Americans, whites, etc.) on the basis of color and cultural characteristics, according to Feagin and Feagin (2008), the term was originally used to describe "descendants of a common ancestor, emphasizing kinship linkages rather than physical characteristics such as skin color, hair type, or facial features" (p. 4). However, by the late eighteenth century, the term began to be used to describe "physical characteristics transmitted by descent" (p. 4). The German anatomist Johann Blumenbach played a significant role in this change by creating a racial classification system in his doctoral thesis, "On the Natural Variety of Mankind" (published in 1775). Blumenbach's system included a hierarchy of the races, listing them in the following order: Caucasians (Europeans), Mongolians (Asians), Ethiopians (Africans), Americans (Native Americans), and Malays (Polynesians).

Just as the concept of race is not new, racism, which is the use of race as the basis for discriminating against another group of people, also has a long history. Gossett (1963) documented that, while the term "race" is of recent origin, acts of racism are of ancient origin. Pointing to India and Egypt as some of the first places where the distinction of race was noted, he wrote that "the racism of ancient history, even though it had no science or biology or anthropology behind it, was real, however difficult it may be for us to judge the extent of its power" (p. 3). Gossett described some early illustrations of race prejudice in India and Egypt. Over 5,000 years ago in India, he noted, the sacred text of Hinduism, the Rig-Veda, refers to "an invasion by Aryas, or Aryans, of the valley of the Indus where there lived a dark-hued people" (p. 3). Quoting from the Rig-Veda, Gossett wrote that Indra, the god of the Aryans, "[blows] away with supernatural powers the might from earth and from the heavens the black skin which Indra hates" (pp. 3–4). In the end, Indra conquers the land for the Aryans and decrees that the defeated blacks be whipped (p. 4).

In Egypt, as early as 1350 BC, pictures in tombs portrayed people using four colors. Red was used to represent the Egyptians, while yellow represented "their enemies to the east." White was used to represent people from the north and black for Negroes. As noted by Gossett (1963):

> Color prejudice . . . depended on which ethnic group held sway. When the lighter-skinned Egyptians were dominant they referred to the darker group "as the evil race of Ish." On the other hand, when the darker-skinned Egyptians were in power, they retorted by calling the lighter-skinned people "the pale, degraded race of Arvad."
>
> (p. 4)

Even with this long global history of racism, Frederickson (2002) has suggested that only within the last century have "overtly racist regimes" emerged. Such societies have five distinguishing features. First, the ideology of the society must be explicitly racist. Expanding on this feature, he wrote:

> Those in authority proclaim insistently that the differences between the dominant group and the one that is being subordinated or eliminated are permanent and unbridgeable. Dissent from this ideology is dangerous and is likely to bring legal or extralegal reprisals, for racial egalitarianism is heresy in an overtly racist regime.
>
> (p. 101)

Another distinguishing feature is that the racist regime codifies its beliefs by outlawing interracial marriages to create "racial purity" and a caste system based on racial differences (p. 101). The third feature of a racist regime is that social segregation is mandated by law, the purpose of which "is to bar all forms of contact that might imply equality between the segregators and the segregated" (p. 101). The fourth feature is when "outgroup members are excluded from holding public office or even exercising the franchise" (p. 101). The final feature is when the subordinated group has such limited access to resources and opportunities that most of them "are either kept in poverty or deliberately impoverished" (p. 101).

In Frederickson's view, while there have been racialized societies where race prejudice has contributed to social stratification, none of those prior to the twentieth century constituted "overtly racial regimes." During the twentieth century, he classified "Jim Crow" laws in the American South, South Africa under apartheid, and Nazi Germany as "ideal types" of "overtly racist regimes" (p. 101).

Even if Frederickson is correct, the racist regimes that have existed were significant contributors to the globalization of racist doctrines that, as noted throughout this book, serve as a central component of various racist criminological doctrines.

Crime

On crime, the eminent French sociologist Emile Durkheim (1938/1895) stated:

> Crime is present not only in the majority of societies of one particular species but in all societies of all types. There is no society that is not

confronted with the problem of criminality. Its form changes: the acts this characterized are not the same everywhere; but, everywhere and always, there have been men who have behaved in such a way as to draw upon themselves penal repression.

(pp. 65–6)

Given this suggestion, Durkheim felt crime must be normal. A glance at world history suggests that his assertion has some merits (for an alternative view, see Christie 2004). Therefore, while the nature and extent of crime have varied and continue to vary among societies, there is no society in which it has not been found. As a consequence, over time, most societies have generally defined certain behaviors as wrong or, as we now refer to them, criminal. Given this fact, most societies have sought to address crime through various programs and practices. Similarly, over time, even with Durkheim's pronouncement, scholars have sought to explain why people violate the norms (or laws) constructed by individual societies. Such explanations (also referred to as theories or perspectives) have been diverse in both nature and scope.

In more recent times, scholars have also become interested with the over-representation of racial and ethnic minorities in arrest and victimization statistics in white-dominated and previously colonized countries around the globe (for examples, see Bowling and Phillips 2002; Chan and Mirchandani 2002; Gabbidon 2009; Gabbidon and Taylor Greene 2013; Glynn 2014; Hawkins 2011; Higgins 2009; Marshall 1997; Mosher 1998; Rowe 2012; Saleh-Hanna 2008; Tonry 2011; Walker, Spohn, and DeLone 2011). Predictably, irrespective of the country where the interest in racial and ethnic disparities has originated, formulating and testing the utility of theories to understand the scope and nature of the criminality and victimization have been a central focus of scholars. Before reviewing some of these perspectives, the rudimentary aspects of theory are reviewed next.

The Foundations of Theory

According to Bohm (2001), "A theory is an explanation" (p. 1). Some theory can be found in practically everything we do. When it comes to explaining crime, just about every society has scholars who have an opinion on the subject. All of these insights, however, might not qualify as scientific theory. Curran and Renzetti (2001) state that, to qualify as scientific, "a theory is a set of interconnected statements or propositions that explain how two or more events or factors are related to one another" (p. 2). Furthermore, they point out that theories are usually logically sound and empirically testable.

Theories can further be categorized by whether they are macrotheories, microtheories, or bridging theories (Williams and McShane 2014). Macrotheories focus on the social structure and are generally not concerned with individual behavior; conversely, microtheories look to explain crime by looking at groups (but in small numbers) or at the individual (p. 7). Bridging theories "tell us both how social structure comes about and how people become criminal" (p. 7). Many of the theories reviewed in the following chapters fit some of these criteria; although others fall short they nonetheless provide useful insights into race and crime. Thus, there is some discussion of nontraditional perspectives that speak to race and crime but have not been folded into the mainstream of scientific criminological theory.

Theories are valuable for a number of reasons. Curran and Renzetti (2001) provided an important summary of the usefulness of theory:

> Theories help bring order to our lives because they expand our knowledge of the world around us and suggest systematic solutions to problems we repeatedly confront. Without the generalizable knowledge provided by theories, we would have to solve the same problems over and over again, largely through trial and error. Theory, therefore, rather than being just a set of abstract ideas, is quite practical. It is usable knowledge.
>
> (p. 2)

There are several paradigms within criminological theory that are reviewed here; for example, biological approaches, some of which look to genetic inheritance to explain crime. Other theories have their foundations in the American social structure, culture, or one's gender. Yet other theories, such as the labeling and colonial perspective, have psychological foundations. In recent years, more theorists have also sought to integrate some of these approaches (Agnew 2005; Barak 2009; Godinet and Vakalahi 2009; Messner et al. 1989; Miethe and Meier1994; Robinson and Beaver 2009). As one might expect, many of these theories have been applied to explain racial and ethnic disparities related to crime. Even before such theories were being formally postulated, race and crime were connected primarily through religious doctrines. This connection is explored next.

Early Religious Connections of Race and Crime

At some point in history, the concepts of race and crime became enmeshed; persons of a darker hue were saddled with the criminal badge. While no exact date of this connection likely exists, the general ideology under which it initially flourished, I believe, was religious in origin. On the connection between crime and spirituality, Bernard et al. (2010) noted that "primitive people regarded natural disasters, such as famine, floods, and plagues as punishments for wrongs they had done to the spiritual powers" (pp. 2–3). As religion became more formalized and documented, holy books such as the Bible took a central place in the search for those who were to be considered "evil" and criminal.

Eventually, the Hamatic myth, which linked this "evil" and criminality to black people, was developed (Jablonski 1997; Sanders 1969). The myth centers on Genesis 9 and 10 in the Bible. The first key passage notes that Noah and his sons were given the responsibility of repopulating the world after the great flood. Genesis 9 identifies Noah's sons as Shem, Ham, and Japheth. In Genesis 10, Noah plants a vineyard and gets drunk. Naked and drunk in his tent, Noah is seen by his son Ham, who tells his brothers to look at him. However, instead of looking at their father, Ham's two brothers covered their father with a blanket. When Noah awakened, he realized what had happened and declared,

> Cursed be Canaan [son of Ham]; a servant of servants shall he be unto his brethren . . . Blessed be the Lord God of Shem; and Canaan shall be his servant . . . God shall enlarge Japheth, and he shall dwell in the tents of Shem; and Canaan shall be his servant.
>
> (King James Bible 1992, p. 31)

The central point here is that Ham is believed to have been a black person (Emanuel 1992, p. 25) (see Figure 1.1) and his cursed son Canaan would have been the producer of generations of cursed offspring. Following the path of the myth, the Canaanites were described as wicked people whose temples were said to feature "prostitutes, orgies, and human sacrifice. Relics and plaques of exaggerated sex organs hint

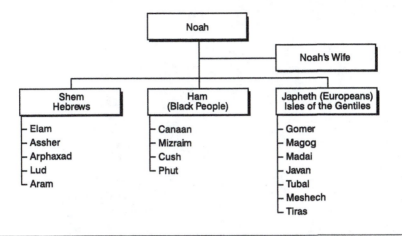

Figure 1.1 People of color in the Bible. (From W. G. Emanual, *People of Color in the Bible Series*, Vol. 1, Schuylkill, PA: Faith of Jesus Publishers, 1992. With permission.)

at the morality that characterized Canaan" (King James Bible 1992, p. 228). In addition, it is believed that

> Canaanite gods, such as Baal and his wife, Anath, delighted in butchery and sadism. Archeologists have found great numbers of jars containing the tiny bones of children sacrificed to Baal. Families seeking good luck in a home practiced "foundation sacrifice." They would kill one of their children and seal the body in the mortar of the wall.
>
> (pp. 228–9)

Such a virulent myth set in motion the belief that all black people were "evil" and criminal.

Seeking the origin of the use of this myth to denigrate black people, Frederickson (1981) found that "Johan Boemus, a German Hebraic scholar, argued as early as 1521 that all barbarous people descended from Ham, while all civilized men were the issue of Shem and Japheth" (p. 10). From this point forward, the myth was used to justify the enslavement and colonization of blacks around the globe. Given the myth's connection to the "evil" Canaanites, it was also implicitly used to explain blacks' involvement in deviant or criminal activities (Sanders 1969).

The next logical step was to move the myth from the religious sphere to a sphere more "scientific" in character. This sphere came in the form of biological theories. The origin and nature of biological perspectives on race and crime are the focus of Chapter 2.

2
BIOLOGICAL PERSPECTIVES ON RACE AND CRIME

In this chapter, the coverage of biology, race, and crime spans several areas. First, the chapter examines those works that look at primarily physical characteristics to explain crime (e.g. body type, head shape, etc.). Reviewing some of the earliest writings on biological criminology, the chapter aims to illustrate the global reach of Cesare Lombroso's work connecting biology, race, and crime. Second, the chapter examines literature in the emerging and controversial area of biosocial perspectives. Finally, the chapter also examines those theories that focus on intelligence, which though psychological in origin, are often discussed under the umbrella of biological perspectives. All of these areas provide the bases for the current arguments linking biology, race, and crime.

Early Connections of Biology, Race, and Crime:
Lombroso's Global Influence

In general, the connection between biology and crime has its roots in Europe. Of the origin of this connection, Reid (1957) wrote that "[in] the year 1843 a Spanish physician Soler was [the] first to [mention] the concept of the born criminal" (p. 772). It was also Europe where phrenology, the study of the external shape of the head, was first popularized (Vold et al. 1998, pp. 41–2). The publication of Darwin's *On the Origin of Species* (1859) and *The Descent of Man* (1871) were also quite influential in this era. Once Cesare Lombroso, a doctor in the Italian Army in the nineteenth century and the so-called father of criminology, read Darwin's texts, he drew on them and began studying army personnel from the southern portions of Italy where, in addition to being considered inferior beings, the citizens were thought to be "lazy, incapable, criminal, and barbaric" (Vold et al. 1998, pp. 42–3). Lombroso's assessment was largely based on his belief that it was the presence of Africans and Eastern elements that contributed to this situation in southern Italy (Gibson 1998). His views were also largely the product of biological determinism and his feelings about the inferiority of black people.

In an early work, *White Man and Colored Man: Lectures on the Origin and Variety of the Human Races* (1871), Lombroso presented an evolutionary theory espousing that

> blacks represented the lowest and most primitive race, from which all others—including intermediary groups like the Semites and the Asians—had sprung under the positive influence of temperate climates. But the African had changed little for millennia, still displaying "that infantile and monkey-like manner of smiling and gesturing."
>
> (as quoted in Gibson 2002, p. 107)

Seeking an explanation for what he felt was the intellectual inferiority of blacks, Lombroso turned to the following physical explanation: "the brain is undeveloped in the back and weighs less than ours. As for the skull that holds it, the face predominates over the forehead as [their] passions drown [their] intelligence" (as quoted in Gibson, p. 107).

Five years later Lombroso published his first major work, *The Criminal Man* (1876). The crux of Lombroso's thesis was that criminals were different from noncriminals. In his view, the difference could largely be traced to their biology. He concluded that most criminals fell into one of four categories. First, there were those who were atavistic (born criminals) or were primitive in their genetic makeup. While too numerous to list here, some of these atavistic characteristics included:

> the slight development of the pilar system; low cranial capacity; retreating forehead; highly developed frontal sinuses, great frequency of Wormian bones; early closing of the cranial sutures; the simplicity of sutures; the

thickness of the bones of the skull; enormous development of the max-
illaries and the zygomata; prognathism; obliquity of the orbits; greater
pigmentation of the skin; tufted and crispy hair; and large ears.

(Lombroso 1911/1968, p. 365)

Lombroso's three other categories of criminals included insane criminals, occasional criminals, and criminals by passion. The insane criminals included those he categorized as idiots, imbeciles, alcoholics, and
epileptics (see Lombroso 1876/1911, pp. 74–99). The occasional criminals or criminaloids, as he referred to them, were fairly normal (with
few physical anomolies), intelligent (in contrast to born criminals), and
typically offended later in life (see Lombroso 1876/1911, pp. 100–21).
Lastly, criminals by passion

are in complete contrast with the born criminal, both in the harmonious
lines of the body, the beauty of the sole [sic], and great nervous and emo-
tional sensitiveness, as well as in the motives of their crimes, always noble
and powerful, such as love or politics. Nevertheless, they show some
points of resemblance with epileptics, such as their tendency to excess,
impulsiveness, suddenness in their outbreaks, and frequent amnesia.

(Lombroso 1911/1968, p. 376)

Throughout Lombroso's works, he made clear the importance of
race in explaining crime. He mentioned that some tribes in parts of
India and Italy had high crime rates due to "ethnical causes" (Lombroso
1876/1911, p. 140). He added that "the frequency of homicide in Cal-
abria, Sicily, and Sardinia is fundamentally due to African and Oriental
elements" (p. 140). When Lombroso took on the task of explaining
criminality among women, he again saw race as being an important
contributor to crime. In his view, Negro women and American Indian
women were seen as manly looking (a sign of atavism), which contributed to their criminality. More specifically, after presenting pictures of
both types of women (see Figure 2.1), he wrote: "It is difficult to believe
that these are really women, so huge are their jaws and cheekbones, so
hard and thick are their features. The skulls and brains of savage women,
too, often resemble those of men" (Lombroso and Ferrero 1893/2004,
pp. 149–50).

Negro Woman   Red Indian Woman

Figure 2.1 Negro and American Indian women. (From C. Lombroso and G. Ferrero, *Criminal Woman, the Prostitute and the Normal Woman*, Durham, NC: Duke University Press, 2004. Originally published in 1893. With permission.)

In another publication, Lombroso had the following to say about American Negroes:

> The principal thing is always . . . the stifling of the primitive, wild instincts. Even if he (the Negro) is dressed in the European way and has accepted the customs of modern culture, all too often there remains in him a lack of respect for life of his fellow men, the disregard for life which all wild people have in common. To them, a murder appears as an ordinary occurrence, even a glorious occurrence when it is inspired by feelings of vengeance. The mentality is furthered in the Negro by his scorn of his white fellow-citizens, and by bestial sexual impulses.
>
> (as quoted in Bonger 1943, pp. 48–9)

Building on Lombroso's work, Enrico Ferri (1895), another celebrated Italian criminologist, felt that race was more relevant for explaining the more serious offenses. As he put it, "The Negro does not have a bad but only an unstable character like a baby, but with the difference that it is linked with mature physical development; thus this instability is the consequence of an incomplete cerebral development" (as quoted in Gibson 1998, p. 106). A student of Ferri's, Alfredo Niceforo, seeking to explain the difference in offending throughout Italy, conducted an analysis of Nuorese skulls and found that the trends in Nuorese crime could be traced to the fact that their skulls resembled those of Africans (Gibson 1998, p. 108).

Other writers of the period, such as Rowlands (1897), also turned to race and physical characteristics to explain crime:

> The criminal is further to be recognized by his tastes and occupation; he is fond of alcohol, cards, and sexual vices; he dislikes regular work, and is sentimental, religious, or superstitious; he is given to write poetry on the walls of his cells or on the kitchen utensils; he is both stupid and cunning; he is frequently tattooed, and generally justifies his misdeeds on high moral principle. And, finally, the typical criminal would have "projecting ears, thick hair, and thin beard, projecting frontal eminences, enormous jaws, a square and projecting chin, large cheek bones, and frequent gesticulation," and would in type resemble the Mongolian or sometimes the Negroid."
>
> (p. 245)

As is evidenced by these early publications, Lombroso's works were widely hailed and adopted. Most of his work was also translated into other languages. By the time Lombroso's works were translated into English, biological determinism had already taken hold internationally. This doctrine, which preached the superiority of whites over other racial groups, had serious consequences for people of color. Racists used the race and crime connection proposed in Lombroso's work to show the inferiority and inherent criminality of people of color around the globe.

For example, an early writer who pointed to the international relevance of Lombroso's work in explaining race and crime was one of Lombroso's collaborators (and son-in-law) Guglielmo Ferrero. Specifically, Ferrero (1900) pointed to the primitiveness, laziness, and criminality of Tupis (people of Brazilian origin) and Africans. Of the criminality of the Tupis of South America, he wrote that, "if they happened to tread on a stone, [they] became so furious that they would begin to bite the latter like a dog" (p. 96). As for Africans, he commented, "In Africa we find a proverbial giddiness and levity among the Hottentots. They are so little given to labor that they almost all live by begging and are reduced to a state of extreme muscular debility" (p. 96). He also wrote that "[another] important characteristic of the African [N]egro is the ease with which he passes from one extreme to the other, and the sudden violence and brevity of his fits of rage" (p. 96).

In line with Lombroso's ideas, Ferrero (1900) noted that 18 centuries earlier the Teutonic (German) race had gone through a similar stage, but was now "universally reputed [as being] calm and tenaciously laborious" (p. 96). Put succinctly, in Ferrero's view, the Tupis and Africans were still atavistic while Germans had long evolved from such a state and no longer exhibited the criminal characteristics associated with atavism.

Criminologists have likely underestimated the reach of Lombroso's work. It is well known that European and American scholars adopted Lombroso's approach, but scholars in understudied countries such as Latin America also embraced his doctrines. Graham (1990) writes: "It was Fernando Ortiz in Cuba and Nina Rodrigues in Brazil, pioneer students of Afro-Latin American culture, who endorsed the idea of innate black criminality" (p. 5). Rodrigues was a Brazilian who studied Lombroso's work and applied it to his country. Skidmore (1990), highlighting the various facets of Rodrigues's work, wrote that

> he also studied the social behavior of blacks and mixed bloods in the light of Lombrosian theory. Criminal tendencies among blacks, for example, were explained by analyzing their skulls. His approach to criminal medicine—which clearly followed dominant European theories—greatly influenced the succeeding generation of anthropologists and sociologists . . .
>
> (p. 11)

Moreover, Skidmore wrote that "to appreciate how far he carried Lombrosian theory, one need only remember that he recommended different treatment of convicted criminals according to their race" (1990, p. 11).

Because of the "triracial" nature of Cuba, Helg (1990) noted that Fernando Ortiz, who is recognized as Cuba's first ethnologist, found it an ideal place to study black delinquency (pp. 48, 52). Among those who influenced Ortiz were Lombroso, Ferri, and Garofolo. In fact, four years after writing his doctoral thesis at the Universidad Central in Madrid in December of 1901, he began regular communications with Lombroso, who also directed and published some of Ortiz's work on crime among blacks in Cuba (Orovio and Mulero 2005). According to Helg, Ortiz felt that "Africans were inferior because of their lack of integral civilization and morals" (Ortiz as cited in Helg 1990, p. 52). Other characteristics Ortiz used to describe African inferiority included that "they were lascivious lovers, given to polygamy, and had no cohesive families; their religion led them to human sacrifice, anthropophagy (cannibalism) and the most brutal superstitions" (p. 52). Drawing on these observations, Ortiz concluded that African criminality ". . . differed from the white criminality theorized by Lombroso . . . [t]he criminality of Africans . . . was explained by the complete primitives of their collective psyche, incapable of moral discernment" (p. 52). At its core, Ortiz felt that Cuban criminality was the product of "African superstitions, organizations, languages, and dances . . ." (p. 52).

These ideas are highlighted in his well-known work, *Hampa Afro-Cubana, Los Negros Brujos* (1906). In Ortiz's view, the brujos or sorcerers were main contributors to crime-related concerns (di Leo 2005). Consequently, Ortiz's proscription for solving the crime problem in Cuba was to eradicate the negative African traits and culture. To do so, he dreamed of a "penitentiary city" where he felt that "if there were a true criminal colony in Cuba, the problem [of the isolation of the brujo] would almost be solved as brujos could take up special tasks, isolated from the other categories of criminals" (p. 42).

These two case studies illustrate that, in the late 1800s, Lombrosian ideals were being espoused not only in Europe and North America, but around the globe where racial and ethnic groups were the focus of ideas that inferior "stocks" were polluting societies. After the publication of Lombroso's work, linking bad "stock" to crime became the standard progression. Some of the most virulent attacks were reserved for African Americans. Books such as Charles Carroll's *The Negro a Beast* (1900) and *In the Image of God* (1900) spoke to the fact that African Americans were not human; they were more akin to apes. Relying heavily on biblical interpretations, such as those presented in Chapter 1, Carroll sought to show why the white race was superior to African Americans. Around the same time, it was thought that, because of their genetic inferiority, African Americans would eventually die off (Hoffman 1896).

Even early American sociologists, such as Charles Henderson (1901) of the University of Chicago, picked up on the connection of biology, race, and crime and wrote:

> There can be no doubt that one of the most serious factors in crime statistics is found in the conditions of the freedmen of African descent, both North and South. The causes are complex. The primary factor is racial inheritance, physical and mental inferiority, barbarism and slave ancestry and culture.
>
> (p. 247)

Though Henderson also discussed the importance of sociological factors, he clearly prioritized the role of genetic inheritance. Analyses such as Henderson's predominated in America and other countries during the first few decades of the twentieth century. Noting the over-representation of people of color in the crime statistics, scholars continued to look to racial and ethnic diversity to explain these differences.

Criticisms of Lombroso's Work

While race and biological inferiority doctrines were vigorously challenged in America and abroad, such ideas predominated in late nineteenth- and early twentieth-century literature and gave rise to the global racist eugenics movement, which was also targeted at racial and ethnic groups (Goode 2005). American scholars such as W.E.B. Du Bois (Atlanta University) and Frances Kellor (University of Chicago) were among the earliest to respond to the doctrines based on Lombroso's work. Du Bois (1898/1982) acknowledged the "mass of theory" based on the biological approach, but noted such theories were based on "the flimsiest basis of scientific fact" (p. 50). Kellor also criticized Lombroso's work based on her belief that theories developed in European countries were not applicable to the United States because, as she put it, "The United States does not resemble [European] countries to sufficiently warrant their adoption. It must have its own facts because of its heterogeneous population, nature of soil, climate, government, and industrial and economic conditions" (1901a, p. 61). Kellor then presented the results of her own research on American Negroes, which provided little support for Lombroso's assertions (1901b, 1901c, 1901d).

Later, Dutch criminologist Willem Bonger (1943) also countered the Lombrosion approach with the following observation:

> Criminality is not a characteristic. It is neither a physical quality such as the possession of blue eyes, nor the spiritual one such as musicality. No

one comes into the world with "criminality," in the way in which one is born with a certain color of eyes, and so forth. Crime is something completely different.

(p. 27)

In Bonger's view (1943), the notion of criminal and noncriminal races was ridiculous. On this point, he opined, "The truth is naturally, that crime occurs in all races, and, by the nature of things, is only committed by a number (generally very limited) of individuals in each race. In principle the races do not differ" (p. 28). As for Lombroso's assertions about black Americans, Bonger dismissed them with the following: "As is usually the case in Lombroso's work, nothing but assertions are offered, and these rest, moreover, on a gross ethnological blunder" (p. 49).

On the whole, there were, and continue to be, several recurring criticisms of Lombroso's work. One of the more obvious criticisms relates to his use of the term "race." Lombroso's use of the term was clearly too broad and often without clear definition. Thus, while he argued that Africans were biologically inferior, at times he used similar arguments for other groups as well. Discussing the contradictions of Lombroso's use of the term, Gibson (2002) wrote:

Although Lombroso took race for granted as an important determinant of behavior, he was slipshod in his definition of the term. In *Criminal Man*, he sometimes divided Europe into two large groups designated the "Germans" and the "Latins" or, alternatively, the "blondes" and the "dark-haired." In other instances he multiplied the number of races, dividing Italy into three parts: the Semetic South; the Latin Center; and the Germanic, Liguarian, Celtic, and Slavic North.

(p. 105)

It is noteworthy that, on occasion, he labeled Jews as a race and while he noted their distinctive traits, he took a different position on their criminality, which he explained in more environmental vis-à-vis racial and biological terms (Gibson 2002, pp. 106–7). This was likely linked to the fact that, besides being the founding father of biological criminology, Lombroso was also of Jewish heritage (Gibson 2002).

Lombroso's work was also "characterized by haste, slipshod logic, and a tendency to ignore data that did not fit support his theories" (Gibson

2002, p. 28). Other problems include weak sampling approaches, inadequate use of control groups, unsophisticated statistical analyses, no differentiation between causation and correlation, and the use of anecdotal illustrations (p. 29).

Even with these persistent criticisms, Lombroso's work set the stage for contemporary criminologists who turn to biology to explain crime and for the development of scientific criminology (Beaver, Barnes, and Boutwell 2015; Wright et al. 2008). On this point, in a recent translation of Lombroso's *Criminal Woman* (originally titled *The Female Offender*), Gibson and Rafter (2004) wrote:

> Lombroso's work is historically valuable despite its scientific and logical naiveté. In fact, it is vulnerable partly because it so clearly reveals scientific and scientistic vulnerabilities, making them available for study. For better or worse, moreover, one outstanding quality of Lombroso's work is its magnificent tangle of brilliance and nonsense . . .
>
> (p. 31)

While retrospectively it might seem innocent to praise Lombroso's contributions, it is equally important for scholars to remember that his work, with its pungent racism, began the linkage of biology, race, and crime, which has persisted until modern times—a fact that, since the publication of his earliest works over a century ago, has resulted in misery for countless people of color. The next section looks at one of the more comprehensive tests of Lombroso's ideas in twentieth-century America.

Crime and the Man: An Ode to Lombroso

During the 1930s, Dr. Ernest A. Hooton conducted research to test some of Lombroso's (whom he admired) ideas (Hooton 1939a, 1939b; for an extended review of Hooton's work, see Rafter 2004). Based on a review of more than 17,000 criminals, Hooton set out to see whether physical and sociological difference did, in fact, matter (see Figures 2.2–2.4; Hooton 1939a, pp. 69, 96). In his work he examined old Americans or persons whose parents were also born in America. After considering a host of physical features (e.g. facial, cranial, etc.) and sociological factors (regional variations, previous convictions, marital status, etc.), he concluded that anthropometric and morphological features were significant, noting that "crime is not an exclusively sociological phenomenon, but is also biological" (Hooton 1939a, p. 75). Hooton went on to document the differences between native-born criminals of foreign parentage and foreign-born criminals. Some of these differences, which are highlighted in Figures 2.2–2.5, include those related to face structure, ear length, and jaw angles.

In Chapter VII, Hooten discussed white criminals of various ethnic backgrounds (he referred to them as "races"). Here again, he combines analysis of sociological factors and anthropological measurements to determine whether there are any differences among the groups. From his results, Hooton (1939a) concluded:

> Race is definitely associated with choice of crime, and with sociological status. There is, however, no implication whatsoever that these racial differences in criminal propensities are evidences that one race is superior to another ... Each produces its pitifully few men of genius, its hordes of the mediocre, its masses of morons, and from the very dregs of its germ plasm, its regiments of criminals.
>
> (p. 252)

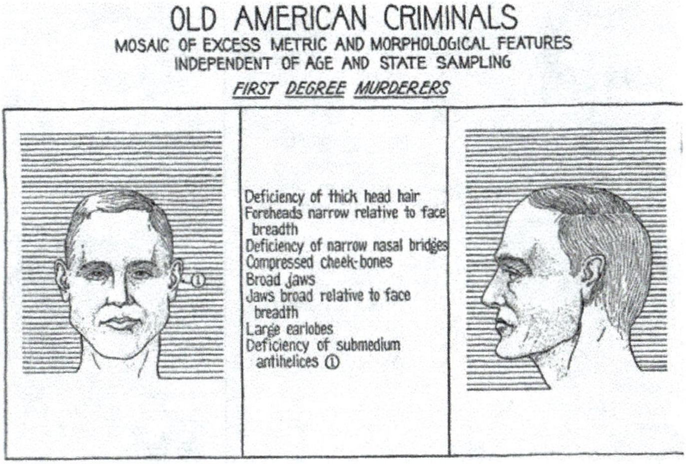

Figure 2.2 Facial structure of native-born criminal guilty of first-degree murder whose parents were also born in America. (From E. A. Hooton, *Crime and the Man*, Cambridge, MA: Harvard University Press, 1939. With permission.)

Figure 2.3 Facial structure of native-born criminal guilty of second-degree murder whose parents were also born in America. (From E. A. Hooton, *Crime and the Man*, Cambridge, MA: Harvard University Press, 1939. With permission.)

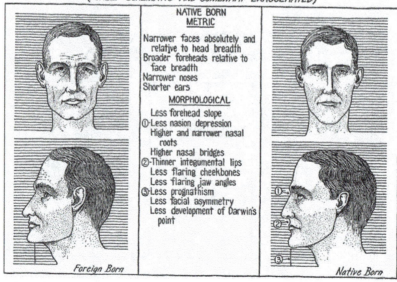

Figure 2.4 Differences in facial features between native-born criminals of foreign parentage and foreign-born criminals. (From E. A. Hooton, *Crime and the Man*, Cambridge, MA: Harvard University Press, 1939. With permission.)

and morphological features were significant, noting that "crime is not an exclusively sociological phenomenon, but is also biological" (Hooton 1939a, p. 75). Hooton went on to document the differences between native-born criminals of foreign parentage and foreign-born criminals. Some of these differences, which are highlighted in Figures 2.2–2.5, include those related to face structure, ear length, and jaw angles.

In Chapter VII, Hooten discussed white criminals of various ethnic backgrounds (he referred to them as "races"). Here again, he combines analysis of sociological factors and anthropological measurements to determine whether there are any differences among the groups. From his results, Hooton (1939a) concluded:

> Race is definitely associated with choice of crime, and with sociological status. There is, however, no implication whatsoever that these racial differences in criminal propensities are evidences that one race is superior to another ... Each produces its pitifully few men of genius, its hordes of the mediocre, its masses of morons, and from the very dregs of its germ plasm, its regiments of criminals.
>
> (p. 252)

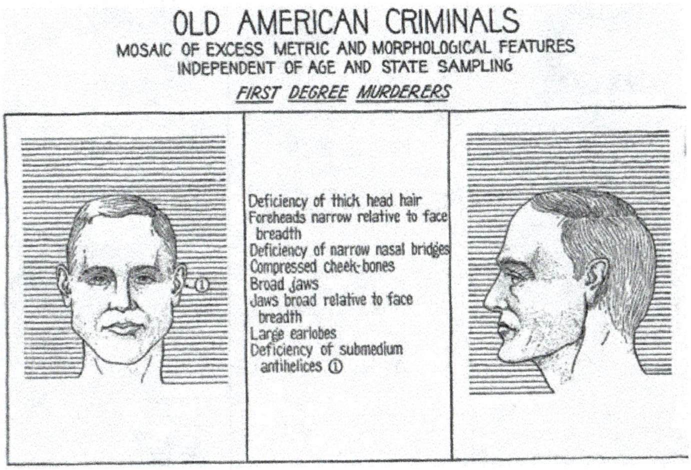

OLD AMERICAN CRIMINALS
MOSAIC OF EXCESS METRIC AND MORPHOLOGICAL FEATURES
INDEPENDENT OF AGE AND STATE SAMPLING
FIRST DEGREE MURDERERS

Deficiency of thick head hair
Foreheads narrow relative to face breadth
Deficiency of narrow nasal bridges
Compressed cheek-bones
Broad jaws
Jaws broad relative to face breadth
Large earlobes
Deficiency of submedium antihelices ①

Figure 2.2 Facial structure of native-born criminal guilty of first-degree murder whose parents were also born in America. (From E. A. Hooton, *Crime and the Man*, Cambridge, MA: Harvard University Press, 1939. With permission.)

OLD AMERICAN CRIMINALS
MOSAIC OF EXCESS METRIC AND MORPHOLOGICAL FEATURES
INDEPENDENT OF AGE AND STATE SAMPLING

SECOND DEGREE MURDERERS

Low absolute head height
Low length-height index
Low breadth-height index
High nasal bridges
Facial wrinkles
Bilateral chins ①

Figure 2.3 Facial structure of native-born criminal guilty of second-degree murder whose parents were also born in America. (From E. A. Hooton, *Crime and the Man*, Cambridge, MA: Harvard University Press, 1939. With permission.)

NEW AMERICAN CRIMINALS
GENERALIZED CRANIOMETRIC AND MORPHOLOGICAL DIFFERENCES BETWEEN NATIVE
BORN CRIMINALS OF FOREIGN PARENTAGE AND FOREIGN BORN OF SAME STOCKS
(PURELY SCHEMATIC AND SOMEWHAT EXAGGERATED)

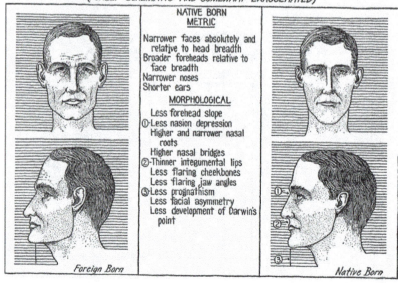

NATIVE BORN
METRIC

Narrower faces absolutely and
relative to head breadth
Broader foreheads relative to
face breadth
Narrower noses
Shorter ears

MORPHOLOGICAL

Less forehead slope
①-Less nasion depression
Higher and narrower nasal
roots
Higher nasal bridges
②-Thinner integumental lips
Less flaring cheekbones
Less flaring jaw angles
③-Less prognathism
Less facial asymmetry
Less development of Darwin's
point

Foreign Born

Native Born

Figure 2.4 Differences in facial features between native-born criminals of foreign parentage and foreign-born criminals. (From E. A. Hooton, *Crime and the Man*, Cambridge, MA: Harvard University Press, 1939. With permission.)

In two later chapters (IX and X), Hooton turned his attention to Negro (pure blood) and Negroid (mixed blood or mulatto) criminals.

Using a subsample of 4,100 Negro and Negroid offenders from prisons and reformatories around the country, Hooton (1939a) found very slight differences regarding offending patterns and occupational background (pp. 298, 302–3). The physical differences noted included differences related to height, weight, shoulder breadth, nose breadth, hair texture, etc. These differences are highlighted in Figure 2.5, which was presented in Hooton's work. In Hooton's second chapter devoted to Negro and Negroid criminals, he compares them with civilians. Hooton's comparison of these groups revealed slight differences related to age (criminals were older) and weight (criminals were heavier). Given these minor differences, Hooton stated he was unable to conclude that "criminals of African descent . . . represent the biological dregs of their population" (p. 356). At the close of the chapter, Hooton made the following final statement:

It is rather difficult to avoid the conclusion that a depressed physical and social environment determines Negro and Negroid delinquency to a

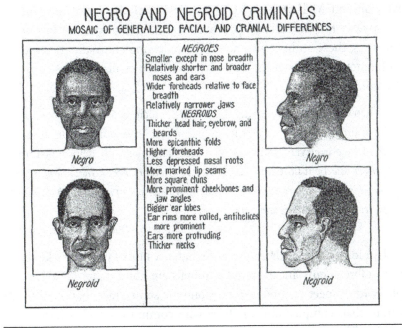

Figure 2.5 Physical differences between Negro and Negroid offenders. (From E. A. Hooton, *Crime and the Man*, Cambridge, MA: Harvard University Press, 1939. With permission.)

much greater extent than it does in the case of whites. This may be due to the probability that, however wretched the environment of the white may be, that of the Negro and of the Negroid is, on average, considerably worse. On the other hand, it is possible that Negroes and Negroids racially are more susceptible to criminalistic infection, so that antisocial behavior is likely to manifest itself more commonly than in whites in individuals who are not obviously stunted, undernourished, and of a generally inferior constitutional and biological endowment.

(p. 369)

While Hooton's work clearly drew on Lombroso's ideas, he readily acknowledged the contribution of sociological factors to the manifestation of antisocial behavior. Even so, though Hooton also readily declared that there were no significant differences regarding crime among whites of different races, he stayed true to his Lombrosian ideals, as evidenced by his closing statement, in which he saw Negroes and Negroids in a different light; they remained biologically inferior to whites.

There were numerous criticisms of Hooton's works published in anthropological and sociological journals (for a summary, see Rafter 2004, pp. 753–4), but the most prominent criticism came from Robert Merton and M.F. Ashley-Montagu (1940). Besides the usual methodological and definitional problems found in the work of biological theorists, these authors also noted the following contradictions related to Hooton's analysis of the differences between civilians and Negro and Negroid criminals:

When the expected differences do not occur, socio-economic factors may be at times involved; when they do occur, socio-economic factors are on the whole irrelevant and the differences are biologically determined. *In neither case*, be it noted, *is there a close examination of the actual role of these non-biological factors; they are introduced or neglected in accord with the disposition of the investigator.*

(p. 406; italics in original)

In addition, the authors also note that, because of practices like selective enforcement, "incarcerated criminals are not a representative sample (with respect to intelligence, economic status, race, nationality and rural-urban composition) of those who commit crimes" (Merton and Ashley-Montagu 1940, p. 386).

Following Hooton's work, very few major studies incorporating Lombroso's ideas were conducted (Rafter 2004). With the rise of the sociological approach, many such studies were likely to immediately draw the ire of the scholarly community. This "paradigm shift" is considered further in the following section, where contemporary biological perspectives are reviewed.

Contemporary Perspectives on Biology, Race, and Crime

The contemporary biological perspective reviewed here can be separated into two areas: first, those researchers who look to biology and sociological factors to explain criminality and, second, those scholars who look to intelligence to explain crime. In both of these areas, scholars have either infused or alluded to the significance of race.

Echoing the sentiment of Sagarin (1980) from more than two decades earlier, Farrington (2002) has appositely noted that, in previous decades, the discussion of biology and crime was considered taboo. From the early work of Lombroso and others who wrote up to the 1950s and 1960s, the biological perspective was rejected by well-known criminologists; this contributed to its limited long-standing appeal. Recounting the demise of the biological perspective, pioneering biosocial criminologist C. Ray Jeffery (1979) opined: "As I have argued elsewhere, criminology is an interdisciplinary field, but due to historic misfortune sociology captured the field in the 1920s" (p. 7). Thus, once the sociological approach was popularized by the University of Chicago, most scholars turned away from exploring the role that biology might play in criminality. In the past two decades, however, there has been a resurgence in the area (for an early volume during this resurgence, see Marsh and Katz 1985). The discussion here begins by reviewing one of the modern day progenitors of the biosocial approach. More than 20 years ago, in 1985, James Q. Wilson and Richard Herrnstein resurrected the biology and crime debate with their publication of *Crime and Human Nature: The Definitive Study of the Causes of Crime.*

Crime and Human Nature

Early in their tome *Crime and Human Nature* the authors declared that the aim of their work was "to explain why some persons are more likely than others to do things that all societies condemn and punish" (Wilson and Herrnstein 1985, p. 23). When they begin to lay the foundations of their perspective, they inform readers that "we believe that criminal behavior, like all human behavior, results from a complex interaction of genetic and environmental factors" (p. 70). After proffering that there are differences related to race found in most societies, they argued that differences in individual criminality should be based "on factors that are common to all societies" (p. 29). In their view such factors include constitutional, familial, educational, economic, neighborhood, and historical factors.

They also noted that "there is no reason to believe that the genes determining one's skin pigmentation also affect criminality" (Wilson and Herrnstein, p. 29). They further added that, "if racial or ethnic identity affects the likelihood of committing a crime, it must be because that identity co-varies with other characteristics and experiences that affect criminality" (p. 29). After providing these statements, Wilson and Herrnstein devoted 18 chapters to constitutional factors; developmental factors; social context; history and culture; and crime, human nature, and society. Under the section heading "history and culture," Chapter 18 is devoted to race and crime. In this chapter, Wilson and Herrnstein pointed to constitutional factors that may contribute to the over-representation of blacks in crime; such constitutional factors, as they noted earlier in the work, relate

> to factors, usually present at or soon after birth, whose behavioral consequences appear gradually during the child's development. Constitutional factors are not necessarily genetic, although they may be. A genetic factor, if not a mutation, is inherited from one or both parents. There is no "crime gene" and so there is no such thing as a "born criminal," but some traits that are to a degree heritable, such as intelligence and temperament, affect to some extent the likelihood that individuals will engage in criminal activities.
>
> (p. 69)

Continuing in their description of constitutional factors, Wilson and Herrnstein wrote:

> And some constitutional factors may be the result of prenatal or perinatal accidents. If, for example, the mother smokes heavily, takes drugs,

is malnourished, or is exposed to environmental toxins while pregnant, this may affect the infant in ways that influence the chances of later displaying aggressive and criminal behavior. Similarly, if the infant experiences some trauma during birth—sustained oxygen deprivation, for instance—or is improperly fed and cared for immediately after birth, some organic damage may result that also may affect subsequent behavior, including criminal behavior.

(pp. 69–70)

Drawing on the foundations of William Sheldon's research on somatotyping (Sheldon 1949; for an excellent review of Sheldon's work, see Rafter 2007), which looked to body types (skinny, muscular, or fat) to partially identify criminals, Wilson and Herrnstein suggested that black males tended to be more mesomorphic (muscular) than white males. In addition, because blacks have higher scores on the MMPI (Minnesota Multiphasic Personality Inventory) than whites, this shows they are "less normal." In a section of the chapter titled "Net Advantage," they also posited that "it is possible, however, that the greater prevalence of early delinquency among blacks is due to their having learned to anticipate bleaker economic prospects than whites—that long before they encounter the labor market, they sense crime will pay more" (p. 473). Referring to the available scholarly literature, the authors review other factors that might contribute to black criminality, including low IQ, inadequate socialization, and subcultural deviance (Wilson and Herrnstein 1985, pp. 470–84).

As with their predecessors, Wilson and Herrnstein have had their critics. Most notably, there were concerns about the clarity of concepts and other measurement issues. Another concern related to their exclusive use of the theory to explain crime in the streets, not "crimes in the suites." This obviously speaks to race and crime because it is clear that these conservative thinkers have more interest in explaining crimes associated with racial minorities than those overwhelmingly committed by middle- and upper-class whites (Lilly et al. 2002).

Diana Fishbein's Biobehavioral Perspectives

Two more recent works by well-known scholars in the area, Diana Fishbein (2001) and David Rowe (2002), provide excellent overviews of the emerging literature in biology and crime. It is striking, though, that while Fishbein tackles the concerns related to race, nowhere in Rowe's work does he devote any substantive discussion to race—even though many biological and biosocial theorists speak directly or indirectly to the question of biology, race, and crime.

Early in her work, Fishbein (2001) informed readers about the contentious nature of the subject:

> There is fear that research into genetic contributions to behavior will undermine our conception of free will and will foster the idea that all behavior is due to biological factors. Even more disturbing is the belief that the study of behavioral genetics is inherently racist and may reinforce racial stereotypes, prejudice, and discriminatory practices by the criminal justice system and society-at-large.
>
> (pp. 2–3)

Her primer presents the cornucopia of biological perspectives that have been used to explain crime; most include the contribution of behavioral, cognitive, and psychological traits (Fishbein 2001, p. 2). Moreover, her review postulated that "abnormalities in certain areas of brain function can heighten sensitivity to negative environmental circumstances, increasing the risk for an antisocial outcome" (p. 3). The key here is that current biological-oriented criminologists now argue that environment does matter and can either mediate or aggravate one's chances of engaging in or refraining from antisocial behavior. In other words, as she noted, the question is no longer whether "nature" (biological causes) or "nurture" (social causes) explains human behavior; it is more about how the two interact to influence one's life (p. 13).

Other biological areas that Fishbein tackled included brain chemistry, hormones, skin conductance (electrical activity in the skin), heart rate, and cognitive and neuropsychological "which involve information processing, memory, and assessment of environmental cues" (Fishbein 2001, p. 55); when not performing normally, all of these can result in behaviors that are associated with antisocial behavior. The race component of the theory is implicit in the discussion on socioenvironmental contexts.

Because one general premise of biological approaches is that inheritable traits such as impulsivity, attention deficits, aggressiveness, and cognitive and conduct disorders are triggered by poor socioenvironmental contexts, urban residents, particularly blacks, have a greater chance of expressing antisocial behavior. These environments are characterized by the physical environment and stressors such as prenatal influences (e.g. alcohol, tobacco, and drug abuse during pregnancy), maternal social conditions (e.g. maternal stress), and perinatal complications such as "prematurity and delivery difficulties such as oxygen loss, infectious disease, prolapsed cord delivery, irregular heart beat in child during delivery, and late-stage drug use" (p. 70). Other environmental factors of concern noted by Fishbein include bonds between caregiver and child, too little stimulation, child abuse and other traumatic experiences, trauma during adolescence and adulthood, and observing violence (pp. 70–6; see Figure 2.6).

In response to this obvious suggestion regarding the implications of sociobiological research for African Americans, Fishbein (2001) noted:

> Critics argue vehemently that biological research must be seen in the context of our racial history and racist attitudes. In our society, any research that links criminal behavior to biological features may be mistakenly seen as implicating the African American community and contribute to its stigmatization.
>
> (p. 94)

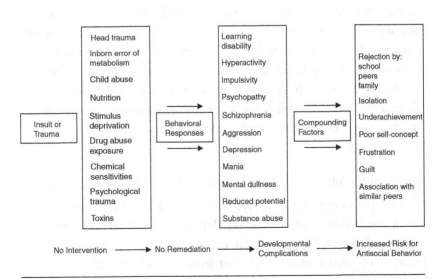

Figure 2.6 Developmental stages of antisocial behavior. (From D. Fishbein, *Biobehavioral Perspectives on Criminology*, Wadsworth, a division of Thomson Learning, 2001. With permission.)

To this she added:

> Defenders of the research, however, deny that it must be captive to our
> racial history, and argue that it will ultimately do far more to *alleviate*
> [emphasis in original] than exacerbate racial tensions . . . More specif-
> ically, over two hundred years of racial discrimination has resulted in
> the relegation of a large proportion of our African American citizens
> to impoverished and underserved communities. No where do we see a
> greater concentration of "environmental triggers" and adversity in these
> neighborhoods, which contributes in substantial ways to maladaptive
> behaviors, irrespective of genetic or biological traits.
>
> (p. 94)

As such, Fishbein believes that advances in biological perspectives
will help disadvantaged African American residents who, because of
biological and environmental factors, are disproportionately at risk to
develop antisocial behaviors. Illustrative of this point is research conducted by John Wright et al. (2008) who studied the impact of prenatal
and postnatal exposure to lead in a sample largely comprised of African American women from Cincinnati. Based on their examination of
lead levels of these residents who lived in lead-infested housing, the
researchers found "that early lead exposure is a risk factor for criminal behavior, including violent crime" (p. 740). These important results
support Fishbein's contention regarding ethnic and racial minorities
being at risk for exposure to harmful environmental contaminants.

In recent years, scholars have sought to test the validity of the biosocial perspectives. Much of this research uses Terri Moffitt's (1993)
adolescence-limited and life-course-persistent antisocial behavior theories. Her theories and some tests of them specific to race and crime are
reviewed next.

Terri Moffitt's Adolescence-Limited and Life-Course-Persistent Theories

In her frequently cited 1993 article, "Adolescence-Limited and
Life-Course-Persistent Antisocial Behavior: A Developmental Taxonomy," Terri Moffitt presented two theories meant to explain the
behavior of youths who (1) commit antisocial acts in their adolescent
years that continue into adulthood; and (2) only commit antisocial acts
during their adolescent years. Moffitt labels the first type of offender

life-course-persistent and links his or her criminality to complications related to neuropsychological development. As previously noted, such things would be brought on through things such as maternal drug use, poor prenatal nutrition or pre- or postnatal exposure to toxic agents, and delivery complications. Also, as previously noted, these sorts of complications in a disadvantaged environment can contribute to the early onset of antisocial behavior.

The adolescence-limited approach is based on the premise that the antisocial behavior "is motivated by the gap between biological maturity and social maturity, it is learned from antisocial models who are easily mimicked, and it is sustained according to reinforcement principles of learning theory" (Moffitt 1993, p. 685). Most importantly, Moffitt feels that, for a variety of reasons including maturity and having good social and academic skills, after a period of time, youth who fall under this category age-out of their antisocial behavior.

As for the role of race in her theory, Moffitt (1994) recognized that black Americans had higher rates of crime than whites, and began her explanation by stating: "The race difference may be accounted for by a relatively higher prevalence of both *Life-Course-Persistent* and *Adolescence-Limited* subtypes among black Americans because the putative causes of this type are elevated by institutionalized prejudice and by poverty" (p. 38; emphasis in original). She continued:

> Among poor blacks, prenatal care is less available, infant nutrition is poorer, and the incidence of fetal exposure to toxic and infectious agents is greater, placing infants at high risk for the nervous system problems that research has shown to interfere with prosocial child development.
>
> (p. 39)

She also suggested that high-risk children who have weak family bonds and parents who are stressed, according to previous research, are likely to exhibit aggressive interpersonal behavior (p. 39). As for the role of schools in this process, she wrote: "To the extent that poor black children attend disadvantaged schools, there is less chance for correction of the learning disabilities that research has shown to contribute toward underemployment and recidivistic crime" (p. 39).

There has been considerable research on Moffitt's theory in both the psychology and criminology literature and there have been several tests of her supposition regarding blacks. Early and more recent research has been supportive of Moffit's suppositions (Bellair, McNulty, and Piquero 2014; Gibson et al. 2000; Piquero et al. 2002; Piquero and White 2003). Nonetheless, at least one study using multiracial/ethnic samples has shown mixed results (Donnellan et al. 2000).

Haynie et al. (2008) investigated the economic aspects of Moffitt's theory in which she argues that a part of the reason why blacks are more likely to be life-course-persistent is because of their limited employment prospects. In short, the researchers explored "whether participation in legitimate employment opportunities and a relative sense of economic well-being in young adulthood accounts for the observed race difference in criminal offending and persistence in offending in young adulthood" (p. 600). The authors found that racial differences in violent offending disappear over the life-course when controls are included for economic and employment prospects (Haynie et al. 2008, p. 617).

A core area of Moffitt's theory relates to intelligence (cognitive abilities). However, the purported connection of intelligence, race, and crime is not new. For nearly a century scholarship has either alluded to or directly pointed to such a connection. Reviewed next are some of the historical and contemporary statements on this relationship.

Intelligence, Race, and Crime

Henry Goddard's Intelligence Determinism

With the development and acceptance of intelligence tests, another linkage was developed: intelligence and crime (Gould 1996). Much of the early literature suggested that criminals were of low intelligence or "feebleminded." This line of thinking was based on the early work of Richard Dugdale's nineteenth-century Juke study (see Dugdale 1877), which chronicled the genealogy of a family that had generations of immorality and criminality.

Building on the Juke study, Henry H. Goddard, director of research at the New Jersey Training School for the Feeble-minded Girls and Boys (1906–18) and later a professor at Ohio State University, studied the lineage of the Kallikak family, who he suggested started out as a fine middle-class family, but, with the introduction of "bad blood" into one branch of the family lineage, a series of feebleminded family members emerged. Based on his observations, Goddard (1912) wrote:

In the good branch of the Kallikak family there were no criminals. There were not many in the other side, but there were some, and, had their environment been different, no one who is familiar with feebleminded persons, their characteristics and tendencies, would doubt that a large percentage of them might become criminal.

(p. 59)

While Goddard was sensitive to the role of environment, in his classic, *Feeble-mindedness: Its Causes and Consequences* (1914), he made his position clear:

Environment will not, of itself, enable all people to escape criminality. The problem goes much deeper than environment. It is the question of responsibility. Those who are born without sufficient intelligence either to know right from wrong, or those, who if they knew it, have not sufficient will-power and judgment to make themselves do the right and flee the wrong, will ever be a fertile source of criminality.

(p. 7)

Goddard continued by declaring:

The criminal is not born; he is made. The so-called criminal type is merely a type of feeblemindedness, a type misunderstood and mistreated, driven into criminality for which he is well fitted by nature. It is heredity feeblemindedness not heredity criminality that accounts for conditions. We have only seen the end product and failed to recognize the character of the raw material.

(p. 8)

Goddard goes on to provide case studies of various cases of feeblemindedness. When he presented his case studies, only two involved "colored people," and, in these instances, their race is not given any significance (1914, pp. 219–20, 384–5). Therefore, regardless of race, Goddard was quite emphatic in his belief that "every feebleminded person is a potential criminal . . . Whether the feebleminded person actually becomes a criminal depends upon two factors, his temperament and his environment" (pp. 514–15). From his various studies, Goddard suggested that as much as 50 percent of institutional populations were feebleminded.

In later works, Goddard continued with a similar line of thinking, but he began to write with a tone of intellectual determinism. That is, he wrote as though simply having knowledge of one's intelligence could solve all of society's problems. Furthermore, equally as troubling was his belief that intelligence should dictate one's place in society. In *Human Efficiency and Levels of Intelligence* (1922), for example, he writes about the military and how IQ provided a useful barometer as to the rank each soldier should hold. He transitioned to a discussion of civilian society with the following: "We wish to maintain the thesis that a knowledge of the intelligence level and a conscious effort to fit every man to his work in accordance with his intellectual level, is the surest way of promoting social efficiency" (p. 48).

Goddard's work was later criticized on a few fronts. First, in some of Goddard's research, his assistant, Elizabeth S. Kite, used some questionable practices to conduct the IQ testing (Knepper 2001, p. 79). Second, Gould (1996) found that Goddard had altered some of the pictures in the Kallikak book. Of this discovery, he wrote: "It is now clear that all the photos of noninstitutionalized kakos were altered by inserting heavy dark lines to give eyes and mouths their diabolical appearance" (p. 201). Finally, Goddard's policy recommendations have been particularly criticized. Because he felt feeblemindedness was inherited, he argued for the sterilization of the feebleminded, limiting immigration of foreigners, segregation, and/or colonization of those found to be feebleminded.

Unfortunately, by the time serious criticism of Goddard's work arose, some states, such as Virginia where, after the *Buck v. Bell* Supreme Court decision upholding Virginia's sterilization law, more than 7,500 men and women were sterilized between 1924 and 1972, had already been convinced of the potential of sterilization of the "feebleminded and antisocial—including unwed mothers, prostitutes, petty criminals, and children with disciplinary problems" (Gould 1996, p. 365).

Intelligence, Race, and Crime: 1920s to the 1970s

From the very beginning, the notion has been that intelligence, race, and crime have been linked and, after Goddard's work, a plethora of studies connecting these variables emerged. Modeling Goddard's approach, during the 1920s, some studies noted the differences in the intelligence and offending patterns of blacks, whites, foreign-born, and army personnel (Doll 1920; Stone 1921); still others simply looked at intelligence, race, and crime (limited to blacks and whites), taking into consideration a host of factors.

During 1925 and 1926, several such studies were conducted by pioneering psychologist Carl Murchison. From this research he found the following:

- Blacks confined in their home states had more intelligence than blacks confined outside their home states (Murchison and Burfield 1925a).
- Blacks scoring lower on intelligence tests committed more serious crimes (Murchison and Burfield 1925b).
- Black recidivists were of higher intelligence than first-time offenders (Murchinson and Nafe 1925).
- Black females had lower intelligence scores than black males (Murchison 1926a).
- Black offenders with higher levels of intelligence had worked in occupations requiring more training or apprenticeship (Murchison and Gilbert 1925a).
- Black offenders with higher levels of intelligence had worked in occupations requiring more training or apprenticeship (Murchison and Gilbert 1925b).
- Blacks incarcerated for more than two years scored higher on intelligence tests than those who were incarcerated for less than two years (Murchison and Pooler 1925).
- Unmarried criminals were more intelligent than married criminals (Murchison and Gilbert 1925b).

In 1926, Murchison's work culminated in the publication of his book, *Criminal Intelligence*. Two things stand out from Murchison's publications: first, he provided no context or serious explanation for his results; second, in none of these publications does he report a level of low mental ability (feeblemindedness) that would meet the 50 percent reported by Goddard.

At the beginning of the 1930s, noted criminologist Edwin Sutherland weighed in on the topic of intelligence and crime and, after reviewing numerous papers on the subject, concluded that feeblemindedness was likely one factor of many that might be used to explain delinquency.

More specifically, Sutherland (1931) noted: "The significance of feeble-mindedness apparently can be determined only when studied in relation to a great many other personal and situational factors" (p. 373). Even with Sutherland's skepticism of the intelligence and crime literature, during the 1930s, there were additional substantive studies conducted examining intelligence, race, and crime. Beckman (1933) and Lichtenstein and Brown (1938) both looked to contextualize intelligence scores by conducting studies in urban areas. From such analyses, Beckman, whose study examined three cities—New York (which recorded the highest IQs of the three cities), Baltimore, and Washington, D.C.— found that delinquents had lower IQs than the matched control groups; however, of larger significance was his finding that "socioeconomic status is significant in the intelligence of colored adolescents" (p. 89). Lichtenstein and Brown (1938) focused on the intelligence and achievement of children in delinquency areas and reported that only 10 percent of them were feebleminded (p. 20).

Other studies during the period noted the relationship between educational attainment and crime (Barnhart 1933) and, as in the earlier period, two studies simply examined the role of IQ and race in explaining delinquency (Lane and Witty 1935; McClure 1933). McClure's findings were similar to those studies conducted in the earlier period: the level of intelligence among black delinquents in Toledo was lower than that of white delinquents (1933, p. 42). Conversely, after studying intelligence in relation to race, recidivists and nonrecidivists, types of offenses, delinquency areas, broken homes, socioeconomic status, and several other variables related to family relationships, Lane and Witty (1935) did not find any significant relationships within their sample of 700 Illinois youth. In their closing remarks, the authors opined:

> The writers feel that their search for factors associated with the intelligence of delinquents has been rather unsuccessful. They cannot point to a single item which seems significantly related to intelligence test results. However, they have demonstrated rather conclusively the falsity of many assertions regarding the role which intelligence assumes in the behavior and the lives of delinquent children.
>
> (p. 10)

By the end of the decade, Simon H. Tulchin published his classic, *Intelligence and Crime* (1939), which dealt a considerable blow to the proponents of the intelligence, race, and crime connection. Tulchin's research examined over 10,000 inmates incarcerated in three Illinois state prisons and reformatories from 1920 to 1927. After comparing the intelligence of native-born whites, foreign-born whites, and Negroes with a sample of Army personnel, Tulchin found that,

> with but one exception, individuals of all grades of intelligence are found in all crime groups. For nearly all nativity and race groups the highest median Alpha scores are men committed for fraud, and the lowest scores by men committed for sex crimes.
>
> (p. 155)

Of Tulchin's findings and mirroring the sentiments expressed earlier in the decade by Sutherland, noted criminologist Edward W. Burgess, wrote: "The findings of this careful and painstaking investigation demonstrate conclusively that criminologists must look to other factors than differences in intelligence for an explanation of crime" (1939, p. ix).

The 1940s saw more researchers studying intelligence, race, and crime. Some continued to simply make note of the nature of the relationship among intelligence, race, and crime (Armstrong and Heisler 1945; Fox 1946), while others found few differences between delinquent and nondelinquent Negroes in a variety of areas including IQ (Watts 1941). Of the latter finding, the author clearly showed a hint of concern regarding the potential policy implications if differences had been noted, stating: "This investigation indicates the impossibility of differentiating between delinquent and non-delinquent Negro boy[s], and probably of detecting those who are likely to become delinquent" (p. 207).

The literature on intelligence and crime diminished precipitously in the 1940s and 1950s. Some have argued that this occurred because of Sutherland's previously discussed critical review of the intelligence and crime literature (see Herrnstein and Murray 1994; Hirschi and Hindelang 1977), but it is likely that it was a combination of Sutherland and Tulchin's work that contributed to the virtual disappearance of the topic from the criminological literature until the 1970s. Some of the contemporary literature on intelligence, race, and crime is reviewed next.

Intelligence, Race, and Crime: Contemporary Perspectives

In the late 1970s, two prominent criminologists, Travis Hirschi and Michael J. Hindelang (1977), conducted a review of the literature on intelligence and crime. On the issue of race, they wrote: "There can be no doubt that IQ is related to delinquency within race categories" (p. 575). From their research, they concluded that students with low intelligence had difficulty in school and, as a result, were more likely to engage in delinquency. Ergo, given that blacks have traditionally scored lower on IQ tests, they are likely to commit more crime. The debate lingered with a few publications here and there, until Richard Herrnstein and Charles Murray published their controversial work, *The Bell Curve: Intelligence and Class Structure in American Life*, in 1994.

The Bell Curve: The Return to Intellectual Determinism

The publication of *The Bell Curve* caused a national stir in America. The book, which rose to several bestseller lists and spawned several volumes rebuking *The Bell Curve*'s basic premise (see Devlin et al. 1997; Fraser 1995; Jacoby and Glauberman 1995; Kincheloe et al. 1996), picked up the intelligence and crime debate where it had left off decades earlier. Herrnstein and Murray (1994) argued that low IQ contributed to a host of things, including crime, poverty, illegitimacy, unemployment, welfare dependency, etc.

The chapter devoted to crime, though brief, provided some insights into their underlying thinking. After reviewing the crime trends, the authors note how intelligence has an impact on the risk of committing crime. They begin using similar reasoning as Hirschi and Hindelang (1977) regarding low intelligence contributing to school failure, which leads some to crime (Herrnstein and Murray 1994, p. 240). A second explanation proposed that low IQ results in persons who lack foresight and "raises the attractions of the immediate gains from crime and lowers the strength of deterrents, which come later (if they come at all)" (p. 240).

They also suggest that low IQ might contribute to someone being drawn to danger and having "an insensitivity to pain or to social ostracism, and a host of derangements of various sorts" (p. 240). Such characteristics combined with IQs, in their view, might also "set the stage for a criminal career" (p. 240). The final suggestion regarding the link between intelligence and crime related to the belief that people with low IQs are unable to follow ethical principles. In Herrnstein and Murray's words:

> [Persons with low IQs] find it harder to understand why robbing someone is wrong, find it harder to appreciate values of civil and cooperative social life, and are accordingly less inhibited from acting in ways that are hurtful to other people and to the community at large.
>
> (pp. 240–1)

Herrnstein and Murray (1994) continue their review of the topic using a race-based analysis solely looking at white males. Their analysis noted that white males with the highest IQs were less likely to encounter the criminal justice system. They point to the relationship between socioeconomic background and crime, which they suggest is statistically insignificant after controlling for IQ (p. 249). Other areas they examine include the role of broken homes and education in white criminality. In each case, the authors argue that, while these factors might have some explanatory power, IQ is also a powerful explanatory variable (pp. 249–51).

While the authors never refer to other racial/ethnic minorities in the chapter on crime (they do make mention of crime disparities in Chapter 14, pp. 338–9), implicit in their coverage of the subject is that such groups, because of their generally lower IQs, are likely to be at higher risk for criminality. Even so, rather than argue that the solution lies in increasing IQ scores, the authors, in their policy suggestions, allude to the fact that IQ is immutable. As such, their overall approach mirrors the earlier work of Goddard in that they adhere to a similar form of intellectual determinism. That is, since IQ scores are fixed, we should work with individuals on their level. In the end, they propose that "the criminal justice system should be made simpler. The meaning of criminal offenses used to be clear and objective, and so were the consequences. It is worth trying to make them so again" (Herrnstein and Murray 1994, p. 544).

Overall, there were several critics of the *The Bell Curve*'s arguments related to crime. Haymes (1996), for example, argued that in limiting their sample to whites, Herrnstein and Murray attempt to mislead readers into believing that they have no interest in race. Yet, it is clear that race is "the primary category utilized to differentiate between people . . ." (p. 243). Haymes further noted the implicit suggestions in Herrnstein and Murray's work:

> they conclude that the differences in black–white crime [are] explained by IQ differences. Their assumption is that blacks are more likely to be involved in violent crime because they are allegedly more likely to be of a "lower intelligence" than whites.
>
> (p. 243)

As Haymes correctly concludes, the authors declare that the use of intelligence is a neutral assessment device; thus, as a result, "[they] are able to claim surreptitiously that blacks are biologically predisposed to violent criminal behavior, linking criminality with race" (p. 244).

Another critic, Manolakes (1997), responded to *The Bell Curve* by suggesting that the authors' arguments were "based on an incomplete set of variables and simplistic statistical analyses" (p. 236). He also criticized them for limiting their sample to white males. Because of this, Manolakes believed that the authors "are unable to determine the ways in which the effects of variables differ for separate racial categories" (p. 252). After reproducing the data presented in *The Bell Curve* with additional variables, Manolakes finds that the social environment still holds a key to understanding criminality. From his reanalysis, he concluded:

> Because the social environment is shown to be as influential as IQ in predicting criminal activity, social policy must continue to battle against social, racial, and economic inequalities that pervade life in America if crime rates are ever to be reduced in an effective manner.
>
> (p. 254)

Prominent criminologist Francis T. Cullen and his colleagues, Paul Gendreau, G. Roger Jarjoura, and John Paul Wright (1997), also responded with harsh criticism for *The Bell Curve*'s statements on crime. These critics were concerned about shortcomings that were both methodological and related to Herrnstein and Murray's policy suggestions. Cullen et al. reanalyzed the data presented in the book and concluded that there was model specification error because of the limited number of variables included along with IQ.

After adding additional sociological variables, the authors concluded that "the effects of sociological variables are not eliminated by IQ and, in fact, outweigh the causal importance of intelligence" (p. 394). So, while they readily admit that IQ might play some indirect role on crime, the model used in *The Bell Curve* should have considered additional sociological factors. Moreover, the authors made use of several meta-analyses, which showed that "IQ generally is among the weakest of the risk factors assessed in the meta-analyses" (p. 398). They conclude by referring to Herrnstein and Murray as "cognitively challenged" criminologists (p. 405). Explaining their reasoning for this description, Cullen and colleagues wrote:

> Their failure to consider alternative criminogenic risk factors is inexcusable not only because the research documenting their salience is readily available but also because doing so leads them to justify ill-conceived, repressive crime policies. By portraying offenders as driven into crime predominantly by cognitive disadvantage, Herrnstein and Murray mask the reality that stronger risk factors not only exist but are also amenable to effective correctional intervention.
>
> (p. 406)

Following the publication of *The Bell Curve*, the American Psychological Association (APA), felt a need to form a task force to examine the state of knowledge on IQ (Neisser et al. 1996). The final report from the task force noted several key findings including the consensus that IQ tests ". . . do in fact predict school performance fairly well . . . They also predict scores on school achievement tests, designed to measure knowledge of the curriculum" (Neisser et al. 1996, p. 81). The report also acknowledges that there are differences in IQ by [racial] group (see pp. 92–95). However, after reviewing the empirical evidence, the task force concluded: "[there is] no adequate explanation of the differential between the IQ means of Blacks and Whites" (p. 97). Notably, the task force also felt a need to point out that IQ tests do not cover all forms of intelligence including creativity, wisdom, practical sense, social sensitivity, and other facets of intelligence. In other words, those using the test to make assertions about intelligence and crime should understand that the test does not fully capture all the dimensions of intelligence.

Therefore, those scholars using this framework should proceed with caution. In fact, some scholars have pointed out that since persons with high levels of intelligence commit white-collar and political crimes, there are problems linking low intelligence to crime (Hacker 1995, pp. 102–3; Lanier and Henry 1998). There has also been some debate about whether differences in IQ are genetic or related to one's environment (Onwudiwe and Lynch 2000). On this point, the APA task force noted that while IQ is highly heritable, there remained questions as to the role of culture and environment in explaining the differences in scores by racial group (Neisse et al. 1996, p. 95). One final biological approach reviewed is the r/K theory, which has garnered significant attention in recent years.

r/K Life History Theory

One of the more controversial biosocial theories related to race in general and crime in particular is the r/K life history theory. Created by Harvard biologist Edward O. Wilson (1975) to explain population growth and decline in plants and animals, the theory has been adapted to humans by J. Philippe Rushton (1995), the late professor of psychology at Western Ontario University. The gene-based evolutionary theory links much of the differences between the races, including crime patterns, to migrations out of Africa. Rushton agrees with the hypothesis that all humans came out of Africa. It is his contention, however, that there was a split of the population before humans left Africa. This split is responsible for the current position of blacks, whites, and Asians.

As he sees it, those who stayed in Africa (now referred to as black people) were subjected to unpredictable droughts and deadly diseases, which caused them to die young (Rushton 1999, pp. 84–5). Those who migrated to Eurasia (now referred to as whites and Asians) had to deal with other concerns, such as "gathering and storing food, providing shelter, making clothes, and raising children during the long winters" (p. 85). According to Rushton, these tasks were more mentally demanding and required more intelligence. Moreover, "they called for larger brains and slower growth rates. They permitted lower levels of sex hormones, resulting in less sexual potency and aggression and more family stability and longevity" (p. 85).

At the heart of the r/K theory are reproduction, climate, and intelligence. Since Africans were faced with early death, they often had to bear more children to maintain their population, which left them unable to provide significant care for their offspring. Conversely, those falling under the K-strategy—whites and Asians (Rushton acknowledges only three races: Negroid, Caucasoid, and Mongoloid)—reproduced less and generally spent more time caring for their offspring. Rushton's theory relates to race and crime in that aggression, impulsive behavior, low self-control, low intelligence, and lack of following rules are all associated with criminals and, according to Rushton, those who fall under the r-strategy: black people.

To support his approach, Rushton conducted cross-national studies that looked at race and crime (see Rushton 1995; Rushton and Templer 2009; Rushton and Whitney 2002; Templer and Rushton, 2011). Other scholars have also adopted some of Rushton's ideas in the areas of crime (Ellis 1997; Ellis and Walsh 1997, 2000; Walsh 2003, 2004) and skin color and intelligence (Lynn 2002). While few of the available studies attempt to provide empirical support for the r/K theory, Akins and Griffin (2000) did find support for the notion that blacks twin and commit more "street crimes" at a higher rate than whites and Asians. Even so, they noted that "if white-collar crime were as visible as street crime, then twinning rates may indicate little or nothing. Additionally, the role that nutrition, opiate use, fertility drugs, prenatal care, and the primacy of the mother in twinning might be considered for the future development of r/K theory" (Akins and Griffin 2000, p. 21). More recently, in support of Rushton's perspective, Wright (2008) has argued that scholars have ignored "the inconvenient truth" that race is not a social construct. Like Rushton, he argues that evolutionary factors have produced differences among the races that have produced elevated levels of crime and other social problems among blacks across the globe. Notably, his arguments suffer from some of the same weaknesses as Rushton's, which are outlined below.

There have been several notable criticisms of the r/K theory. First, Rushton generally ignores sociological factors. Most of his cross-national comparisons point strictly to numbers, without taking into account variables such as socioeconomic status, discrimination, and other important sociological variables. Second, in the twenty-first century, there are very few "pure" races, especially in the United States, where white male sexual aggression against black females during the slave era produced countless mixed-race offspring. Therefore, the rigorous adherence to the black-white-Asian split is problematic. Third, Roberts and Gabor (1990) also note that Rushton presumes causality regarding the relationship between race and crime when, in fact, he has only shown a correlation or that the variables are related (p. 296).

Fourth, Roberts and Gabor also criticize Rushton for not accounting for changes in crime among blacks over time and also for the within-group differences regarding crime among people of African descent. More specifically, if Rushton's theory were valid, one would see consistently elevated rates of crime among all people of African descent in the Diaspora (1990, pp. 301–3). Based on data presented in their paper, this is simply not the case.

In addition, if Rushton's theory were true, what would explain white aggression as colonizers around the globe? In contrast to Rushton's theory, Bradley (1978) argued that, as a result of migration to colder regions, since the beginning of humanity, whites have been the global aggressors. Gabbidon (2009) has also argued that European colonization (see Chapter 8) has clearly contributed to the plight of blacks and other racial/ethnic groups across the globe. Finally, there have been concerns that Rushton's research returns us to the days of Lombrosoism and the eugenics movement (Roberts and Gabor 1990, pp. 305–9), which as Rafter (2008) has recently noted describing the biocriminology in Nazi Germany, was "criminology's darkest hour."

Conclusion

This chapter critically assessed the numerous biologically based theories that have been posited to explain criminal behavior. It examined more than a century of scholarship that has, at numerous points in time, applied biological theories to racial minorities. Implicit in such theories has been the notion of white supremacy—both physically and intellectually. The most recent biological theorists have moved towards the integration of biological and sociological factors. Such perspectives argue that one's biological makeup and one's environment intersect to provide key clues to understanding the etiology of criminal behavior in all communities, but particularly in those heavily populated by racial minorities. After reviewing the numerous perspectives, it was revealed that they all suffer from a variety of shortcomings; some have more glaring weaknesses than others.

In sum, many of the biologically oriented theories reviewed either directly or indirectly point to some race and crime linkage. Nevertheless, for over a century, opponents of such approaches have countered with alternative sociological perspectives; some are reviewed in the next chapter.

3

SOCIAL DISORGANIZATION
AND STRAIN PERSPECTIVES
ON RACE AND CRIME

This chapter aims to illuminate those social disorganization and strain perspectives that have been used to explain racial and ethnic differences in offending and victimization patterns. To begin, the chapter discusses W.E.B. Du Bois's pioneering research effort in Philadelphia. Following this review, the chapter focuses on the social disorganization perspective developed at the well-known University of Chicago's "school of sociology." The chapter closes with a review of Robert Merton's strain theory and its derivatives.

Sociological explanations for crime in general have existed for nearly two centuries. The earliest work using this approach is often credited to the "Cartographic School" led by A. M. Guerry and Adolphe Quetelet (Sutherland and Cressey 1960, p. 53). In fact, Quetelet is believed to have produced the first scientific work on crime (see Quetelet 1833/1984). In his later scholarship, Quetelet (1842) examined the social correlates of crime including age, social class, poverty, education level, and race. On the topic of race, Quetelet (1842) noted the dispersion of distinct racial groups within France. He then highlighted the unique characteristics of each racial group and how they were tied to their involvement in crime. It is noteworthy that several decades after the publication of Quetelet's work, biological notions related to crime were being espoused internationally.

Numerous later scholars from around the globe also criticized and countered the biological approach with sociological analyses of social problems, including crime. In Europe, Charles Booth's *Life and Labour of the People in London* (1889) represented an early comprehensive sociological analysis of social problems. In the Caribbean, Haitian scholar Antenor Firmin produced the pioneering volume, *The Equality of the Human Races* (1885), to dispel the prevailing biological determinism, which, as noted in Chapter 2, argued the innate inferiority of persons of African descent. In the United States, Jane Addams, social activist and scholar, with her publication of the *Hull House Maps and Papers* (1895) used a distinctively sociological approach to examine and contextualize the conditions of those persons residing in the Chicago settlement homes that she cofounded for the underprivileged (Moyer 2001, pp. 300–4).

In response to the growing concerns in urban cities in America, universities began to create departments of sociology to study the mounting social problems. The first set of sociology departments founded in America before 1900 included those at the University of Chicago (1892) and Atlanta University (1897) (Himes 1949; Green and Driver 1976). This was significant because some of the pioneering early sociological works related to race and crime emanated from these two departments. In the late 1890s, Atlanta University hired W. E. B. Du Bois, who was finishing up his pioneering volume on Philadelphia (Du Bois 1899), to head its sociology department and direct sociological research on African Americans.

W. E. B. Du Bois and the Development of Sociological Criminology

Described as a founding father of American sociology (Anderson 1996) and of criminology (Gabbidon 2001; Hayward, Maruna, and Mooney 2009; Jones 2009), Du Bois's research, first in Philadelphia and then in Atlanta, paved the way for the development of sociological criminology in general (Gabbidon 2002, 2007) and, more specifically, sociological perspectives on race and crime. Du Bois was invited to Philadelphia in the late 1890s at the urging of Quaker Susan Wharton, who convinced her neighbor Dr. Charles Custis Harrison, the acting provost of the University of Pennsylvania, to hire Du Bois to carry out a study of the notorious Seventh Ward of the city. After hiring Du Bois as a temporary "assistant in sociology," Lewis (1993) noted that "Harrison drew up Du Bois's charge: 'We want to know precisely how this class of people live; what occupations they follow; from what occupations they are excluded; how many of their children go to school; and to ascertain every fact which will throw light on this social problem'" (p. 188).

According to Lewis, "Du Bois knew that his sponsors held a theory about the race to be studied" (p. 189). What was that theory? Du Bois felt that the concern emanated out of the belief that "[t]he city was 'going to the dogs because of the crime and venality of its Negro citizens. Something is wrong with a race that is responsible for so much crime,' the theory ran, and 'strong remedies are called for'" (Du Bois as quoted in Lewis 1993, p. 189). Even with this in mind, Du Bois was intent on conducting a comprehensive study. After living in the area and studying the community for more than a year, he pointed to several possible explanations for crime among African Americans. First, he wrote:

> Crime is a phenomenon of organized social life, and is the open rebellion of an individual against his social environment. Naturally then, if men are suddenly transported from one environment to another; the result is lack of harmony with the new conditions; lack of harmony with the new physical surroundings leading to disease and death or modification of physique; lack of harmony with social surroundings leading to crime.
>
> (1899/1996, p. 235)

Du Bois felt that the mass migration from the south to the north produced problems of adjustment for African Americans who were previously only familiar with southern life. His ideas were in line with the concept of social disorganization, which is discussed later. Like Quetelet earlier, Du Bois, after laying out and mapping the characteristics of the ward (see Figure 3.1), also pointed to variables such as age, unemployment, and poverty to explain criminality in the Seventh Ward. Du Bois also pointed to discrimination, noting that blacks were arrested for less cause than whites, served longer sentences for similar crimes, and were subject to employment discrimination (see Du Bois 1899, pp. 235–68, 350–2).

On the matter of race prejudice and crime, Du Bois wrote: "It would, of course, be idle to assert that most of the Negro crime was caused by prejudice" (1899, p. 350). However, he continued by asserting:

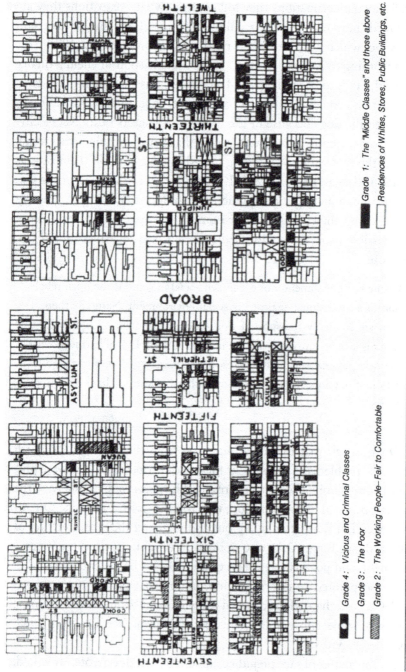

Figure 3.1 Du Bois's mapping of the characteristics of the Seventh Ward.

Grade 1: The "Middle Classes" and those above

Residences of Whites, Stores, Public Buildings, etc.

Grade 4: Vicious and Criminal Classes

Grade 3: The Poor

Grade 2: The Working People– Fair to Comfortable

[I]t is certain that Negro prejudice in cities like Philadelphia has been a vast factor in aiding and abetting all other causes which impel a half-developed race to recklessness and excess. Certainly a great amount of crime can be without a doubt traced to the discrimination against Negro boys and girls in the matter of employment. Or to put it differently, Negro prejudice costs the city something.

(p. 351)

Du Bois closed this discussion by declaring the futility of emphasizing education when getting one, at least for Negroes, will only lead to "disappointment and humiliation." Moreover, he posed the following two questions to readers (1899, p. 351): "How long can a city teach its black children that the road to success is to have a white face? How long can a city do this and escape the inevitable penalty?"

Other early studies of African American communities conducted largely by black scholars would echo similar sentiments on crime (Miller 1908; Work 1900; Wright 1912/1969), with some scholars going as far as to suggest that because of the deep-seated societal discrimination contributing to crime in African American communities, whites were the "ultimate criminals" (Grimke 1915). Only recently, though, have contemporary mainstream white scholars begun to take notice of Du Bois's pioneering work on crime and justice (see, for example, Bursik 2009; Hanson 2010; Rafter 2009; Unnever et al. 2009; Unnever and Gabbidon 2011).

Before Du Bois completed the manuscript based on his research in Philadelphia, as noted earlier, he was approached by Horace Bumstead, the president of Atlanta University, to direct a research program centered on exploring various aspects of African American life. Prior to his arrival in 1897, two studies had been completed, but according to some observers, they paled in comparison to the type of research program Du Bois envisioned and eventually carried out at Atlanta University (see Wright 2005). During his tenure there, he continued to write about crime with his analyses becoming more conflict oriented in nature (these views are presented in Chapter 6). Furthermore, according to Gabbidon (1999, 2007), Williams (2005, 2006, 2009), and Wright (2002a, 2002b, 2002c, 2005, 2006, 2008, 2012), Du Bois's program at Atlanta University produced the first school of social scientific research, which was later duplicated at the University of Chicago. As evidenced by Du Bois's earlier passages from *The Philadelphia Negro*, the major theoretical underpinning of his work was social disorganization, which also became the primary theoretical foundation of the research in Chicago.

Social Disorganization

The Chicago School: Social Disorganization and the Ecological Approach

During the late 1800s and early 1900s, northern cities such as Chicago were also experiencing the same social problems as Philadelphia because of population booms caused by "waves of immigrants, displaced farm workers, and blacks fleeing the rural south" (Lilly et al. 2002, p. 32). With unparalleled philanthropic support from numerous foundations (Blumer 1984), by the 1920s the University of Chicago had put together a formidable cadre of scholars to investigate the social ills plaguing the city. Together, these scholars combined their ideas to formulate what is now known as the "Chicago School."

One of the scholars recruited to Chicago was Ernest W. Burgess, who, before coming to Chicago, had previously conducted a study examining juvenile delinquency in a small city (Burgess 1915). From this early work one sees the foundations of the Chicago program. Burgess examined the seven wards of the small city and pointed to the following to explain the high levels of delinquency in the fourth ward: "low-grade" home conditions, poverty, and the "distracting" and "demoralizing" influence of the business on the city's youth (p. 726). A decade later, outlining the ecological approach, as it became known, Burgess (1925) stated that towns and cities "expand radially from its central business district—on the map" (p. 50).

In conjunction with the ecological approach, another mainstay of the Chicago School was the use of the concept of social disorganization to explain the etiology of delinquency in urban areas (e.g. Frazier 1932). According to Elliott and Merrill (1934), social disorganization is defined as "a breakdown in the equilibrium of forces, a decay in the social structure, so that old habits and forms of social control no longer function effectively" (p. 20). Combined, the ecological approach and social disorganization were shown to be a popular and powerful explanation for crime and delinquency in African American communities

(Brinton 1932; Diggs 1940; Frazier 1937; Moses 1936), as well as other diverse communities such as Honolulu, where the population included Hawaiians, Portuguese, Puerto Ricans, Koreans, Japanese, Chinese, and numerous other ethnic groups (see Lind 1930a, 1930b).

According to the combined theory, Zone I, the "Loop," is where the central business district is located (Burgess 1925, p. 55; see Figure 3.2). Zone II is the "zone in transition" or the "slum," where there is a mixture of residences and businesses. Zone III is the workingman's zone, where workers who previously lived in Zone II now reside. Zone IV is the residential zone. This is where you would find "high-class apartment buildings or exclusive 'restricted' districts of single-family dwellings" (p. 50). Zone V is the outer commuters' zone or the suburbs, which are typically "within a thirty- to sixty-minute ride [from] the central business district" (p. 50). As predicted by the theory, the further one

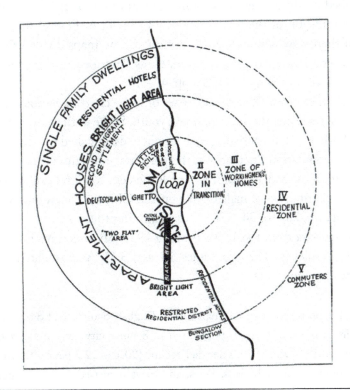

Figure 3.2 Urban areas. (From R. E. Park, E. W. Burgess, and R. D. McKenzie, *The City.* Heritage of Sociology Series. University of Chicago Press, 1925, 1967. With permission.)

moves away from the center city or Zone I, the more crime will decrease (Burgess 1925). More specifically, Burgess notes that Zone II or the "zone in transition" will produce the most social problems. He wrote: "Where mobility is the greatest, and where in consequence primary controls break down completely . . . there develop areas of demoralization, of promiscuity, and vice" (p. 59). Further, he observed that "in our studies of the city it is found that areas of mobility are also the regions in which are found juvenile delinquency, boys' gangs, crime, poverty, wife desertion, divorce, abandoned infants, vice" (p. 59).

Using the aforementioned postulates as their foundation, Clifford Shaw and Henry D. McKay, who worked at the University of Chicago's Institute for Juvenile Research but were not faculty members, put the theory to test by examining juvenile delinquency. From their efforts they produced *Juvenile Delinquency and Urban Areas* (1942), which was described by Burgess as "a magnum opus in criminology" (1942, p. ix). In the tradition of the earlier work by Quetelet in France, they made use of their now famous maps of Chicago. The maps divided the city into several concentric circles or zones, as described in the previously reviewed work of Burgess (1925, pp. 47–62).

In all, there were 20 different types of maps charting various aspects of Chicago's residents and delinquent youth. Some of the maps outlined neighborhood characteristics, such as where demolished buildings were located, population fluctuations, the percentage of families on welfare, distribution of median monthly rentals, percent foreign born or Negro, and the distribution of male delinquents in Chicago (Shaw and McKay 1942, pp. 25, 28, 30, 34, 35). After examining these various maps and reviewing data from the 1880s through 1930, Shaw and McKay found striking results (p. 152; see Tables 3.1 and 3.2). As postulated by the theory, they found that

> . . . the proportions of Germans, Irish, English-Scotch, and Scandinavians in the foreign-born population in 8 inner-city areas underwent, between 1884 and 1930, a decided decline (90.1 to 12.2 per cent); while the proportions of Italians, Poles, and Slavs increased . . . the 8 areas maintained, throughout these decades, approximately the same rates of delinquents relative to other areas.
>
> (pp. 150–1)

Table 3.1 Distribution of nationalities in the foreign-born population at intervals from 1884–1930 for eight Chicago areas combined[a]

Country of Birth	1884[b]	1898	1920	1930
Germany	46.2	35.9	7.2	6.2
Ireland	22.2	18.7	2.8	2.3
England and Scotland	4.8	3.2	1.5	1.6
Scandinavia	16.9	19.8	2.4	2.0
Czechoslovakia	3.5	6.2	2.8	2.8
Italy	0.4	2.4	21.6	25.5
Poland	2.6	4.2	29.2	34.0
Slavic countries	3.1	2.2	19.6	14.0
All others	2.3	7.4	22.9	11.6
Total	100.0	100.0	100.0	100.0

[a] These have been areas of first immigrant settlement throughout the period studied.
[b] Area 91 is not included in computations for this column because it was outside the boundaries of Chicago in 1884.
(From C. Shaw and H. D. McKay, *Juvenile Delinquency and Urban Areas*, University of Chicago, 1942. With permission.)

Table 3.2 Percentage distribution of delinquent boys by fathers' countries of birth for each fifth year 1900–1930[a]

Country of Father's Birth	1900	1905	1910	1915	1920	1925	1930
U.S. white	16.0	19.0	16.5	16.5	22.0	21.7	19.5
U.S. Negro	4.7	5.1	5.5	6.2	9.9	17.1	21.7
Germany	20.4	19.5	15.5	11.0	6.3	3.5	1.9
Ireland	18.7	15.4	12.3	11.7	6.1	3.1	1.3
Italy	5.1	8.3	7.9	10.1	12.7	12.8	11.7
Poland	15.1	15.7	18.6	22.1	24.5	21.9	21.0
England and Scotland	3.4	3.0	2.5	2.6	0.9	0.7	0.6
Scandinavia	3.8	5.6	2.9	2.8	2.3	0.5	0.8
Austria	0.1	0.3	0.9	1.3	0.8	2.2	1.7
Lithuania	0.1	0.3	1.1	2.9	2.2	3.9	3.8
Czechoslovakia	4.6	4.3	5.5	3.0	2.2	2.8	4.2
All others	8.0	4.5	11.8	10.8	9.1	9.8	11.8
Total	100.0	100.0	100.0	100.0	100.0	100.0	100.0

[a] Juvenile Court of Cook County.
(From C. Shaw and H. D. McKay, *Juvenile Delinquency and Urban Areas*, University of Chicago, 1942. With permission.)

In the end, they concluded that the higher delinquency rates in Zones I and II were caused by the presence of social disorganization. More specifically, these areas were characterized by the following conditions: (1) fluctuating populations; (2) significant numbers of families on welfare; (3) families renting; (4) several ethnic groups in one area; (5) high truancy rates; (6) high infant mortality rates; (7) high levels of unemployment; (8) large numbers of condemned buildings; and (9) a higher percentage of foreign-born and Negro heads of families (Shaw and McKay 1942, Chapters 2–7). They closed by stating:

> The fact that in Chicago the rates of delinquents for many years have remained relatively constant in the areas adjacent to centers of commerce and heavy industry, despite successive changes in the nativity and nationality composition of the population, supports emphatically the conclusion that the delinquency-producing factors are inherent in the community.
>
> (p. 435)

While often overlooked by scholars, Parts III and IV of Shaw and McKay's 1942 work examined the utility of social disorganization for explaining delinquency in other major cities across the United States (e.g. Philadelphia, Boston, Baltimore, etc.). The results from research in these varying cities found support for social disorganization and the ecological approach. Only in those cities from the Pacific Northwest where there were heavy concentrations of Orientals (Asian Americans) were there any divergences from the theory.

In later studies, Norman Hayner, a 1923 graduate of the University of Chicago, used social disorganization to explain crime among Asian Americans. Hayner (1938) compared the situation of the Japanese, Chinese, and Filipinos in the Pacific Northwest. Overall, he noted each of the groups had little criminality in comparison to whites. However, he decided to look at variations among the three Asian American populations. According to Hayner, the Japanese had low rates of crime and delinquency because of their closely integrated families, the efficiency and organization of the community, and the lack of acquaintance with American ways. The closely integrated families were a characteristic from their home countries. The organization of the community reflected the concern of the community for their youth. At that time, they maintained language schools to keep youngsters busy after their regular school days. Community attitude concerning crime was so strong that, according to Hayner's research, those caught engaging in crime would likely commit suicide before facing the community (1938, p. 911). Finally, some Japanese steered their youth away from American traditions because there was the belief that increasing Americanization would lead to increasing levels of crime and delinquency (p. 911). In general, the other two groups had more crime than the Japanese; this was explained as a result of their becoming too Americanized or of a population imbalance between males and females, often due to earlier government immigration restrictions. Hayner's (1942) research a few years later on Native Americans also found that increased Americanization resulted in increased crime.

Following these early pioneering studies, the social disorganization perspective and ecological approach continued to be relevant for researchers seeking to explain crime in urban areas and/or race and crime (see Cavan 1959; Cochrane 1949; Diggs 1950; McKeown 1948; Moses 1947; Toby 1957; Wattenberg 1954; Wattenberg and Moir 1957). However, few additional major tests of the perspective were conducted until the 1980s. The next section reviews some of the contemporary studies that have reinvigorated the perspective.

Contemporary Research on Communities and Crime

Since these early articles, scholars have continued to explore the viability of social disorganization to explain crime, particularly in urban areas (Bursik and Grasmick 1993a, 1993b). Sampson (1987) found a connection between black male joblessness and economic deprivation and violent crime. This connection was an indirect one mediated by family disruption (e.g. female-headed households). Another important article by Sampson and Groves (1989) expanded the theory and found considerable support for it. Building on this prior research and the important research of William Julius Wilson (1987), Sampson and Wilson (1995) posited a theory targeted at explaining race and crime with structural and cultural constructs. As they stated:

> [Our] basic thesis is that macro social patterns of residential inequality give rise to the social isolation and ecological concentration of the truly disadvantaged, which in turn leads to structural barriers and cultural

adaptations that undermine social organization and hence the control of crime. This thesis is grounded in what is actually an old idea in criminology that has been overlooked in the race and crime debate—the importance of communities.

(p. 38)

The theory draws heavily on two of Wilson's concepts from *The Truly Disadvantaged* (1987). The first, concentration effects, speaks to the fact that whites and blacks live in considerably different areas. In his research, Wilson found that many African Americans live in areas where there are significant concentrations of poverty. Once neighborhoods reach this point, working-class and middle-class African Americans abandon these areas. This removes important "social buffers" (role models) who show neighborhood kids that there are successful people who go to work day in and day out. When all the "social buffers" have abandoned a community, Wilson suggested the remaining individuals are in a state of "social isolation," which he defined as "the lack of contact or of sustained interaction with individuals and institutions that represent mainstream society" (p. 60). The notion of social isolation adds the cultural component to the theory. By not being exposed to mainstream individuals and institutions, socially isolated people tend to develop their own norms within these isolated areas. In a series of articles, Lauren Krivo and Ruth Peterson have tested some of the ideas of Wilson (1987, 1996) and Sampson and Wilson (1995) and found considerable support for them (see Krivo and Peterson 1996, 2000; Peterson and Krivo 1993, 1999, 2010).

Sampson and Bean (2006) called for a revision of the theory to account for the following protective mechanisms related to concentrated immigration (most notably, involving Latinos): extra-neighborhood and city-wide spatial dynamics, which they believe "create[s] racial inequalities that are potentially more consequential than the ones already in play within neighborhoods" (p. 32); and, "unproductive cultural" practices that are in line with the work of Elijah Anderson (for more on Anderson's work, see Chapter 4).

Scholars have also applied social disorganization to nonurban areas and with populations other than African Americans. For example, studies have found both strong (Bachman 1991) and mixed support (Lanier and Huff-Corzine 2006) when social disorganization has been applied to Native Americans.

Latino Criminology

In addition to Native Americans, social disorganization theory has also been applied to Latinos. Ramiro Martinez, along with his colleague Matthew Lee, has led the way in the development of what might be termed "Latino criminology" (see Russell 1992 for an explication of black criminology). That is, Martinez and Lee have led the way in adding analyses of people of Latino descent into the lexicon of criminology (Peterson and Krivo 2005, p. 345). Moving beyond the traditional research on Latinos, which has tended to focus on gangs (in and out of prisons), these scholars have paved the way for the consideration of the nature and scope of Latino involvement in crime and violence. Three areas of this research have made a significant contribution to the race/ ethnicity and crime literature.

First, Martinez examines violence among multiple racial/ethnic groups and finds that, contrary to conventional wisdom, Latinos do not commit homicides at levels as high as those of blacks or as low as those of whites. Referred to as the "Latino Paradox" this recurring finding reveals that even though Latinos typically face similar social disadvantage as other groups they do not suffer the same negative effects, including elevated levels of crime (Sampson 2008). For example, after examining homicide trends in five cities (Houston, Chicago, El Paso, Miami, and San Diego), Martinez, in his pioneering work, *Latino Homicide* (2002), consistently found that their patterns typically fell between the two groups. Of this he wrote "*Latinos have lower homicide rates than African Americans because they exhibit higher levels of social integration, especially as measured by labor market involvement*" (p. 137; emphasis in original). So while this research has found some support for social disorganization and relative deprivation models (see Martinez 2003; Lee and Martinez 2002), it is clear that there are differences among racial/ethnic groups that have previously been ignored (Cancino et al. 2009).

The role of immigration on crime trends is the second area that has benefited from the work of these scholars. Citizens and public officials expressed concern about crime waves that were believed to be linked to

Latino immigrants. However, Martinez and his collaborators (Martinez and Lee 1998; Martinez 2000; Lee et al. 2001; Martinez and Valenzuela 2006) have found that the current trends regarding the immigration/crime linkage mirror past research on the topic (see Abbott 1931; Taft 1933, 1936; von Hentig 1945), for which Martinez (2002) noted: *"the major finding of a century of research on immigration and crime is that while immigrants occasionally displayed tremendous variations across time and place in their criminal involvement, contrary to popular opinion they nearly always exhibit lower crime rates than native groups"* (p. 22; emphasis in original).

Current research continues to support the notion that immigration does not increase—but actually reduces some violent crimes in Latino communities (Feldmeyer 2009; MacDonald, Hipp, and Gill 2013; Martinez, Stowell, and Lee 2010; Velez 2009). The final area of significance relates to labeling theory, which is presented in Chapter 5.

Collective Efficacy

In the late 1990s, Sampson et al. (1997) conducted research to determine why urban communities differ in their levels of crime. From their research, they concluded that crime was related to the amount of collective efficacy found in a particular community. They defined collective efficacy as "social cohesion among neighbors combined with their willingness to intervene on the behalf of the common good" (p. 918). In short, in the communities where residents do not retreat behind their locked doors, but rather actively look out for one another, there is a diminished likelihood that they will have many of the ills found in similar urban areas. Sampson and his colleagues put their idea to the test and found support for the role of collective efficacy (Sampson et al. 1999; Morenoff et al. 2001; Sampson 2012; see also Browning 2002). Other researchers have also found support for collective efficacy in general (Rukus and Warner 2013; Warner 2014), as well as research involving Asian American intimate homicides (Wu 2009). Moreover, some researchers have applied the concept to racial profiling and shown its importance in explaining the prevalence of such practices in certain communities (Parker et al. 2004). Additional tests of collective efficacy have shown either mixed (Almgren 2005; Sabol et al. 2004; St. Jean 2007) or no support (Kirk 2008).

Social Disorganization and Mass Incarceration

Rose and Clear (1998) also present an important expansion of social disorganization theory. They propose that the recent reliance on the removal of offenders from their communities has not reduced the level of social disorganization in communities. Conversely, they argue that, in some communities, the removal of offenders actually exacerbates the level of social disorganization. More specifically, Rose and Clear argue that mass incarceration increases social disorganization in three ways. First, it exerts an impact on the "socioeconomic composition of the neighborhood by influencing vital local resources, such as labor and marriage markets" (p. 450). Second, they suggest that incarceration influences mobility in and out of the neighborhood: "Every entrant into prison is someone exiting a neighborhood; every release from prison returns someone to a neighborhood" (p. 450). Finally, they note that incarceration affects the heterogeneity of communities. Here, while Rose and Clear suggest that there is generally racial homogeneity in the poor and minority communities where many of these offenders return, they propose that incarceration actually affects the cultural heterogeneity. As a result of individuals' exposure to prison, Rose and Clear (1998) surmise that "upon their return to the community, the stronger deviant orientation of prison releases increases local cultural heterogeneity, thereby increasing disorganization" (p. 450). Rose, Clear, and colleagues have tested the basic premise of their modifications of the theory and found support (Clear et al. 2001; Clear et al. 2003). In recent years there have been attempts to further clarify both the inequalities in the justice system as well as the detrimental impact of mass incarceration on communities of color (Alexander 2010; Christian and Thomas 2009; Clear 2007; Mauer 2006; Wakefield and Wildeman 2014; Western 2006; Western and Wildeman 2009).

Social Disorganization and Middle-Class Communities

Both social disorganization and collective efficacy generally speak to high crime in urban areas. Because not all African Americans live in high-crime urban areas, some have wondered if those in middle-class areas also encounter higher crime rates than those in similarly situated white areas. To investigate this very question, Pattillo (1998) conducted participant observation and 28 in-depth interviews in one such area of

Chicago. She found that "middle class black areas tend to be nestled between areas that are less economically stable and have higher crime rates" (p. 751). In addition, many of those black residents who make it to these middle-class areas are "unstable" middle-class residents and struggle to maintain their status. In some instances, they cross over the line into crime to do so. Therefore, Pattillo also found that such residents were "given a degree of latitude to operate in the neighborhood" (p. 770). Based on the premise of social organization, which, along with being goal oriented, "stresses the importance of kin and neighborly ties for the social control of crime and disorder," Pattillo showed how these communities maintain order while allowing "the integration of licit and illicit networks both working toward common goals, with variant strategies" (p. 770).

Hassett-Walker (2009) recently examined delinquency among black middle-class youth. Using both cross-sectional and longitudinal data, her research found differences for contributors to delinquency among middle-class and more affluent youth. As she noted, "Parenting variables—particularly positive parenting (e.g., playing together, helping with homework, praising child)—had more of an impact on Black youth from mid-class families" (p. 202). In higher income families, she found that conflict with their parents and the social capital of their parents influenced delinquency. Additional analyses found that positive parenting practices served as a protective factor against delinquency for all middle-class youth regardless of race/ethnicity (p. 202). In contrast to the research of Pattillo, Hassett-Walker (2009) also found that "neighborhood factors may play less of a role in influencing the behavior of middle class Black youth" (p. 204). In line with differential association theory, her longitudinal research found that having a delinquent peer was a significant predictor of crime (p. 206). In closing, Hassett-Walker called on criminologists to devote more research to the study of middle-class crime.

General Criticisms of Social Disorganization Theory

All in all, there has been considerable support for social disorganization theory. There have been several persistent criticisms of the theory, however. The most often cited weakness of the social disorganization perspective is the so-called ecological fallacy. This refers to the fact that the perspective is usually tested at the aggregate level but researchers still use the data to make assertions about individuals. The theory also does not explain how certain groups, such as Asian and Jewish communities, maintained low levels of crime and delinquency even though they lived in areas that might be categorized as socially disorganized (Bohm 2001; Lanier and Henry 1998). Moreover, while there are high levels of delinquency in urban areas characterized by social disorganization, the theory does not explain why, in general, most juveniles in these areas do not become delinquent.

Scholars have also noted that the theory "tends to downplay the significance of ethnic and cultural factors" (Shoemaker 1996, p. 83). A related criticism is that some scholars have taken issue with the term "disorganization." Of this concern, Miller et al. (2008) have noted that "to suggest that a community is disorganization might be inappropriate if poor and lower-class neighborhoods are simply differently organized. . . . Crime then is merely a byproduct of the culture . . ." (p. 98). Finally, the theory does not fully transfer to other international contexts (Ebbe 1989; Ouimet 2000).

Felson (2008) has also argued that social disorganization cannot explain why there "are racial differences in violent crime and not crime generally" (p. 3). After posing the question, Felson (2008) then argues that "Perhaps one can make the argument that violent crime tends to be more serious and, for some reason, disorganized communities only produce serious crime" (p. 3). He notes, however, that this is not supported by the respected and widely analyzed Add Health dataset. In the end, he points to the need for a theory of violence to explain racial differences in offending (see also Felson et al. 2008).

Despite these criticisms, social disorganization theory remains popular and has continued to be supported by the empirical literature. Another sociological perspective that has garnered significant attention is strain theory. Robert Merton formulated his anomie theory just as the Chicago School was reaching prominence. Even so, the perspective emerged as a classic perspective and has had a wide influence on the social sciences. The theory is reviewed in the following section.

Strain/Anomie Theory

In the same year as the publication of Sellin's classic work on culture conflict (see Chapter 6), another important theory was presented. The 1938 publication of Robert K. Merton's "Social Structure and Anomie" produced what is likely one of the most cited theories in criminology: strain or anomie theory (Lilly et al. 2002). The theory was influenced by the classic work of Emile Durkheim, who first made use of the word anomie in a criminological sense. According to Akers (2000), "Durkheim (1951[1897]) used the term anomie to refer to a state of normlessness or lack of social regulation in modern society as one condition that promotes higher rates of suicide" (p. 143). Merton's (1938) work showed that in every society, there are "culturally defined goals, purposes, and interest" (p. 672). He also suggested that there are generally "acceptable modes of achieving these goals" (p. 673).

Figure 3.3 shows a schematic representation of Merton's theory. In the figure, when someone accepted a particular tenet of his perspective he denoted it with a plus sign (+), and when they did not, he referred to it as "elimination" or rejection, which was denoted by a minus sign (−). In addition, according to Merton's scheme, a plus and minus sign combined (±) represented "rejection and substitution of new goals and standards" (Merton 1938, p. 676). Merton argued that the majority of persons in most societies were "conformists" or citizens who adhered to the cultural goal of economic success and the institutional means to achieve it (e.g. work, education, etc.). Even so, he suggested that "innovators" were those citizens who adhered to society's cultural goal but found an alternative means to achieve this goal (e.g. crime).

	Culture Goals	Institutionalized Means
I. Conformity	+	+
II. Innovation	+	−
III. Ritualism	−	+
IV. Retreatism	−	−
V. Rebellion	±	±

Figure 3.3 Merton's typology of modes of individual adaptation. (From R. Merton, "Social Structure and Anomie," *American Sociological Review*, 3: 672–82, 1938. With permission.)

Ritualists were those persons who participated in the institutional means for success, but were not actively in pursuit of the American Dream. Another adaptation included "retreatists," who Merton (1938) wrote were

> *in* society but not *of* it. Sociologically, these constitute the true "aliens." Not sharing the common frame of orientations, they can be included within the societal population merely in a fictional sense. In this category are *some* of the activities of psychotics, psychoneurotics, chronic artists, pariahs, outcasts, vagrants, vagabonds, tramps, chronic drunkards and drug addicts.
>
> (p. 677; emphases in original)

Finally, those falling under Merton's (1938) last mode of adaptation, rebellion, were people who sought to "introduce a 'new social order'" (p. 678). Such a new social order would involve a radical change to the existing social structure, which would likely deemphasize economic success.

In general, Merton recognized that "the extreme emphasis upon the accumulation of wealth as a symbol of success in our own society mitigates against the completely effective control of the institutionally regulated modes of acquiring a fortune" (p. 675). In short, in pursuit of the "American Dream," some people turn to alternative means to secure this cultural goal (Merton 1938). When applying the theory to race and crime, Merton recognized the special case of African Americans, writing:

> Certain elements of the Negro population have assimilated the dominant caste's values of pecuniary success and advancement, but they also recognize that social ascent is at present restricted to their own caste almost exclusively. The pressures upon the Negro which would otherwise derive from the structural inconsistencies we have noticed are hence not identical to those upon lower class whites.
>
> (p. 680)

Merton understood that the strain experienced by African Americans was unlike any other in American society. Basically, no matter how much they sought to achieve the American Dream, they could never "legitimately" reach the status of whites, so they maintained lower aspirations and were resigned to achieving a lower level of success and advancement. Such a situation likely contributed to a strain that resulted in some of them becoming innovators and "retreatists."

Testing Merton's Strain Theory

Early tests of Merton's classic theory were generally supportive (Cole and Zuckerman 1964; Hill 1959; Wyatt 1943). Epps's 1967 test of the theory was revealing. Using a racially diverse sample of high school students from Seattle (159 white students, 111 African Americans, and 76 Asian Americans), he tested several hypotheses that looked at whether there were differences in delinquency and aspirations by race and class (Epps 1967, p. 25). Epps did find some differences between the occupational expectations and aspirations, and the educational aspirations of the students. In all cases, whites and Asian Americans had higher aspirations and expectations than African Americans (p. 24).

More than 30 years after Epps's research, Cernkovich et al. (2000) tested whether African Americans still subscribe to the American Dream and whether this is related to their involvement in criminal behavior. Making use of longitudinal data involving African Americans and whites from private households and an institutional sample (both from Toledo, Ohio), the authors found that

> African Americans maintain a very strong commitment to the American dream. Blacks report higher levels of commitment to economic success goals than do their white counterparts and indicate that they are prepared to work harder and sacrifice more to realize them. Even though the young black adults in our study report low incomes and are more likely to be unemployed than are whites, they continue to maintain a very strong commitment to the American dream.
>
> (pp. 158–9)

Their study, which also partially tested social control theory, found support for strain theory—but only in the case of whites. That is, many of the variables used to test strain theory "were significant correlates of crime among . . . Whites in our sample but not among African Americans" (Cernkovich et al. 2000, p. 161)—a finding that the authors could not explain, but curiously implied that the African American participants might not have been forthright with their answers (p. 161).

Applying strain theory to Latinos (primarily Mexican and Puerto Rican), whites, and African Americans, McClusky (2002) used the Denver (n = 345) and Rochester (n = 578) youth surveys to test a variety of hypotheses connected to Merton's strain theory, and Cloward and Ohlin's well-known expansion of the theory (1960), which is discussed in Chapter 4. Her overarching goal "was to test the assumption that strain theory is generalizable to all ethnic groups" (p. 184). Taking into account Latino culture (e.g. family involvement, acculturation, religiousness) and things such as marginality and discrimination, McClusky found that "the theory has been accepted as a general explanatory model, and for the most part, it provided an adequate explanation of delinquency when all males were examined as a whole" (p. 198). However, when McClusky analyzed each group separately, she reported that there was a "weakened delinquent peer influence within the Latino population. In addition, the adequacy of traditional strain theory in explaining Latino delinquency is relatively weak" (p. 198). This led her to conclude that there were differences among ethnic groups that might require the development of a more culturally specific model (p. 198).

Maximization and the Expansion of Strain Theory

Murphy and Robinson (2008) have expanded Merton's original typology related to strain theory. The authors suggest that lacking in Merton's original formulation is a mode of adaptation that takes into account the situation in which individuals simultaneously use "legitimate or institutionalized means and illegitimate means in pursuit of the so-called American Dream" (p. 502). To fill this hole in Merton's theory, the authors create an additional mode of adaptation, maximization (see Table 3.3). This is the person who might work in a legitimate job and also engage in illegal activities. Much of the examples the authors use to highlight maximization includes corporate crimes that typically involve legitimate industries—often owned and operated by whites—that engage in deviant activities in pursuit of making more money to achieve the American Dream (Robinson and Murphy 2009).

In their discussion of the mode of adaptation, Murphy and Robinson suggest that citizens tend to be sympathetic to these corporate

Table 3.3 Merton's modes of adaptation to anomic strain, expanded to include non-institutionalized means

Modes of adaption	Cultural goals	Institutional means	Criminality
Conformity	Accept	Accept	Reject
Innovation	Accept	Reject	Accept
Ritualism	Reject	Accept	Reject
Retreatism	Reject	Reject	Accept
Rebellion	Reject/Replace	Reject/Replace	Accept
Maximization	Accept	Accept	Accept

offenders—even in the face of evidence that their actions have, at times, resulted in death. Though in its infancy, this expansion likely also has relevancy to contextualize the activities of some racial and ethnic minorities who often, because of high unemployment rates, move between legitimate and illegitimate activities, but likely go for periods where they use both in pursuit of the American Dream. More research is needed to flesh out the nuances of this application of maximization. Even so, the authors have presented a fresh new direction for strain theory.

General Criticisms of Strain Theory

Several weaknesses have been leveled at Merton's strain theory. In an exhaustive critique of sociological theories, Kornhauser (1978) argued that the pursuit of monetary success is not culturally induced. In her view, such a pursuit is a natural part of most societies. In addition, her review of the extant literature revealed little empirical support for the theory. While Bernard (1984) countered some of her criticisms and found support for the theory in the empirical literature, others have noted some additional concerns. Bohm (2001) noted that anomie theories have a middle-class bias; they presume that lower-class individuals commit crimes in an effort to reach middle-class status. As was seen by some of the research reviewed, and the emphasis on corporate offenders by Murphy and Robinson (2008) in their application of maximization, this is not always the case.

Another persistent criticism is that the theories do not explain white-collar and government crimes. Given that people at this level have already achieved middle-class status, why, then, do they engage in crime? Even in its various incarnations, the theory is generally silent on this issue. Bohm also suggested that the theory suffers from over-prediction. As he put it: "If strain is caused by the inability to achieve the American dream and is as widespread as Merton implies, then there ought to be much more crime than occurs" (p. 80). Given the numerous criticisms of Merton's theory, Robert Agnew revised the theory.

Agnew's General Strain Theory

Robert Agnew's popular revision (1992, 2006) of Merton's theory has also been used to explain race and crime (see Figure 3.4). Agnew's General Strain Theory (GST) renewed interest in strain by adding that the removal (or loss) of positive or introduction of negative stimuli into an environment can cause a strain such that, as with blocked opportunities, the removal or loss of positive stimuli from an individual can result in criminal behavior. As for the removal of positively valued stimuli, Agnew (1992) specifically pointed to the following: "loss of a boyfriend/girlfriend, the death of or serious illness of a friend, moving to a new school district, the divorce/separation of one's parents, suspension from school, and the presence of a variety of adverse conditions at work" (p. 57).

Turning to the presentation of negative stimuli, Agnew (1992) pointed to the following: child abuse and neglect; criminal victimization; physical punishment; negative relations with parents; negative

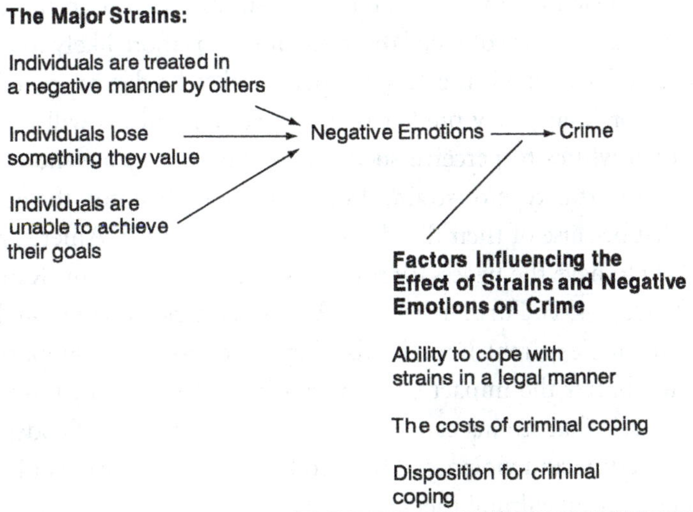

The Major Strains:

Individuals are treated in a negative manner by others

Individuals lose something they value ———→ Negative Emotions ———→ Crime

Individuals are unable to achieve their goals

Factors Influencing the Effect of Strains and Negative Emotions on Crime

Ability to cope with strains in a legal manner

The costs of criminal coping

Disposition for criminal coping

Figure 3.4 The central propositions of General Strain Theory

relations with peers; adverse or negative school experience; stressful life events; verbal threats and insults; physical pain; unpleasant odors; disgusting scenes; noise; heat; air pollution; personal space violations; and high density (pp. 58–9). Nearly a decade later in an article that specifies the strains most likely to result in crime and delinquency, he includes prejudice/discrimination (see Agnew 2001, pp. 346–7).

Race and GST

Kaufman et al. (2008) have offered a more complete discussion of how GST can explain racial differences in criminal offending. The authors argue that "A GST explanation of racial differences in offending . . . implies that African-Americans experience disproportionate strain in the social environment and/or have fewer resources for coping with strain in conventional ways" (Kaufman et al. 2008, p. 424). More specifically, they argue that African Americans are more likely to experience the following strains more than other groups: economic strain (poverty, high unemployment, etc.), family strain (exposure to poor parenting practices), educational strain (poor grades, unfair discipline, interpersonal problems with students and teachers, etc.), criminal victimizations, discrimination (in all facets of life), and community strain (high levels of economic disadvantage and violence) (Kaufman et al. 2008, pp. 425–30; see also Kaufman 2005).

Kaufman et al. (2008) also weigh in on whether there are racial differences in reactions to strain. Here, they surmise that if an individual loses their job because of racial discrimination it is more likely to lead to criminal activity than if the loss was perceived to be due to some legitimate factor. Thus, they predict that African Americans will be more likely than whites to perceive such differences so they are more likely to encounter this type of strain. As for coping with strain, the authors argue that because of their disadvantaged status African Americans are less likely to have the necessary resources to cope with strain (Kaufman et al. 2008, p. 431). Further, because African Americans are more likely to live in single-parent households, they have less social support that can often buffer the impact of noxious stimuli and strains. Lastly, the authors posit that strains can also lead to the adaptation of codes conducive to crime and violence. These codes are tied to ideas outlined in Chapter 4 on subcultural theory.

Research on Race and GST

Using Agnew's GST as their theoretical foundation and data from the National Survey of Black Americans (comprising a sample of 2,107 adult African Americans), Jang and Johnson (2003) tested and found support for the core tenets of GST. They also found that religiosity served as an effective buffer of negative emotions (see also Jang and Johnson 2005) and that social support can serve as an effective buffer against depression and anxiety (Jang and Lyons 2006).

Simons et al. (2003) examined the relationship between racial discrimination and delinquency, also using Agnew's GST. Using discrimination as a stressor (or strain), an analysis of data from 718 African American children and their caregivers in Georgia and Iowa found that experiencing discrimination was a significant predictor of delinquency, even after the authors "controlled for quality of parenting, affiliation with delinquent peers, and prior conduct problems" (p. 848). Furthermore, the results showed "that . . . anger and depression fostered by discrimination increase[d] delinquent behavior" (p. 850). The research findings also made clear that "delinquency is [not] an effective strategy for attenuating these negative feelings" (p. 850).

Eitle and Turner (2003) also tested GST and the role of stress exposure, race, and crime among a diverse sample of Hispanics, African Americans, and whites. The research revealed that "African Americans report the highest proportion of self-reported crime, the lowest group levels of self-esteem and mastery, and the second lowest group level of social support" (p. 252). Even so, there were few significant differences among all the groups except in the area of peers involved in crime and exposure to major events within one's lifetime (e.g. violence or some other traumatic event). Strikingly, additional analysis of their data showed that

> . . . racial differences in crime may largely or even entirely be explained by differences in the level of exposure to stressors—African Americans are more likely to be involved in crime because they are exposed to greater levels of stressors (particularly lifetime negative events) than other racial/ ethnic groups.
>
> (p. 254)

They conclude by noting that "race does not matter except as a marker of increased risk for stress exposure" (p. 258).

Additional tests of Agnew's strain theory have also been supportive. Rocque (2008) used Agnew's theory to show how it can be applied to American slavery and this early form of confinement of African Americans. More specifically, he shows how strains during the slave era such as those related to health/mortality, overwork and mistreatment, sexual and physical exploitation, and the people as property mentality, all fit Merton's notions of strain. Furthermore, he points to the coping mechanisms used during slavery such as social support, religion, pursuit of skills/ownership/education, and overt resistance as ways slaves "dealt" with their enslavement. On the whole, the author makes a strong case for the use of Agnew's perspective to understand the strains associated with being black in America during the slave period (for examples of research related to the stressors of being black in America during contemporary times, see Blitstein 2009; Gabbidon and Peterson 2006; Geronimus et al. 2006; Geronimus and Thompson 2004; Walton, Dawson-Edwards, and Higgins 2014).

Perez et al. (2008) apply General Strain Theory to Hispanics. Their analysis researched whether ethnic-specific strains such as acculturation to Anglo culture impacted on Hispanic involvement in violent delinquency. Specifically, among a variety of findings that were supportive of general strain theory, the researcher noted that "in both low and high Hispanic concentration areas, as the adolescents' perception of anti-Hispanic discrimination increased so did the likelihood of violent delinquency" (Perez et al. 2008, p. 564; see also Jennings et al. 2009).

Other studies testing general strain with Latino samples have found that Latino youth are less likely to commit delinquency due to strain than a sample of white youth (Rodriguez and Belshaw 2010). Notably, an additional study involving a sample of university students found that out of several stressors, race discrimination was one of three found to have a significant effect on engaging in violent deviance (Moon et al. 2009, p. 104).

Conclusion

This chapter reviewed two of the leading sociological theories that have been used to explain crime. The chapter began with a portrait of the pioneering work of Du Bois. This was followed by a review of the well-known research program that developed at the University of Chicago, where the focus was on social disorganization theory and the ecological approach. The many variations of the theory were reviewed. The chapter concluded with a review of strain theory and its persistent criticisms. Of particular concern were the strain theories of Merton and Agnew. As was seen, both social disorganization and strain perspectives have been successfully used to contextualize crime in minority communities. After the appearance of social disorganization and strain theory, subcultural theories, some of which integrated strain theory, emerged in the criminological literature. As with other criminological theories, they have also been applied to racial/ethnic minorities. Chapter 4 focuses on subcultural perspectives.

4
SUBCULTURAL PERSPECTIVES
ON RACE AND CRIME

Beginning in the 1950s, several theories were formulated that tied criminality to the development of subcultures among urban youth. Since this early period, scholars have continued to refine and reframe subcultural perspectives, many of which were, and continue to be, aimed at explaining crime among mostly urban racial/ethnic minorities. The chapter begins by reviewing the early subcultural perspectives and highlighting their race-related themes, after which, tests of these theories as they relate to race and crime are reviewed. The chapter then moves on to examine the one of the most popular subcultural perspective: Wolfgang and Ferracuti's (1967) subculture of violence thesis. Following a review of the literature in this area, Anderson's "code of the streets" perspective is reviewed, which is followed by the presentation of some additional subcultural perspectives on race and crime.

Early Subcultural Perspectives

Albert Cohen, in his work, *Delinquent Boys* (1955), draws on Merton's strain theory to create a general theory of subcultures in which he argued that gang delinquency was associated with juveniles being unable to achieve status among their peers ("status frustration"). When they are unable to meet established white middle-class standards or what he referred to as the "middle-class measuring rod" (p. 84), they establish their own values, which generally involve activities and behaviors in conflict with middle-class values. Such middle-class values include: ambition; individual responsibility; educational achievement; "worldly asceticism" or deferred gratification; rationality (exercise of forethought, conscious planning, budgeting of time, etc.); "manners, courtesy, and personability" (p. 90); avoidance of aggression and violence; pursuit of constructive hobbies; and a "respect for property" (pp. 88–93).

Cohen's theory speaks very little to race, but he does suggest the difficulty of formulating a "general" or all inclusive theory because

> each age, sex, racial and ethnic category, each occupation, economic stratum and social class consists of people who have been equipped by their society with frames of reference and confronted by their society with situations which are not equally characteristic of other roles.
>
> (p. 54)

Cohen notes additional complications of formulating a general theory considering the limitations placed on each particular group within society:

> The problems and preoccupations of men and women are different because they judge themselves and others judge them by different standards and because the means available to them for realizing their aspirations are different. It is obvious that opportunities for the achievement of power and prestige are not the same for people who start out at different positions in a class system; it is perhaps a bit less obvious [what] their levels of aspiration in these respects [are] and therefore what it will take to satisfy them are likely also to differ.
>
> (p. 55)

So, like Merton before him, Cohen recognized that certain characteristics, such as race and ethnicity, mattered in the formulation of a general sociological theory.

Miller's Focal Concerns Theory

After examining lower-class areas in Boston (comprising primarily Negroes and whites), Walter Miller (1958) created a subcultural theory. Based on more than three years of research and "over eight thousand pages of direct observational data on behavior patterns of group members and other community residents" (p. 144), Miller, a cultural anthropologist, formulated his theory of "focal concerns" among lower-class culture. In his view, delinquent gangs or subcultures were formed within all social groups; however, in the case of lower-class youth, their subculture adhered to lower-class ideals, which he called "focal concerns" (or what scholars from other disciplines might refer to as "values").

Miller's focal concerns included trouble, toughness, smartness, excitement, fate, and autonomy. According to the theory, trouble is "a dominant feature of lower-class culture" (1958, p. 145). Trouble represents things such as fighting or "sexual adventures" among males, while for females, it represents "sexual involvement with disadvantageous consequences" (p. 146). Depending on the circumstances, both law-abiding and law-violating behavior might be valued within the lower classes.

Toughness represents the second focal concern. Being tough requires that one adhere to the "tough guy" image. Such an image is represented by being "hard, fearless, undemonstrative, skilled in physical combat— [and] is represented by the movie gangster of the thirties, the 'private eye,' and the movie cowboy" (Miller 1958, p. 147). Smartness refers to the importance of "street smarts" in acquiring material goods and personal status. The fourth focal concern, excitement, refers to the search for "thrills" within lower-class culture (p. 149). Fate represents the fifth focal concern and relates to the belief that "many lower-class individuals feel that their lives are subject to set forces over which they have very little control" (p. 150). Autonomy represents the final focal concern. Here Miller argued that, among lower-class youth ". . . there is a strong and frequently expressed resentment of the idea of external controls, restrictions on behavior, and unjust coercive authority" (p. 151). Throughout the presentation of his theory, Miller also stressed the important role of the absence of male father figures for those males who adopt these focal concerns.

Cloward and Ohlin's *Delinquency and Opportunity*

Two years after Miller's work, Richard Cloward and Lloyd Ohlin's *Delinquency and Opportunity* (1960) pointed to the opportunity structure as the key to understanding gang activities. As with Cohen's perspective, Cloward and Ohlin's ideas owed much to Merton's strain theory. Their theory, however, suggested that when there are limited opportunities, youth join gangs with one of three orientations. Those who cannot find legitimate opportunities join criminal gangs or subcultures whose primary aim is to make money through a variety of illegitimate avenues (e.g. theft or extortion). If, however, there remain few illegitimate opportunities, the youth might join a "conflict" gang. Such gangs primarily engage in violent activities, doing whatever is necessary to maintain their status in the streets (pp. 24–5). Youth who end up in "retreatist" gangs are what Cloward and Ohlin refer to as "double-failures." Because such youth did not make it in either legitimate or illegitimate opportunities, they retreat to drug usage.

Cloward and Ohlin (1960) did address the issue of race and ethnicity in their theory. First, they wrote that ". . . little evidence is currently available on the distribution of these three types of delinquent subcultures in lower-class areas . . . certain types seem to be especially prevalent among certain racial and ethnic groups" (p. 29). Drawing on data from New York, they assert:

> Criminal groups oriented toward "the rackets," such as gambling, vice, narcotics peddling, etc. tend to be found most often in Italian neighborhoods, while criminal groups oriented toward professional burglary, robbery, and theft are most likely to be found in areas of mixed nationality. Conflict and retreatist groups appear to be especially prevalent in Negro and Puerto Rican neighborhoods.
>
> (p. 29)

As with the previously reviewed subcultural perspectives, they noted that

> a Negro may find it difficult to maintain his faith in the ideology of equality under social conditions which conspicuously bar members of his 'race' from access to legitimate opportunities for achieving success. Indeed, Negroes are even at a disadvantage in the illegitimate world . . .
>
> (Cloward and Ohlin 1960, p. 121)

On the latter point, the authors noted that "political and rackets structures in the Negro communities of New York are now dominated principally by Italians and Jews; most Negroes have been relegated to minor roles in these structures although they aspire to rise" (pp. 199–200).

Thus, even in the illegitimate areas of crime, African Americans were relegated to the lower rungs of organized crime groups, which were obviously within the realm of Cloward and Ohlin's conception of gangs.

At the time of the publication of their work, Cloward and Ohlin pointed to structural changes in urban areas that led them to believe that the experience of Negroes would be different from those of ethnic immigrants who previously resided in urban areas. As such, they predicted the development of criminal subcultures would also be different for Negroes. In their words:

> Present conditions of urban life are different in certain significant respects from those of an earlier time, when the Italian immigrant occupied a status similar to that of the Negro today. Vast changes have taken place in urban politics, organized crime, and the general character of lower-class life. For the most part, these changes have resulted in the disorganization of slums, restricted opportunity, and lessened social control. Thus the pattern of ascent to illegal wealth and power by Negroes may be somewhat different from the pattern that was followed by Italian and other groups.
>
> (1960, p. 202)

So what did Cloward and Ohlin foresee for these urban areas? In short, they predicted that there would be more violence in these areas. More specifically, they wrote, "We predict that delinquency will become increasingly aggressive and violent in the future as a result of the disintegration of slum organization" (p. 203). Given the special circumstances surrounding the condition of and restrictions placed on Negroes and other racial/ethnic minorities, one must presume that they would constitute a large share of Cloward and Ohlin's "double-failures" in retreatist gangs. Following the appearance of their theory, some early tests of their perspective using a diversity of samples were mixed (Jessor et al. 1968; Short and Strodtbeck 1965), while others were less supportive (Velez-Diaz and Megargee 1971).

With the emergence of criminological perspectives such as labeling theory (Chapter 5), conflict theory (Chapter 6), control theory (Chapter 7), in the 1960s and early 1970s, strain-based subcultural perspectives fell out of favor (see Bernard 1984; Kornhauser 1978). However, in the late 1980s, Simons and Gray (1989) returned to Cloward and Ohlin's theory to examine whether perceived blocked opportunities contributed to delinquency among a sample of lower-class black males. Using data from nine American cities, the authors

> ... hypothesized that the relationship between perceived blocked occu-
> pational opportunities and delinquency would be rather strong for
> lower-class blacks, somewhat lower for lower-class whites, and insignifi-
> cant for middle-class whites and blacks.

(p. 93)

The authors found perceived opportunities to be lower among lower-class whites and blacks than both groups of middle-class respondents. They noted that this could be the case because lower-class youth start out with lower aspirations (Simons and Gray 1989, p. 98; cf. Wendling and Elliott 1968). The authors also suggest that both lower-class and higher-status youth "... are likely to anticipate failure to realize their occupational aspirations" (Simons and Gray 1989, p. 99). However, according to Cloward and Ohlin's theory, it is the differential response to this failure that is at the heart of the theory. Unable to achieve their aspirations, lower-class minority youth are likely to blame the "system" and engage in delinquency. Given that there was a moderate relationship between perceived chance for occupational success and delinquency among only the lower-class blacks, support was found for the theory.

The same year in which Walter Miller published his theory on focal concerns, noted criminologist Marvin Wolfgang published *Patterns in Criminal Homicide* (1958). This was significant because, as an outgrowth of this pioneering work, less than a decade later, he, along with Franco Feracutti, formulated the subculture of violence theory, which has been used to explain homicide, particularly in the African American community. The theory is reviewed next.

The Subculture of Violence Theory

In the United States, African Americans and Latinos continue to be over-represented in several violent crime categories (Gabbidon and Taylor Greene 2013; Martinez 2002; Walker et al. 2011). An abundance of early scholarly literature focused on violent crime, with a particular emphasis on homicide among African Americans (for early examples of such research, see Allredge 1942; Barnhart 1932; Brearley 1930, 1932; Garfinkel 1949; Spirer 1940; Sutherland 1925; von Hentig 1940). In the late 1950s, though, while studying homicides in Philadelphia, Wolfgang (1958) conducted one of the most thorough examinations of race and homicides. Based on case files from 588 homicide victims and 621 offenders in Philadelphia from 1948 to 1952, Wolfgang's efforts produced a landmark effort in the study of homicide. The research showed the racial characteristics, sex differences, victim-offender relationships, weapons involved, temporal patterns, and motives of the homicides.

It was in this volume that Wolfgang (1958) introduced the notion of victim-precipitated homicides or those instances ". . . in which the victim is a direct, positive precipitator in the crime" (p. 252). The volume also included one of the most comprehensive reviews of literature on homicides, which revealed that African Americans were over-represented not only in Philadelphia homicides (as victims and offenders), but also in most of the previously conducted homicide research leading up to Wolfgang's study. After looking at the dynamics of the African American homicides in Philadelphia, where they comprised 73 percent of the victims and 75 percent of the offenders, Wolfgang hinted at the formulation of a theory related to his findings.

Drawing on Sellin's culture conflict theory (reviewed in Chapter 6), Wolfgang (1958) wrote:

> Our analysis implies that there may be a subculture of violence which does not define personal assaults as wrong or antisocial; in which resort to physical aggression is a socially approved and expected concomitant of certain stimuli; and in which violence has become a familiar but often deadly partner in life's struggles.
>
> (p. 329)

He continued, noting that while the subculture likely exists among the lower class, it was "especially comprised of males and Negroes" (p. 330). A replication of Wolfgang's work in another metropolitan area (Chicago) a decade later overwhelmingly confirmed many of his earlier findings (see Voss and Hepburn 1968).

Less than a decade after his pioneering research, Wolfgang and his colleague, Franco Ferracuti, who had also conducted homicide research in Italy, formulated the subculture of violence theory (Wolfgang and

Ferracuti 1967). Their theory draws from several other criminological theories and consists of seven propositions. These propositions speak to a range of factors that encapsulate the subculture of violence. Some of them include the fact that those invested in the subculture of violence are not violent all the time; while the subculture is found in all age segments of society, it is found most in those in the late-adolescence to middle-age categories. Since those vested in the subculture do not see violence as an "illicit conduct," they have no feelings of guilt toward their actions (pp. 158–61). During the mid-1970s, Curtis (1975) and Silberman (1978) argued in favor of a subculture of violence among blacks.

Darnell Hawkins (1983) provided one of the earliest and most comprehensive critiques of the theory. In doing so, he also provided an alternative perspective. We begin with a summary of his critique; then, we turn to a brief overview of his alternative theory.

Hawkins (1983) pointed to the following five major weaknesses of the theory (pp. 414–15):

- There is an extreme emphasis on mentalistic value orientations of individuals—orientations that, in the aggregate, are said to produce a subculture.
- The theory lacks empirical grounding and indeed is put in question by some empirical findings.
- Much of the theory has tended to underemphasize a variety of structural, situational, and institutional variables that affect interpersonal violence. For blacks, these variables range from historical patterns developed during slavery to the immediate social context of an individual homicidal offense to the operation of the criminal justice system, past and present.
- Subcultural theory underemphasizes the effects of the law on patterns of criminal homicide.
- There are other plausible ways, apart from the inculcation of values, by which the economic, political, and social disadvantages of American blacks may produce high rates of homicide.

Hawkins's alternative theory provided three propositions that were meant to address the holes in the subculture of violence theory (see

Figure 4.1). Proposition one states, "American criminal law: Black life is cheap but white life is valuable" (p. 415). Here, Hawkins believes that, based on history, black lives have taken on less value than white lives; as a result, African Americans can kill other African Americans without fear of being punished. In line with this argument, Hawkins expands the work of Johnson (1941) and presents a hierarchy of homicide seriousness that punctuates the least serious and most serious types of homicides (see Figures 4.2 and 4.3).

Hawkins's second proposition states: "Past and present racial and social class differences in the administration of justice affect black criminal violence" (1983, p. 422). This proposition speaks to the lack of attention paid to prehomicide behaviors in black communities. Hawkins believes that since various prehomicidal assaults in the African American community do not receive the attention they deserve, homicides that could be prevented are not. Such inattention is also a product of the poor relationship between African Americans and police agencies. As a product of these poor relations, in some instances, response times are slower and, at some point, African Americans lose faith in the police and refuse to call on them for assistance in certain instances. Furthermore, once a homicide is committed and the police are called, the lack

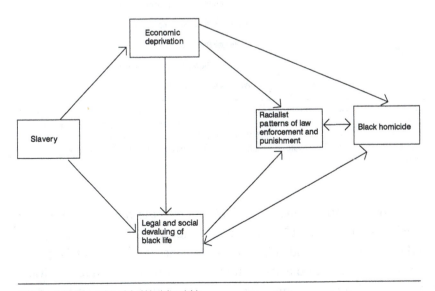

Figure 4.1 A causal model of black homicide

Rating	Offense
Most serious	Negro versus White
	White versus White
	Negro versus Negro
Least serious	White versus Negro

Figure 4.2 Johnson's hierarchy of homicide seriousness. (From D. F. Hawkins, "Black and White Homicide Differentials: An Alternative to an Inadequate Theory," *Criminal Justice and Behavior*, 10(4): 407–40. Reprinted by SAGE Publications. With permission.)

Rating	Offense
Most serious	Black kills White, in authority
	Black kills White, stranger
	White kills White, in authority
	Black kills White, friend, acquaintance
	Black kills White, intimate, family
	White kills White, stranger
	White kills White, friend, acquaintance
	White kills White, intimate, family
	Black kills Black, stranger
	Black kills Black, friend, acquaintance
	Black kills Black, intimate, family
	White kills Black, stranger
	White kills Black, friend, acquaintance
Least serious	White kills Black, intimate, family

Figure 4.3 Hawkins's hierarchy of homicide seriousness: Most serious to least serious types of homicides. (From D. F. Hawkins, "Black and White Homicide Differentials: An Alternative to an Inadequate Theory," *Criminal Justice and Behavior*, 10(4): 407–40. Reprinted by SAGE Publications. With permission.)

of serious attention provides no deterrent effect to the community. The final proposition—that "economic deprivation creates a climate of powerlessness in which individual acts of violence are likely to take place" (p. 429)—speaks to the association between socioeconomic disadvantage and violence, a connection generally lacking in the subculture of violence theory, but was incorporated into a well-known unsuccessful test of the theory (Sampson 1985).

After some preliminary studies on black female violence in the 1980s (see Laub and McDermott 1985; Mann 1987; McClain 1981), the 1990s saw tests of the subculture of violence theory to determine its applicability to black women. Mann (1990) examined homicide data from six major cities and found black women to comprise more than three-quarters of the female murderers. However, after taking all factors into consideration, she concluded, "These women are not part of a 'subculture of violence' but of a 'subculture of hopelessness.' Their fierce independence, their tendency to batter or to kill when battered and their almost insurmountable economic obstacles represent a constant struggle" (p. 198). When Melvin Ray and Earl Smith (1991) took up the subject the following year, they noted that if there is a "subculture of violence" among African American females, there must also be one among white females who had identical offending patterns, primarily committing homicides against males of the same race with whom they have a close relationship (p. 150).

Although additional tests during the 1990s continued to find no support for the theory (see, for example, Cheatwood 1990), researchers began to examine the perspective from new angles. Using the previously reviewed work of William Julius Wilson (1987), Bernard (1990) created a subcultural perspective on the "truly disadvantaged." His perspective aims to explain angry aggression or "aggression that is motivated by the intent to harm (i.e. to reduce the target's well-being)" among inner-city residents (p. 76). At the center of his perspective is the notion that social factors such as urban environment, low social position, and racial ethnic discrimination, combined with Wilson's concept of social isolation, result ". . . in a highly aggressive environment" (p. 87).

Notably, in contrast to other subcultural perspectives, Bernard's model does not portend that such aggression is valued in these communities; it argues that, given the social factors highlighted, angry aggression among the "truly disadvantaged" is likely. He also notes that, on an individual level, biological and psychological factors

> could be used to explain individual differences in angry aggression within similar social situations. They would not be useful in explaining the

distribution of angry aggression among social groups . . . unless it could be demonstrated that they are distributed similarly among social groups. No formal tests of the theory have been conducted. (1990, p. 89)

Harer and Steffensmeier (1996) examined the subculture of violence thesis in the context of prison violence. Using misconduct data from the Federal Bureau of Prisons, the authors found a strong race effect on prison violence, with "blacks [being] more than twice as likely to be found guilty of violent misconduct than . . . whites, net of controls" (Harer and Steffensmeier 1996, p. 339). As predicted by the authors' hypotheses, they found that ". . . black inmates have significantly lower levels of prison alcohol/drug misconduct than white inmates, net of controls" (p. 340). As they aptly note, some of the racial differences could be attributable to racial bias in the reporting of misconduct. After considering this caveat and other possible limitations, the authors remained convinced that their results were supportive of the subculture of violence thesis.

Using data from the 1980s and 1990s, Cao et al. (2000) tested the subculture of violence thesis and concluded:

Based on our data and analyses, there is enough evidence to conclude that blacks in the general U.S. population are no more likely than whites to embrace values favorable to violence. Our findings thus repudiate the idea that the causes of black crime are rooted in unique aspects of black culture.

(p. 58)

They suggest that given the limited support for the theory, for scholars to continue to promote it as an explanation for racial differences in violence implies that all African Americans are violent—something that is "unfair and potentially racist in nature" (Cao et al. 2000, p. 58). Other criticisms have also been leveled at the theory. Covington (2003) noted that supporters of the theory "fail to explain how [the] black subculture of violence came to be more combative than the white subculture of violence" (p. 258). Psychologists have also argued that Wolfgang and Feracutti (1967) "ignore the psychological underpinnings of [the] subculture" (Poussaint, as cited in Covington 2003, p. 259). Even with these criticisms, scholars continue to investigate the veracity of the subculture of violence approach. As a recent example, Staff and Kreager (2008) tested whether disadvantaged youth gain status through violence that places them at risk for dropping out of school. Notably, the authors did find support for subcultural theory; however, they make clear that "low SES Blacks who gained prestige within violent groups were not significantly more likely than other low SES males to drop out of high school" (Staff and Kreager 2008, p. 461). In short, they did not find support for a unique *black* subculture of violence thesis. Another important study tested whether adherents to the subculture of violence mindset favor violence over general offending (McGloin et al. 2011). There was no support for this underlying tenet of the subculture of violence thesis.

Another recent paper related to the subculture of violence thesis investigated whether Latinos adhere to a culture of honor and have different attitudes towards violence than African Americans and whites (Rose and Ellison 2014). Relying on data from a poll of more than 1,400 Texans, the researchers found that "Latinos do, in fact, hold distinct views about the appropriateness of violence" (p. 14). In particular, ". . . non-Hispanic Whites residing in Texas . . . expressed the most agreement with all measures of violence—Latinos, and to some extent African Americans, were less likely to agree with the appropriateness of violence to prevent future violence and the right to kill another in self-defense" (p. 14).

A derivative of the general subculture of violence thesis is the southern subculture of violence thesis. The thesis suggests that there is an elevated level of violence in the south that dates to white southern violence originating in the colonial period (see Butterfield 1995). Some of the early and more contemporary scholarship pertaining to the thesis is reviewed below.

Southern Subculture of Violence Thesis

Hackney (1969) and Gastil (1971) produced two early papers in support of the notion of a southern subculture of violence, while other early scholarship in the area by Ball-Rokeach (1973) and Loftin and Hill (1974) were less supportive of the perspective. However, further tests during the 1980s found mixed results (Shoemaker and Williams 1987), with some again showing support for the theory (Messner 1983; Lichtenstein 1984) and others continuing to find that poverty is the most important and consistent predictor of the types of homicide . . . Evidence of a southern culture of violence that influences homicide is absent, and although at least two types of homicide are significantly related to racial composition, this variable does not assume the importance . . . that others have claimed for it in attempting to understand the predictors and causes of homicides in the U.S.

(Parker 1989, p. 1000)

Clarke (1998) examined lynching and capital punishment in the American South. Drawing on historical data, which showed that before the Civil War the majority of those lynched were white, Clarke's analysis also found that, following the Civil War, southern blacks became the primary targets of such violence. Using Wolfgang and Ferracuti's (1967) propositions as his guide, Clarke showed how lynching was a manifestation of the southern subculture of violence. In addition, his data showed the over-representation of blacks as victims of lynching in the former slave states and that, after the decline of lynching, capital punishment was substituted for the practice of lynching and became what southerners referred to as "legal lynchings" (p. 284). Clarke's data on state executions from the former slave states clearly support the notion that the southern subculture of violence persisted under the guise of capital punishment (for a similar analysis, see Zimring 2003). Keil and Vito (2009) also tested what is referred to as the substitution thesis (replacing lynchings with state-sanctioned executions) using data from Kentucky and found mixed support.

Lee et al. (2008) examined two key ideas related to the southern culture of violence. First, they studied whether "structural deprivation may be attenuated as a correlate of crime under a southern culture of violence because the strains generated by failure to achieve universally held goals are not experienced as acutely by this group" (p. 83). They also studied "whether structural deprivation may be amplified under a Southern culture of violence" (p. 83). Using county-level data, structural *and* cultural factors were found to impact white homicide rates.

In a recent paper, Doucet, D'Antonio-Del Rio, and Chauvin (2014) tested whether the southern culture of violence extends to southern girls. Using official data sources including homicide data from the 1970s, the authors found support for the southern culture of violence among females. Specifically, "southern subculture . . . is positively and significantly associated with female-perpetrated homicides" (p. 816). The authors surmise that while the strong patriarchal system in the south likely does not condone violence by females, both males and females are socialized into the same attitudes towards violence (p. 818).

The Code of the Streets

A subcultural theory approach that has some connections to several earlier approaches (see particularly the work of Kobrin 1951 and Miller 1958) is the "code of the streets" (Anderson 1994, 1999). Based on his research in Philadelphia, Elijah Anderson, an urban ethnographer, published a highly acclaimed article, "The Code of the Streets." The article focused on interpersonal violence in impoverished inner-city communities (such as Philadelphia) and how residents in these areas adopt "the code of the streets" to survive. Anderson (1994) believes that "at the heart of the code is the issue of respect—loosely defined as being treated 'right,' or granted deference one deserves" (p. 82).

In such an environment, something that has little meaning to one person might be interpreted as "dissing" someone else and result in a confrontation that could lead to violence. Being able to defend yourself is also an important part of the code. Within these depressed neighborhoods, Anderson suggested that there are "decent" and "street" families. Decent families "tend to accept mainstream values more fully and attempt to instill them in their children" (1994, pp. 82–3). Such families are also strict and teach their children to respect authority and act in a moral way. In addition, they are not seriously tied to the code.

On the other hand, Anderson (1994) described "street families," who loosely supervise their children and in many cases are unable to cope with them. Unlike the decent families, "they believe in the code and judge themselves and others according to its values" (p. 83). Subsequently, their lives "are marked by disorganization" (p. 83). In such families, children learn early on they must fend for themselves. This produces a cycle in which they also become invested in the code and take to the streets to prove their "manhood," which involves securing pretty women, being able to defend themselves, and being able to support themselves "by any means necessary."

There has been considerable support for some of Anderson's ideas in studies focusing on blacks (Baumer et al. 2003; Berg, Stewart, Schreck, Simons 2012; Brezina et al. 2004; Chilton 2004; Intravia, Wolff, Stewart, and Simons 2014; Matsueda, Drakulich, and Kubrin 2006; Stewart et al. 2002), Hispanics (Lopez et al. 2004), young black women (Brunson and Stewart 2006; Jones 2004, 2008, 2009), and the role of rap music in the perpetuation of the code of the streets (Kubrin 2005). One study, however, found that, in contrast to Anderson's theory, adhering to the code increases not decreases the likelihood of victimization (Stewart et al. 2006). Another study examining black masculinity found that black males that fit Anderson's definition of "decent" were no more likely than whites and blacks classified as "street" to drop out of boot camp (Beckley 2008).

Parker and Reckdenwald (2008) tested portions of Anderson's thesis. They explored whether the presence of employed "old heads" who serve as positive male role models decreases violence in nearly 200 U.S. cities (see also Wilson's 1987 concept of social buffers in Chapter 3). The authors found that "the presence of traditional male role models mediates the influence black concentrated disadvantage has on violent arrests of black juveniles within urban areas" (Parker and Reckdenwald 2008, p. 724). Stewart et al. (2008) also suggest that, along with reinvesting in communities, politically empowering residents, and alleviating poverty, reducing violence associated with the code requires "improving police–community relations and providing peaceful dispute resolution options" (pp. 142–3). Additional support for the theory was reported by Mears et al. (2013) whose research found that the importation of street codes to prison settings led to increased inmate violence.

Besides the need for continued replications, there have been other concerns expressed about the viability of Anderson's ideas (DeLisi, 2014). Commenting on one of the life histories presented in Anderson's work, Miller (2001) wrote that, based on the way he describes the person's prison experience, it could be that the prison, not the streets, is the more powerful contributor to the development of the code of the streets. Elaborating on this point, he wrote:

I do not feel that Professor Anderson gives enough weight to the influences of prison on the code of the streets. It is no accident that most of the known violent gangs in California developed in the institutions of the California Youth Authority or the California prisons. Leadership is confirmed by a stint in prison. The walk, the "pose," the language, the argot, the dress, the focus of one's eyes, and the studied indifference all bespeak prison.

(p. 157)

Wacquant (2002) provided a more expansive critique of Anderson's work, pointing to the "loose and over expansive definition of the code of the streets" (p. 1491). Another point of concern is that "there is considerable confusion as to the origins and vectors of the code of the streets" (p. 1491). Wacquant further observed:

> Because he starts from an overly monolithic vision of the ghetto and conflates folk with analytic concepts, Anderson cannot relate the *moral distinctions* he discovers in it to its internal *social stratification*. He thus boxes himself into a culturalist position with deeply disturbing political implications insofar as they render ghetto residents responsible for their own plight through their deviant values or role ineptness.
>
> (p. 1500)

In response to Wacquant's criticisms, Anderson (2002) published a detailed rejoinder. Anderson's response rested on the belief that Wacquant had both misread his work and distorted its findings (p. 1533). Furthermore, he argued that Wacquant's critique was ideologically driven. In other words, the critique was motivated by the fact that Anderson's findings in "The Code of the Streets" did not align with Wacquant's conception of inner-city life (p. 1549).

Several years after the initial exchange between Wacquant and Anderson, William Julius Wilson and Anmol Chaddha (2009) weighed in on the debate and concluded that both Wacquant and Anderson had valid arguments. However, Wilson and Chaddha argue on the side of Wacquant regarding one of his criticisms regarding the need for ethnographic research to be guided by some theoretical foundation, as opposed to being strictly inductive. In closing, they acknowledge that the best ethnographic research includes a synthesis of both inductive and deductive approaches (pp. 562–3).

Structural-Cultural Theory

In the 1980s, William Oliver proposed that in order to explain black male criminality, one needs to use an integrated theory combining structural conditions of African Americans and their cultural adaptations to such conditions. In one of his early articles, he explored black males and their "tough guy image" or, as he calls it, the "Black compulsive masculinity alternative." Because of racial oppression, Oliver believes that black males exhibit masculine behavior that places an overemphasis on "toughness, sexual conquest, manipulation, and thrill-seeking" (1984, p. 199). Oliver has argued that black males act this way because of two reasons. First, "lower-class black males who adopt the compulsive masculinity alternative do so in order to mitigate low self-esteem and negative feelings which emerge as a consequence of their ability to enact the traditional masculine role" (p. 199). The second reason relates to the notion that males who adopt the masculine approach pass it on to other males.

In later publications, Oliver applied his theory to sexual conquest and the adaptation of an Afrocentric perspective to ameliorate social problems in the African American community (Oliver 1989a, 1989b), and he has also examined violence among African Americans in barroom settings (Oliver 1994, p. 144). Years after the publication of his original work, Oliver continued to refine his perspective (see Oliver 2003, 2006).

Critiquing the subcultural-structural perspective, Covington (2003) has argued that Oliver's approach makes activities that whites also engage in race specific. For example, many of the functions that bars serve for African Americans also serve the same functions for whites. Finally, Covington noted that, in one of his studies, Oliver's "sample of African-American participants in violent transactions report that many of their fights seem to have been precipitated for non-race-specific reasons that apply equally well to violent whites" (p. 266). In addition to Covington's concerns, the role of low self-esteem—a central component of Oliver's work—as it applies to delinquency among blacks has been challenged (see Ross 1992). Another structural cultural theory is Johnson's (1996) subcultural backlash theory.

Subcultural Backlash Theory

Seeking to explain the over-representation of African Americans in the criminal justice system, Scott Johnson (1996) introduced the theory of subcultural backlash. Based on common themes found in the over-representation literature such as racial inequities in the social structure and discriminatory law enforcement, the subcultural backlash theory argues that these things lead to

> resentment, frustration, and anger in the African American community. The experience with oppression and discrimination leads to an empathy or understanding for members of the group engaged in criminal behavior by other members of the group. In this context, empathy means a personal comprehension of another's suffering or pain; it is not overt pity. These feelings of empathy or understanding cause members of the group to hesitate to condemn or ostracize members for criminal conduct because of the shared experience with racial oppression in certain instances. This is subcultural backlash.
>
> (Johnson 1996, p. 148)

Johnson (1996) noted that because the community refuses to condemn such criminal behavior, the deterrent effect of condemning or reporting such behavior is not present and thus implicitly "endorses either the behavior itself or supports its members against the unique social system. These new crimes worsen the differential involvement of the group in criminal activity, and hence, the over-representation of the group in the criminal justice system" (pp. 148–9). To test the theory, Johnson conducted several homogeneous focus groups comprising both whites and African Americans, drawn from a college and a prison. Though exploratory in nature, his study revealed that African Americans were more likely than whites to interact with actual or suspected criminals. Combined with the fact that they were less likely than whites to "engage" or rely on criminal justice officials when criminal activity was observed (p. 199), this indicated preliminary support for the theory. No additional tests have been conducted.

General Criticisms of Subcultural Theories

In general, a common shortcoming of subcultural theories is that they ignore criminality in the middle and upper classes (Hagan 2002). In addition, as noted in the critiques of Hawkins and Cao and his colleagues, tests of the popular subculture of violence theory have found minimal support. On the other hand, Anderson's "code of the streets" perspective has shown promise. A final persistent criticism of subcultural theories is that, in most instances, they speak only to male criminality (Lilly et al. 2002).

Conclusion

For nearly 60 years subcultural theories have been postulated to explain crime in urban areas. Beginning with the early works of Cohen, Miller, and Cloward and Ohlin, the perspective has considered the role of race/ethnicity in the development of criminal subcultures. But it was the pioneering work on homicide by Wolfgang that led to the development of the popular subculture of violence thesis, which has been used to contextualize violence in inner-city areas, particularly among racial/ethnic minorities. Though popular, the results of research devoted to tests of the perspective have been mixed. Within the last two decades, Elijah Anderson's "code of the streets" perspective has dominated the subculture of violence literature. As was seen from some of the scholarship reviewed, there has been considerable support found for the perspective. One of the well-known but least applied theories used to explain racial differences in offending and victimization is labeling theory. A discussion of this theory is presented in Chapter 5.

5

LABELING PERSPECTIVES ON RACE AND CRIME

This chapter examines the literature related to labeling theory, race, and crime. Labeling theory, which is also referred to as social reaction theory or interactionist theory, has a long tradition in criminology. Rooted in the early work of eminent psychologist William James (Shoemaker 1996), the labeling perspective owes its greatest debt to the work of Charles Cooley and Herbert Mead (Brown et al. 2004; Moyer 2001). In his classic work, *Human Nature and the Social Order* (1902), Cooley presented his concept of the "looking glass self," which argued that our identities are formed based on how others view us (pp. 151–3). It is important to note that, in a later edition of this same work, Cooley also addressed the special circumstances surrounding the identity formation among American Negroes, writing that "there is no understanding [the Negro question] without realizing the kind of self-feeling a race must have who, in a land where men are supposed to be equal, find themselves marked with indelible inferiority" (Cooley 1922/1967, p. 262). He was unmistakably aware that, for American Negroes, the "looking glass self" was polluted with racist images that, in many instances, hindered their opportunity to form normal identities or self-concepts.

The foundation of Mead's work is the concept of symbolic interactionism, which, in line with Cooley's work, pointed to the notion "that human behavior is the product of purely social symbols communicated between individuals. A basic idea of symbolic interactionism is that the mind and the self are not innate, but rather products of the social environment" (Williams and McShane 2004, p. 62). After the work of Cooley, Kelly Miller, in his early work, *Race Adjustment* (1908), presented an early statement on labeling, race, and crime. The chapter begins with a review of Miller's work, which is followed by brief reviews of other early pioneering labeling perspectives formulated by Tannenbaum (1938), Lemert (1951), Becker (1963), and Goffman (1963). The remainder of the chapter provides a sampling of the contemporary literature related to labeling theory, race, and crime.

Miller's *Race Adjustment*

Kelly Miller, who, in 1895, presented the first lectures in sociology at Howard University and later founded their pioneering Department of Sociology (Jarmon 2003, pp. 366–8), was an early African American critic of race relations in America. Describing him, Jones wrote: "Kelly Miller must be labeled the inflammable catalyst who constantly sought to kindle the alleged spark of 'Christian Love' lodged in the white man's breast" (1974, p. 146). Like other prominent African Americans of his era (e.g. Ida B. Wells-Barnett and W. E. B. Du Bois) and those before him (most notably, Frederick Douglass), Miller was an outspoken scholar-activist, especially in matters related to race and crime (particularly the lynching of blacks).

In 1908, many of his early essays were published in *Race Adjustment: Essays on the Negro in America*. In the work, he covers a wide variety of topics. However, in the chapter entitled "An Appeal to Reason," which was a reply to something that had been written by Mr. John Temple Graves, Miller discussed the 1906 Atlanta riot, which he attributed to poor race relations and the "exaggeration" of media accounts of crime in the city. He noted the tense relations in the city and, echoing themes similar to those of his contemporaries, he wrote that "there were assaults or rumors of assaults by black or blackened fiends, upon white women, in and around Atlanta. These were eagerly seized upon and exaggerated by an inflammatory press" (Miller 1908, p. 60).

Later in the work, Miller bluntly declared that southern whites were deliberately spreading propaganda to "place the colored race in evil repute in order to justify iniquitous practices. To make a race odious in the eyes of the world is ample excuse for all forms of outrageous and cruel treatment" (p. 67). On this practice, Miller wrote:

> Assault by a Negro, actual or alleged, is displayed by the press in the boldest headlines, whereas like offenses by white men are compressed within a half inch space, as part of the ordinary happenings of the day. Whenever a Negro is accused of this crime the Associated Press sends the announcement all over the land. The morning papers proclaim it in bold headlines, only to be outdone by their more reckless evening contemporaries. The weekly journals rehash the same with gruesome particularities, until the whole nation becomes inflamed against the race on account of the dastardly deed of a single wretch.
>
> (p. 68)

Miller continued his analysis, arguing that, as a result of the dubious practices of the press, the actions of a few Negroes resulted in the "abhorrence" of 40,000 Negro Atlanta residents. Noting the unfairness of this, he stated: "This is as fragrantly unfair to the Negro as it would be to base the reputation of the population of London upon the deeds of Jack the Ripper . . ." (p. 68).

Miller's analysis is illustrative of the feelings of many African Americans of his period *and* today. It provided a clear portrait of the methods employed to perpetuate negative stereotypes as well as the consequences of such stereotypes. In the end, though, it was the work of white scholars such as Frank Tannenbaum that is credited with the formalization of the labeling perspective. Tannenbaum's work is discussed next.

Tannenbaum's *Crime and the Community*

Early in Frank Tannenbaum's nearly 500-page treatise, *Crime and the Community* (1938), he critiqued the varying definitions that were used to describe acts committed by youth in the community. Tannenbaum described how some activities engaged in by youth (e.g. breaking windows, annoying people, running around porches, playing truant, etc.) might, in their view, be seen as adventurous, full of excitement, and fun, while, on the other hand, residents might classify these same activities as "nuisance[s], evil, [and] delinquency" (p. 17). These conflicting perspectives result in residents calling for the "suppression" of such activities. This call often results in what Tannenbaum referred to as the "dramatization of evil" (pp. 19–21). Such a process usually involved the "tagging" or labeling of the juveniles. Once a child had been tagged, he or she would never be the same and was now "delinquent" or "criminal." Describing this process, Tannenbaum made his now classic statement:

> The process of making the criminal . . . is a process of tagging, defining, identifying, segregating, describing, emphasizing, making conscious and self-conscious; it becomes a way of stimulating, suggesting, emphasizing, and evoking the very traits that are complained of. If the theory of relation of response to stimulus has any meaning, the entire process of dealing with the young delinquent is mischievous in so far as it identifies him to himself or to the environment as a delinquent person.
>
> (p. 20)

Tannenbaum felt that the "dramatization of evil" tended to make matters worse. Therefore, instead of solving the problem, this process turned minor juvenile acts into major events. Handling these activities as major events resulted in the isolation of these newly identified "delinquents." But, as a result of this isolation, the youth were

> force[d] . . . into companionship with other children similarly defined, and the gang becomes his means of escape, his security. The life of the gang gives it special mores, and the attack by the community upon these mores merely overemphasizes the conflict already in existence, and make[s] it the source of a new series of experiences that lead directly to a criminal career.
>
> (1938, p. 20)

Tannenbaum's rendering of labeling theory made no mention of race, but it did provide the foundation for later writers who saw the clear connection among labeling, race, and crime. One such writer was Edwin Lemert.

Lemert's *Social Pathology*

Edwin Lemert's *Social Pathology: A Systematic Approach to the Theory of Sociopathic Behavior* (1951) presents another attempt to formalize labeling theory. While some of the basic tenets from the work of Tannenbaum remain, Lemert presented a formal sequence of events that produced deviant behavior. In general, that sequence involved two processes. First, there was primary deviance or the initial deviant act.

Once the act was committed, over time, if the youth continued to engage in deviant behavior, he or she would become stigmatized "in the form of name calling, labeling, or stereotyping" (p. 77). Once this occurred, it was likely that secondary deviance would occur. At this point, the person begins to identify with the "pathological role" and accepts status as a deviant (p. 76).

Detailing the sequence of events that leads to secondary deviance, Lemert presented the following eight steps:

> (1) primary deviation; (2) societal penalties; (3) further primary deviation; (4) stronger penalties and rejections; (5) further deviation, perhaps with hostilities and resentment beginning to focus upon those doing the penalizing; (6) crisis reached in the tolerance quotient, expressed a[s] formal action by the community stigmatizing of the deviant; (7) strengthening of the deviant conduct as a reaction to the stigmatizing and penalties; (8) ultimate acceptance of deviant social status and efforts at adjustment on the basis of the associated role.
>
> (p. 77)

In general, though, as is illustrated by this process, Lemert felt that one act was not enough to produce the stigmatizing effect that led to secondary deviance; it was the continuation of such acts that led to the "labeling" of the individual as deviant, resulting in secondary deviance.

Turning to a discussion of crime and criminals, Lemert devoted an entire chapter (Chapter 9) to the topic. Within this chapter, Lemert made note of racial and ethnic differences in offending. Here, he first informs readers that "crime is a predominantly male activity, particularly among Caucasoid members of our society" (p. 288). Addressing the over-representation of racial and ethnic minorities in justice statistics, Lemert pointed to the role of bias, discrimination, and "the greater visibility of Negro crime and the greater likelihood and prosecution for their crimes" (p. 289).

However, he cautioned readers against totally discounting the notion that these were the only reasons for the elevated crime rates among Negroes and American Indians. Elaborating on this point, he suggested that more "exacting" or precise studies showed that "there is a real, although as yet not accurately measured, difference between the objective criminal deviation of Negroes and whites and between that of American Indians and whites" (p. 289). His discussion of ethnic groups simply discussed the crime trends and also noted that some groups, such as the Italians and Irish, tended to have higher crime rates (p. 290).

While Lemert said little about the direct ways in which labeling theory intersected with race and crime, by articulating the steps involved in the labeling process, one can easily see its relevance for explaining race and crime. A core concept of Lemert's work is the notion of stereotyping, which, as we will see later in the chapter, remains a concern among criminologists. Over a decade after Lemert's work, two scholars, Erving Goffman and Howard Becker, presented their own labeling perspectives. The chapter continues with a review of Becker's work.

Becker's *Outsiders*

Becker's version of the labeling perspective is based on the premise that within every society there are social rules. When someone is caught violating these social rules ("rule breakers"), they become "outsiders." In his 1963 book, *Outsiders: Studies in the Sociology of Deviance*, Becker noted, though, that not everyone in society will agree with the prescribed social rules and, therefore, there will be those who see rule-makers as "outsiders" (pp. 1–2). In more concrete terms, Becker described his perspective as follows:

> Social *groups create deviance by making the rules whose infraction constitutes deviance*, and by applying those rules to particular people and labeling them as outsiders. From this point of view, deviance is *not* a quality of the act the person commits, but rather a consequence of the application by others of rules and sanctions to an "offender." The deviant is one to whom that label has successfully been applied; deviant behavior is behavior people so label.
>
> (p. 9; emphases in original)

Becker also noted that who was labeled deviant could depend on a number of factors. But, he felt that the most significant criteria for labeling will be determined by who committed the act and who was harmed by it (p. 12). Using middle-class white boys and Negroes as examples, he noted that middle-class white boys who violated legal norms were often not formally processed by the police and were commonly released to the custody of their parents. On the other hand, Negro boys, particularly if their victims were whites, were likely to be formally processed through the justice system (p. 13).

In the second chapter of his work, Becker lays out a typology that describes the various types of behavior (see Figure 5.1). As he noted, there are conformists who obey all societal rules and people expect this of them. In addition, there are pure deviants or rule breakers who will always violate the norms of society. As such, society expects them to continue to do so (pp. 19–20). Becker's typology also has a category for the falsely accused, who are persons who get a "bum rap." Describing such a person, Becker wrote: "The person is seen by others as having committed an improper action, although in fact he has not done so" (p. 20). At the other end of the spectrum is the secret deviant. This is the person who has committed a deviant act but no one knows about it or expects it from the person who is involved. Becker suggested that the number of persons falling into this category "is very sizeable, much more so than we are apt to think" (p. 20).

A final component of Becker's theory draws from Everett C. Hughes's (1945) work on master and auxiliary status traits. Of this, Becker (1963) wrote that "Hughes notes that most statuses have one key trait which serves to distinguish those who belong and those who do not" (p. 32). Borrowing from Hughes's writing, Becker notes that some traits are considered master traits or "master statuses." For example, being a doctor is a master trait. Doctors have been licensed to practice medicine and this separates them from everyone else. However, they are also expected to have "auxiliary traits" such as being "upper middle class, white, male, and Protestant" (p. 32). On the other hand, because of

	Obedient Behavior	Rule-Breaking Behavior
Perceived as Deviant	Falsely Accused	Pure Deviant
Not Perceived as Deviant	Conforming	Secret Deviant

Figure 5.1 Becker's types of deviant behavior. (From H. Becker, *Outsiders: Studies in the Sociology of Deviance*, New York: Free Press, 1963. With permission.)

their race, blacks have a "master status." This means that, even if they graduate from the same medical school as whites, they are considered a black doctor, which, as Becker writes, results in their being "treated as Negro first and . . . [anything else] . . . second" (p. 33).

Like race, Becker saw some deviance as a "master status." That is, once someone committed more serious offenses, he or she was considered deviant first and everything else second. Like Tannenbaum and Lemert before him, he also believed that this "master status" isolated deviants to the point where their status influenced their social identity and resulted in a sort of self-fulfilling prophecy (for a classic discussion of this phenomena, see Merton 1967, pp. 421–36), which results in their consorting with others who have been similarly labeled. In the end, the problem has been aggravated because of the labeling process (Becker 1963, pp. 34–5).

The relevance of Becker's version of labeling theory for race and crime is apparent. First, the notion of secret deviants is very telling for racial minorities. If racial minorities are labeled as "deviants" and receive an added measure of attention from justice system officials, it stands to reason that they are likely considerably represented among the falsely accused; conversely, whites and Asians in America (who have been labeled "model" minorities), who are likely escaping the scrutiny of the same justice system officials, are likely over-represented among secret deviants. In a similar vein, if both race and deviance are "master statuses," then black criminals not only are in the classic "double bind," but also likely represent the worst fears of whites and others who internalize these labels. Unfortunately, these two "statuses" have become enmeshed in the minds of whites and others. As is discussed later in the chapter, this has resulted in considerable consequences for racial minorities who are not criminals, but are "falsely accused" because they cannot avoid being treated in relation to their externally (societal) designated "master statuses."

Goffman's *Stigma*

Goffman's *Stigma: Notes on the Management of Spoiled Identity* (1963) represents another landmark publication on the labeling perspective. His perspective provided another view on the process of labeling. He believed that society was responsible for determining who would be labeled or not. During this process, individuals will have what Goffman refers to as virtual social identities or identities based upon assumptions about a particular person or group. On the other hand, there are also actual social identities, which are the attributes that can be proven regarding an individual or group. Keeping these two characterizations in mind, Goffman outlined the labeling process, which usually occurred when a stranger is present:

> Evidence can arise of his possessing an attribute that makes him different from others in the category of persons available for him to be, and of a less desirable kind—in the extreme, a person who is quite thoroughly bad, or dangerous, or weak. He is thus reduced in our minds from a whole and unusual person to a tainted, discounted one. Such an attribute is a stigma, especially when its discrediting effect is very extensive; sometimes it is also called a failing, a shortcoming, a handicap. It constitutes a special discrepancy between virtual and actual social identity.
>
> (p. 3)

According to Goffman, there were three types of stigmas. First, there were physical deformities. Second were what Goffman referred to as "blemishes of individual character" (1963, p. 4), which he described as things such as dishonesty, addiction, imprisonment, suicidal attempts, and other things that might be considered negative personality traits. The final type of stigma was the "tribal stigma of race, nation, and religion, these being stigmata that can be transmitted through lineages and equally contaminate all members of a family" (p. 4). Those not falling under any of the aforementioned stigmas were referred to as normals (p. 5). It was the attitudes of the normals towards the stigmatized that resulted in "varieties of discrimination, which . . . effectively, if often unthinkingly, reduced . . . [one's] . . . life chances" (p. 5).

Goffman's work expanded on the previous literature in that he argued that there was a transmission of one's stigma from one generation to the next. This is significant for understanding the nature of race and crime because, for racial and ethnic minorities, color and ethnic background continue to be the proxy for criminality and dangerousness. Hence, irrespective of where you were born, who your parents were, where you worked, or how much money you had in the bank, in many instances, the stigma you were born with (being a racial or ethnic minority) trumped all of these things and, at times, resulted in discriminatory treatment throughout society and, of more significance for this work, throughout the criminal justice system.

Following the publication of these classic works on the labeling perspective, some scholars continued to examine the way class-based labeling exerted an impact on how white youth were treated by justice system officials (Chambliss 1973). Others argued that the removal of "individualized justice" and the unfettered discretion in the juvenile justice system would actually improve the system (Schur 1973, pp. 168–9).

Criticisms of Early Labeling Theories

During the mid-1970s, criticisms regarding these early labeling perspectives evolved (Grove 1975a). The most common criticism was that there were no specifically formulated propositions for the theory. As such, it was difficult to test the theory. The few substantive tests conducted up to the 1970s revealed mixed findings (Grove 1975b), with some observers finding limited support for the theory (Hirschi 1975; Robbins 1975; Tittle 1975; Wellford 1975). Other critics found the theory to be tautological. In other words, when labeling theory is tested, no matter what is found, the outcome can still be credited to the theory. Tittle (1975) provides an example of such a situation:

> In considering the postulate that labeling leads to secondary deviance . . .
> if it is found that negatively classified individuals repeat the behavior for
> which they were labeled, proponents will applaud the power of the labeling
> perspective. On the other hand, should it be discovered that those who are
> negatively classified actually engage in the behavior less frequently, propo
> nents will maintain that the label obviously did not stick.
>
> (p. 159)

The period following the publication of these searing critiques of the labeling perspective saw it fall out of favor among criminologists. Recently, though, the perspective has received new life in studies pertaining to the stigma of being an ex-offender (Hirschfield and Piquero 2010). More specifically, researchers have found that the stigma that attaches to being a black ex-offender can result in extreme difficulties finding employment (Pager 2007a, 2007b; Winnick and Bodkin 2009).

On the flip side, this same research suggests that white privilege or simply being white can deflect the impact of being an ex-con (Pager et al. 2009; Winnick and Bodkin 2009). Another important expansion of the labeling approach has been outlined by Wacquant in his work on territorial stigmatization where he has discussed the assorted negative consequences of the stigmatization of entire neighborhoods across the globe (Wacquant 2008; Wacquant, Slater, and Borges Pereira 2014); these consequences include damaged sense of self among residents of these areas, discrimination in employment (e.g. address discrimination), the reduced level of service delivery from social services agencies and the police, the increased reproduction of specialists in symbolic reproduction or persons who shape how people or places are viewed (e.g. journalists, scholars, policy analysts, and politicians), and the development of public policies ". . . that, [combined] with market and other forces, determine and distribute marginality and its burdens" (Wacquant et al. 2014, p. 1275).

All in all, the labeling perspective highlights the potential power of stereotypes/stigma in shaping the societal views and treatment of certain populations (and communities), especially racial minorities. In fact, tracing the origin of the term "black-on-black violence," David Wilson (2005) shows the power of stereotypes in the shaping of national public policy.

Contemporary Labeling Theory: The Power of Stereotypes

In his work, *Inventing Black-on-Black Violence: Discourse, Space, and Representation*, Wilson, a geographer, who considered the nature of the discourse and the spaces that became criminal during the 1980s and 1990s, convincingly argued that, beginning in the early 1980s, the press in most major cities began to focus attention on "waves of violence" in black communities. This attention produced a new phenomenological term: "black-on-black violence." As his research suggested, prior to the 1980s, very few major newspapers used such a term (see Table 5.1). But, according to his research, with the initiation of this term, "'black-on-black violence' thereafter became widely discussed in Congress, public schools, mayoral forums, churches, and presidential speeches" (p. 4). Based on his analysis of newspapers and interview

Table 5.1 Proportion of articles on local violence using the term "black-on-black violence"

Source	1978	1980	1982	1984	1986
San Francisco Chronicle	0	0	2 (4%)	12 (24%)	14 (28%)
Chicago Tribune	0	0	3 (6%)	14 (28%)	18 (36%)
Cleveland Call and Post	0	0	3 (6%)	40 (60%)	31 (82%)
St. Louis Post Dispatch	0	0	1 (2%)	9 (18%)	16 (32%)

Note: Based on a random sample of 50 articles selected for each year. Articles had to have the word "violence" or "crime" in their titles and focus on local affairs. (From D. Wilson, *Black-on-Black Violence: Discourse, Space, and Representation*, Syracuse, NY: Syracuse University Press, 2005. With permission.)

data, Wilson's research found that, during this era, stereotypical views of blacks were used by conservatives *and* liberals to move their agendas forward.

On one side, the conservatives portrayed black families, black inner-city youth, and liberal black politicians as the villains. On the other side, liberals focused on drug-peddling gangs, who were products of "devastated and culturally declining inner cities" (Wilson 2005, p. 82). Liberals also argued that, to solve the "black-on-black violence" problem, racism needed to be eradicated. According to black leaders, another "cure" for the problem required halting of the criticisms of black political leaders "by conservatives and many in the media of corruption and self-aggrandizement" (p. 93). Finally, black culture (also referred to as "inner-city culture," "underclass culture," or the "black subculture") was on the decline. According to the prevailing liberal argument: "This deteriorating glue of values and morals, a crucial communicative element in the discourse, seared residents in a context of deepening poverty and disenfranchisement. These youth and spaces, purportedly decimated by this culture, were profoundly damaged" (p. 99).

After examining both sides, Wilson noted the obvious overlapping themes between the two sides. The most potent was that America was "under siege by a new horde of criminals—the black predator—taking over cities, suburbs, and rural places" (p. 131). As a result of this stereotypical image, beginning with the Ronald Reagan era, national legislation such as the Comprehensive Crime Control Act of 1984, the Anti-Drug Abuse Act of 1986, and numerous other legislative acts during the 1980s (under Reagan and the elder Bush) and 1990s (under

Clinton) translated the fears into punitive policies. He also documented the wave of similar legislation that emanated from local jurisdictions around the country (pp. 143–7). Such legislation, originating from the "black-on-black violence" stereotype (label) at the federal, state, and local levels resulted in the massive incarceration of racial and ethnic minorities (Gabbidon and Taylor Greene 2013; Walker et al. 2011).

At the conclusion of his text, Wilson (2005) surmised that

> [while the] Negro-ape mythology no longer flourishes . . . instead a common understanding of race works through notions of culture and space. Common thought has largely rejected biological determinism but widely substitutes spatial–cultural disposition. Urban African Americans become understood as place-based beings carrying so many cultural attributes that capture an irrefutable essence.
>
> (p. 153)

He also believed that there are new nuances to the way stereotypes are now perpetuated. Of this, he wrote:

> . . . racial stereotypes continue to flourish in a dimly recognized and taken-for-granted process of representing. The dilemma is that even allegedly sensitive, sympathetic depictions of crime and inner city life are tainted by this template of "seeing." Applied by conservatives and liberals, this new racism conceals its existence under the auspices of sensitivity and concern.
>
> (p. 153)

Wilson's analysis clearly reveals how crime-related stereotypes, left unchecked, become labels that have "collateral consequences," especially for racial/ethnic minorities.

Building on the classic work of Lawrence (1987), Armour (1997) examined "Negrophobia" and the incorporation of what has been referred to as "reasonable racism" or the notion that, because of their perceived dangerousness, the irrational fear of blacks might be justified in situations where whites take preemptive action (shooting) to ward off their prospective attacker(s). So, for example, in a situation where a white person shoots a black person who he or she *thought* was a perceived robber, based on statistics and stereotypes that feed into "Negrophobia," Armour argued that some courts might actually buy into such an argument, which one could interpret as the implicit acceptance of "reasonable racism" or "rational discrimination." In other words, given the over-representation of blacks in robbery arrest statistics, it is all right to blow a black man away if he looks like a potential robber. But the obvious problem with such a premise is that, in the socially constructed minds of many whites and some racial minorities, all blacks and Latinos look like potential robbers. In the end, as noted by Covington (1995), crime becomes racialized or, put another way, crime becomes associated with particular racial/ethnic groups.

Katheryn Russell-Brown, in her critically acclaimed work, *The Color of Crime* (1998), created the term the *criminalblackman*. It is her contention that, because of "the onslaught of criminal images of black men ... many [people] incorrectly conclude that most black men are criminal" (p. 3). Because of this negative imagery, Russell argued that racial hoaxes were often perpetrated against blacks (see Russell 1994; 1998, pp. 69–93). She defined a racial hoax as a situation "when someone fabricates a crime and blames it on another person because of his race OR when an actual crime has been committed and the perpetrator falsely blames someone because of his race" (1998, p. 70). After surveying newspapers, Russell found that most hoaxes involved incidents where whites had falsely accused blacks of committing some crime (white-on-black hoaxes). Because the *criminalblackman* image was believable, the black community was often "shaken down" when such hoaxes were perpetrated. So, once again, stereotypes evolved into labels that resulted in black communities being targeted for increased criminal justice attention (see also Fishman 2006; Rome 2004, 2006; Russell-Brown 2006a, 2006b; Stabile 2006; Young 2006). It is widely believed by the public that the 2012 killing of Trayvon Martin provides another example of how the *criminalblackman* stereotypes played a role in the tragic death of a black youth (see Gabbidon and Jordan 2013).

In her book, *Protecting Our Own: Race, Crime, and African Americans* (2006c), Russell-Brown argues that blacks respond to labeling by "protecting their own" in the form of what she refers to as "black protectionism" (pp. 34–5). She defined black protectionism as "the response by large numbers of the black community to allegations that a famous black person has engaged in a criminal act or ethical violation. The response is protective in that it denies, excuses, or minimizes the charges" (p. 2).

Russell-Brown argues that, when conducted in a systematic manner, black protectionism can serve as a way to promote racial justice.

Besides African Americans, Mann et al. (2006), in several editions of their work, *Images of Color, Images of Crime*, have profiled scholarship that examines the role of stereotyping in the lives of other racial/ethnic minorities. Such scholarship clearly illustrates the common impact that stereotypes have on racial/ethnic minorities.

Since the 1990s, scholars began in earnest to quantify the impact of such stereotypes in a variety of settings. This move produced four types of studies:

1. Studies that connected the use of stereotypes in the sentencing process.
2. Studies that examined the stereotypical view that immigrants (particularly Latinos) were causing "crime waves" around the country.
3. Studies that examined the content of media to determine whether the common belief that the media were purveyors of the *criminal-blackman* stereotype was "fact or fiction." (Such studies have also sought to determine whether the content of media has an impact upon emotions such as fear.)
4. Experimental/simulation psychology-based studies that examined how stereotypes affected the behavior of criminal justice professionals.

Illustrative examples of each of these areas of scholarship follow. Given that the first two areas have received considerable attention in the field, they are briefly reviewed next. The latter two areas have only recently become of serious interest to scholars. As a result, more attention is devoted here to these two areas.

Stereotypes and Sentencing Decisions

The role of race in who gets prosecuted and sentenced has been a long-standing topic in the criminological literature (Du Bois 1899). However, most scholars examining this question generally turn to conflict theory (see Chapter 6) to contextualize the disparate treatment of racial minorities. Among the scholars investigating the question of how labeling affects race and sentencing are Darrell Steffensmeier, Jeffrey Ulmer, and John Kramer (1998), who have led the way by examining what they call the "focal concerns" theory of sentencing (a term borrowed from Walter Miller's subcultural theory profiled in Chapter 4).

The theory considers three areas: "the offender's blameworthiness and the degree of harm caused by the victim, protection of the community, and the practical implication of sentencing decisions" (Steffensmeier et al. 1998, p. 766). Taking these things into consideration, these authors also noted that stereotypical views of young black males as a "dangerous class" was a concern. As such, using data from Pennsylvania, they tested several hypotheses to determine whether race, age, or gender had an impact on sentencing outcomes. While the authors' results mirrored previous research in that "the primary determinants of a judge's sentencing decisions are seriousness of the crime committed and the defendant's prior record," there were race, gender, and age effects as well (p. 785). The authors' other results showed that "young black men (as opposed to black men as a whole) are the defendant subgroup most at risk to receive the harshest penalty . . ." (p. 789).

Another research study, published in the same year, examined the role of unemployment and sentence severity and found similar results in Chicago and Kansas City (Nobling et al. 1998). However, the authors of the second study found that, in the courts studied, "unemployment increases the likelihood of incarceration for racial minorities but not for whites" (p. 478).

In later studies by Steffensmeier and Demuth (2000, 2001, 2004), the authors found additional support for the "focal concerns" theory, as well as for the notion that racial minorities receive more harsh sentences than whites in both federal (Steffensmeier and Demuth 2000) and state (Steffensmeier and Demuth 2001, 2004) courts. Notably, though, in these more recent studies, Hispanics were found to epitomize the most serious "threats," which resulted in their receiving the most severe sentences.

Building on the focal concerns perspective, Muniz and McMorris (2002) examined the outcomes of sentences in misdemeanor cases and found similar results in Nebraska. Their study revealed that "Native Americans and Latinos respectively were more at risk in criminal sentencing outcomes as they received higher fines and a two to five times higher likelihood of jail time for misdemeanor convictions in comparison to whites" (p. 255). They contextualized the results by arguing that, because of long-standing stereotypes, Hispanics and Native Americans were seen as the greatest "threats" or as "symbolic assailants." More recent scholarship examining the role of stereotypes and sentencing among Native Americans and found that Native American males were sentenced more harshly than similarly situated white and African American males (Franklin 2013).

Another issue tied to stereotypical views is the topic of immigration and crime. Some of the scholarship, as it relates to Latinos in America, is reviewed next.

Stereotypes and the "Immigration and Crime" Link

It was noted in Chapter 3 that the historical and contemporary scholarship on immigration and crime has clearly revealed that, in most instances, crime among immigrants has been lower than that of native groups (Martinez 2002). Missing from the earlier discussion, though, was the potential impact of such stereotypes or myths (Cisneros 2008). In the last two decades scholars (Hagan and Palloni 1999) have attempted to dissect the "myth" of Hispanic immigrants and crime (Hagan et al. 2008; Hagan and Palloni 1999). While doing so, some of them have observed how such myths result in public policies that contribute to a sort of "self-fulfilling prophecy" (see also Chavez and Provine 2009; Hagan and Palloni 1999).

Building on the classic work of Sutherland (1924) and the more recent work of Tonry (1997), Hagan and Palloni (1999) first note the shortcomings of the "immigration causes crime hypothesis" (p. 618). They argue that "reports of Hispanic imprisonment obscure policies and practices that inflate Hispanic incarceration. That is, high Hispanic incarceration rates are the product of specific immigration and criminal justice policies and practices" (p. 619). In addition, they argue that, when considering incarceration rates, one should take into account age and pretrial detention issues. Such considerations, in their view, are critical to understanding the incarceration rates of Hispanic immigrants.

To examine their suppositions, the authors analyzed data from arrest and citizenship status data from El Paso and San Diego. Their research found: "When we take gender into account, we find Mexican immigrants, the most numerous Hispanic immigrants to the United States, are in state prisons at an adjusted rate that is not strikingly different from U.S. citizens" (Hagan and Palloni 1999, p. 629). Moreover, they found that immigrants in the two areas studied were "at greater risk of being detained prior to trial, and that this results in their increased likelihoods of being convicted and imprisoned" (p. 630). Finally, the authors found that young male immigrants were more likely to engage in petty crimes, which were likely a way to "satisfy basic subsistence needs while moving through the early stages of seeking, finding, losing, and regaining employment" (p. 630). The authors closed by indicating that Mexicans tend "to do as well and sometimes better than [American] citizens" (p. 631). As such, policymakers should place their emphasis "on ways to preserve, protect, and promote the social and cultural capital that Mexican immigrants bring to their experience in the United States" (p. 631).

During the 1990s, as noted previously, Ramiro Martinez published numerous articles on the nature of crime in the Latino community. During this period, he examined whether the concerns regarding Latino violence were fact or fiction (Martinez 2000; Martinez et al. 2001). In one of these studies, using data from the 1980 UCR Supplemental Homicide Reports (SHR) and census data from 111 U.S. cities, his results indicated that, while the contribution of immigration to homicides was low, "Latino immigration increases urban Latino felony homicide. However, for all other types of Latino homicide, acquaintance in particular, the effect of immigration is negative" (Martinez 2000, p. 372). In more recent research Martinez et al. (2008) has continued to find that immigration does not significantly increase violence in Latino neighborhoods. These results suggested that, like other groups residing in urban areas, Latinos were not immune to the effects of social disorganization (p. 373). Even so, their immigration to such areas has saddled them with the "criminal immigrant" stereotype, which has been used by select politicians to push what some consider to be nefarious legislation (Chavez 2013; Mata and Herrias 2006; Podgomy 2009; Stupi, Chiricos, and Getz 2014).

The next section of the chapter provides an in-depth examination of the stereotypical portrayals of racial/ethnic minorities in a variety of media outlets.

Stereotypes and the Mass Media

Research on the portrayal of racial minorities in television dramas (Eschholz 2004), the print (Barlow 1998) and television news media (Dixon 2007, 2008a, 2008b; Entman 1990, 1992; Entman and Rojecki 2000), and reality-based television police shows (Oliver 1994, 1996; Oliver and Armstrong 1998) has revealed the perpetuation of crime-related and other negative stereotypical views of racial minorities. Such research has been conducted by criminologists and other scholars, who have sought to determine whether television was, and remains, the purveyor of stereotypical crime-related views of racial minorities that, if supported, among other things, could exert an impact on the level of fear (Eschholz 2002) and the endorsement of punitive policies (Dixon 2008b). While numerous scholars have looked at some of these questions (for a comprehensive review of such studies, see Chiricos and Eschholz 2002), this section examines research by some of the leading researchers in this area.

Beginning in the mid-1990s, Mary Beth Oliver, a distinguished professor of communications at Penn State University, conducted a series of studies to examine the nature of the content in reality-based television police shows (e.g. *Cops*). In one of her earliest studies (1994), she sought to determine the nature of the types of crimes portrayed in these shows, how often arrests were made in various situations, the representation of ethnic and racial representations of police officers and criminal suspects, and the incidence of aggressive behaviors (p. 180). Following a systematic review of several shows, the research revealed that violent crimes were over-represented in the shows, and arrests were made at a higher rate than as reported in the FBI's Uniform Crime Reports (pp. 184–5).

Looking at her results on race and ethnic representation, it was found that "white characters more often appeared as police officers than they did as criminal suspects, whereas black and Hispanic characters more frequently appeared as criminal suspects than they did as police officers" (Oliver 1994, p. 186). When Oliver compared these results with government statistics, she noted that, while whites were over-represented as police officers, blacks were under-represented. Blacks were slightly over-represented as criminal suspects, but their representation in the commission of violent crimes was in line with national statistics (p. 186).

Finally, when she examined aggression, among the significant results, she found that, in regard to unarmed physical aggression, "blacks and Hispanics [were] more likely to receive this type of aggression than whites" (p. 188).

In two subsequent studies, Oliver (1996; Oliver and Armstrong 1995) examined the components of white viewers' enjoyment of reality-based programs and the roles of authoritarianism (e.g. discipline, patriotism, obedience to authority, etc.) and the portrayals of race in determining the level of enjoyment. In the first of the two studies on predictors of enjoyment of reality-based shows, her research, based on telephone surveys of whites conducted in Virginia and Wisconsin ($n = 358$), revealed that "reality-based programs are most enjoyed by viewers who evidenced higher levels of authoritarianism, reported greater punitiveness about crime, and reported higher levels of racial prejudice" (p. 565).

Building on these findings, Oliver (1996) then directly sought to test the role of authoritarianism and portrayals and race in the enjoyment of reality-based crime dramas. More specifically, using a sample of undergraduate white students ($n = 124$), she examined the following two hypotheses: (1) authoritarianism will be more strongly associated with enjoyment of scenes involving the arrest of African Americans than Caucasian suspects; and (2) authoritarianism will be more strongly associated with unfavorable evaluations of African American than Caucasian criminal suspects (p. 143).

Strikingly, her results revealed that "authoritarianism was . . . associated with greater enjoyment of the video segments and more unfavorable evaluations of criminal suspects provided that the criminal suspect was African-American rather than Caucasian" (p. 147). Of these results, Oliver surmised that it could be that such shows are popular because a portion of the viewing audience has "negative racial attitudes" (p. 147). In more vivid terms, Oliver wrote: ". . . these shows may enjoy viewer approval not only because they provide images of 'bad guys' getting what they deserve, but also because they may cater to associations that some viewers may have between African-Americans and crime" (p. 147).

In 2004, Oliver and her colleagues, Ronald Jackson, Ndidi Moses, and Celnisha Dangerfield, published a paper that examined the role of race-related facial features in the memory of persons shown on the news. Their primary hypothesis was that "memory of Afrocentric features will be most pronounced for news stories pertaining to stereotyped topics, with Afrocentric features most pronounced for news stories pertaining to crime and to violent crime in particular" (Oliver et al. 2004, p. 93). The authors' hypothesis was supported, which was in line with concurrent psychology research showing that, among black defendants, those with more Afrocentric facial features receive harsher sentences than those defendants with less Afrocentric features (Blair et al. 2004; Eberhardt et al. 2006; for illuminating discussions regarding skin tone, see Dixon 2005; Tatum 2000).

A review of several studies conducted by Sarah Eschholz and colleagues revealed considerable agreement with Oliver's work. Chiricos and Eschholz (2002), for example, examined the content of television news programs in Orlando, Florida, to determine whether "crime is stereotypically portrayed as a black phenomenon" (p. 402) and/or "blacks are disproportionately portrayed as criminals" (p. 402; referred to as the criminal typification of race thesis). On the first thesis, the research revealed that the representation of suspects on the news aligned with the demographic of Orlando. Hispanics, however, were slightly over-represented as suspects (p. 409). Blacks were found to be under-represented as criminals and violent criminals on the news, while whites were over-represented. Turning to qualitative assessments of each group, the authors found that the news

> show[s] black suspects and, to some degree, Hispanic suspects in a negative light, especially when compared to whites. For three of four qualitative distinctions, black suspects were shown in a menacing context substantially more often than whites. For two of the qualitative measures, those involving victim and offender characteristics, Hispanic suspects were not only the most likely to be shown in a menacing context but were presented exclusively in that manner.
>
> (p. 412)

In regard to the criminal typification of race and ethnicity, the authors found that blacks were portrayed as criminal suspects "2.4 times greater than whites" (p. 414). Exploring this further, the authors found that "whereas whites were no more likely to be shown as suspects than victims, blacks were 4 times more often shown in the negative role of suspect than in the sympathetic role of victim" (Chiricos and Eschholz

2002, p. 414). Such a finding supported the existence of the criminal typification of race and ethnicity in Orlando news.

Turning to television crime dramas, Eschholz et al. (2004) examined the content of *NYPD Blue* and *Law and Order* to determine the portrayal of offenders, victims, the types of civil rights violations, and other issues, including the role of race and gender on the shows. Comparing the content of the two shows with New York City census data, their research revealed that whites were over-represented in nearly every category (e.g. offenders, violent offenders), while other racial/ethnic groups were under-represented in most categories. Even so, there were other significant findings regarding race:

> Minorities are disproportionately more likely to be cast as offenders than their white counterparts. This is especially true on "Law and Order," where African American offenders are 1.75 times as likely to be shown in handcuffs than white offenders, almost 5 times as likely to be shown as an offender than a victim, and 3.57 times as likely to be shown as an offender than an attorney.
>
> (pp. 173–4)

Moving from simply examining the nature of television dramas and news shows, Eschholz sought to determine the impact of such programs on the fear of crime. Specifically, she tested the hypothesis that "higher concentrations of African-American offenders on television will produce more fear than viewing predominantly white offenders. Based on previous reception research, the findings are expected to be more pronounced for white viewers than for African-American viewers" (2002, p. 45). After analyzing a variety of television dramas, news shows, and reality-television programs, she found that there was a general effect that the more one watched television, the more likely one would be fearful of crime (p. 52). But when she examined a subsample of just whites,

> the racial composition of television offenders significantly increased fear of crime. Television viewing appears to influence fear among all racial categories, but different characteristics of programming may be important for different groups. The introduction of racial composition into regression models of fear of crime produced no significant effects for minorities . . .
>
> (p. 53)

It is significant that, a year later, Eschholz et al. (2003) published a related study on the impact of television and fear, adding an exploration of whether the perception of the racial composition of neighborhoods would influence fear. They found very little support for their model. Such a finding was contrary to well-established scholarship on the racial fears of whites (see, most notably, Skogan 1995).

After reviewing the previous scholarship, one is still left with one pressing question. Does the minority media perpetuate the same stereotypes as the white media? A research study by Lundman et al. (2004) examined this question. Examining the coverage of homicides in an African American newspaper (*Columbus Call and Post*) in Columbus, Ohio, the authors found that homicides were covered differently than they were in white newspapers. According to their review of eight years (1984–92) of homicides and newspaper coverage, the authors found that, unlike the typical coverage in white newspapers where the focus is on interracial homicides (particularly ones involving black males killing white females), "the *Call and Post* data provide no evidence that the black newspaper employs these same typifications and no evidence of systematic attention to interracial homicides, including those where whites murder blacks" (p. 267). In general the authors noted that the African American newspaper did not use "fearsome and racist images" of blacks or whites (Lundman et al. 2004, p. 267). Conversely, their analysis of gender differences in news coverage found that there were distortions in both the white and African American newspapers related to the way in which women were portrayed. The newspapers perpetuated the following myths regarding females: "They are frequent victims of homicide, men regularly kill females, and women do not kill men" (p. 267).

Another study of interest to stereotypes, race, and crime focused on the way in which athletes involved in crime are viewed in the media. Mastro, Belcha, and Seate (2011) studied the contents of the *Los Angeles Times, New York Times*, and *USA Today* over a three-year period and found that: blacks were over-represented as criminals compared to whites; more detail was provided and more negative consequences were noted when black athletes were involved in a crime; and, ". . . crime news coverage of Black athletes was markedly more derisive, accusatory, and sympathetic to the victim" (p. 539). Only in the findings pertaining to discussions of athletic accomplishment, remorse, or guilt, were there no differences found between the descriptions of crimes involving black and white athletes.

After reviewing the diverse literature related to the presentation of stereotypical images related to race and crime, the next step would be to determine whether justice system officials act on such stereotypes. That is, while it is problematic whether the public consumes the negative imagery of racial minorities in assorted mass media outlets, it is quite another proposition if someone working in the system does so and responds to situations obviously based on stereotypical conceptions of "dangerousness." It can be quite difficult to determine whether the actions of criminal justice professionals have been or will be based on such conceptions; however, psychologists have attempted to do so using experimental studies. Some of this pioneering literature is reviewed next.

Stereotypes and the Actions of Criminal Justice Professionals

Ruby and Brigham (1996) conducted one of the earliest studies to determine whether stereotypes might play a role in the decision-making process of law enforcement officials. Making use of a sample of college students and law enforcement officers from Florida, they examined whether the typical criminal "schema" or profile included race and socioeconomic status (SES). Of their three hypotheses, two tested related areas. The first focused on whether the guilt perceptions related to race and SES of law enforcement officers and students differed. The second investigated whether the guilt perceptions of white and black suspects differed by the race and nature of the subject (student or law enforcement officer). The results did not support the first hypothesis. However, there was support found for the second hypothesis. More specifically, "LE officials were . . . more likely than laypersons to view the actions of blacks as guilty" (p. 107).

In 2001, B. Keith Payne published a study that became an instant classic. His study comprised two experiments involving undergraduate students. In the first, he tested the hypothesis that "participants would respond faster to guns when they were primed by a black face compared to a white face" (p. 183). The author did find support for the notion that whites, when shown a black face and given unlimited time, reacted faster to the identification of guns. The author also tested to see how shortening reaction time would affect the identification of weapons. Here, again, race was an important factor: "Black primes caused race-specific errors. Harmless distracters were more likely to be classified as guns when primed by a black face than when primed by a white face" (p. 190). Nearly a decade after Payne's work, psychological research continues to find support for the stereotype that young black men are threatening and dangerous (see Trawalter et al. 2008).

Cornell et al. (2002, p. 184) continued to delve into the role of stereotypes in how people respond to "potentially threatening individuals." In a series of four experiments, they sought to determine whether the decision to shoot in tragic situations such as the one involving Amadu Diallo, who was shot at 41 times and killed by the New York City Police Department, "was influenced by the stereotypic association between African Americans and violence" (p. 1314). Employing the use of video games and a sample of undergraduate students, the authors created a variety of scenarios involving situations where the subjects were required to make decisions to shoot or not shoot. The scenarios involved instances where the suspected perpetrators were armed or unarmed, with the unarmed suspects having a silver-colored aluminum can, a silver camera, a black cell phone, or a black wallet (p. 1315). Throughout the series of experiments, the backgrounds and required response times (the amount of time in which a decision to shoot or not was required) were adjusted to determine the potential role such things might play in errors related to the decision to shoot or not. Summarizing their results from the experiments, the authors wrote:

> In four studies, participants showed a bias to shoot African American targets more rapidly and/or more frequently than white targets. The implications of this bias are clear and disturbing. Even more worrisome is the suggestion that mere knowledge of the cultural stereotype, which depicts African Americans as violent, may produce Shooter Bias, *and that even African Americans demonstrate the bias.*
>
> (p. 1327; emphasis added)

Subsequent studies using undergraduate students have found support for stereotype bias in critical situations (see Greenwald et al. 2003; Payne 2005). In recent years, scholars have also begun to include criminal justice professionals as participants in such studies.

Eberhardt et al. (2004) sought to determine whether "black-ness" serves "as the prototypical associate for a number of ostensibly race-neutral concepts, such as crime, jazz, basketball, and ghetto. These concepts may trigger clear, visual images of black Americans" (p. 877). To test this hypothesis, a series of studies were conducted. These studies made use of students and police officers. In one of the studies, involving 182 police officers, the researchers measured whether stereotypes influenced their judgments of criminality (by examining pictures to determine the criminality of certain facial features). Again, the results were striking. Of their findings, the authors noted the following:

> When officers were given no information other than face and when they were explicitly directed to make judgments of criminality, race played a significant role in how those judgments were made. Black faces looked more criminal to police officers; the more black, the more criminal. These results provide additional evidence that police officers associate blacks with the specific concept of crime.
>
> (p. 889)

Other researchers have continued in this area of inquiry and found some support for these studies (Graham and Lowery 2004; Payne et al. 2005), while others have challenged the studies because they believe that the faces of African Americans trigger positive *and* negative responses; they likely collectively play a role in racially biased policing (Judd et al. 2004).

Even though some researchers have been successful in using simulations to eliminate the bias found in this genre of research (Plant et al. 2005; Plant and Peruche 2005), some of the most recent research in the area has continued to reveal disturbing findings. For example, one such study reported that "participants shot armed blacks more quickly than armed whites, and decided not to shoot unarmed whites more quickly than unarmed blacks. Participants reporting a stronger association between violence and blacks at the cultural level displayed especially biased behavior" (Cornell et al. 2006, p. 126).

These studies have clearly taken the nature of the labeling/stereotype literature to another level. Scholars can now see the power of negative stereotypes on the actions of criminal justice professionals. This is yet another illustration of the interdisciplinary nature of criminology and criminal justice. As revealed by the literature reviewed here, criminologists have much to learn from psychologists in determining the role of stereotypes in justice system outcomes.

Conclusion

After reviewing some of the early classics of labeling theory and noting their relevance to race and crime, this chapter examined the emerging scholarship that focuses on stereotypes. Such literature examines how racial/ethnic stereotypes exert an impact on justice system outcomes. The scholarship reviewed in this area focused on how negative stereotypes potentially affect sentencing, immigration and crime polemics, the portrayal of minorities in the mass media, and the behavior of students and criminal justice professionals in critical situations. In all instances, the research revealed that stereotypes have the power to influence attitudes such as fear and behavioral actions such as the decision whether to shoot a suspect or not. Such research clearly reveals that the labeling perspective is alive and well, though in a different form, and continues to have relevance for understanding race/ethnicity, crime, and justice.

6

CONFLICT PERSPECTIVES
ON RACE AND CRIME

Conflict theory (also referred to as critical theory) likely represents the most popular theoretical framework used to explain race and crime. The theory, which has some seeds in many of those previously discussed, has some of its origins in Germany. Specifically, the works of German scholars Karl Marx, George Simmel, and Max Weber have been credited with providing the impetus for the theory. According to Lilly et al. (2002), "Theories that focus attention on struggles between individuals and/or groups in terms of power differentials fall into the general category of *conflict theory*" (emphasis in the original; p. 126). In short, when applying conflict theory to race and crime, one would look to whether the creation of laws, the enforcement of laws, and distribution of punishment are done in a discriminatory manner. While social class and gender would also be important to investigate (Barak, Leighton, and Cotton 2014), the way in which the white power structure administered justice would be of central concern to conflict theorists.

The chapter begins with a brief overview of the early scholarship related to race, crime, and conflict theory. Next, the development of conflict criminology as it has been applied to race from the 1960s to 1990s is then reviewed. The chapter closes with a review of contemporary conflict perspectives that have been used to contextualize race and crime.

Early Scholarship on Race, Crime, and Conflict Theory

Among the earliest writers credited with founding conflict theory was Dutch criminologist Willem Bonger. In 1905 Bonger wrote his classic text, *Criminality and Economic Conditions*, which was among the texts selected to be translated into English by the American Institute of Criminal Law and Criminology. Appearing in English in 1916, the text, as Austin Turk noted in his introduction to the abbreviated version in 1969, "had become a minor classic, i.e. a book everyone knows about, a few have read, but hardly anyone ever uses" (1969a, p. 4). In Turk's view, the book had "become a 'classic' before its time" (p. 4). In the work, Bonger argues that capitalism, in some way, influences the manifestation of crime in nearly every facet of society. As such, he views the creation of a socialist society as a way to eliminate crime. Notably missing, though, from his 706-page tome is any substantive discussion of race and crime. However, in his preface to the American edition, Bonger addresses this slight by suggesting that the length of the manuscript was the reason for the omission. Of this he wrote:

> In concert with the desire of the Committee I have shortened the text as much as possible. The whole passage about "race and crime" I have omitted because—maintaining in general what I have written about it—I now have much more to say on the subject, but the space therefore [sic] was not at my disposition.
>
> (1916, p. xxviii)

One wonders what those early passages would have stated regarding race, capitalism, and crime, but he did later produce a classic in the area of race and crime (Bonger 1943).

Another early conflict theorist, W.E.B. Du Bois, studied under Weber and produced one of the earliest works that incorporated a conflict analysis (Gabbidon 1999, 2007; Taylor Greene and Gabbidon 2000). In 1901, he published an article on the notorious convict-lease system that operated in the south in the post-slavery era. Du Bois (1901/2002) traced the history of the system whereby, immediately after the passage of the 13th Amendment, states leased convicts out to private landowners, who no longer had the free labor of African American slaves. He wrote about how states strategically enacted various laws (referred to as the "black codes") to snare blacks into the criminal justice system so that they could be returned to the labor force, which helped maintain the power and privileged status of southern white landowners. In the article, Du Bois also rebutted the biological theorists of his day by declaring that

> above all, we must remember that crime is not normal; that the appearance of crime among Southern Negroes is a symptom of wrong social conditions—of a stress of life greater than a large part of the community can bear. The Negro is not naturally criminal; he is usually patient and law-abiding. If slavery, the convict-lease system, the traffic in criminal labor, the lack of juvenile reformatories, together with the unfortunate discrimination and prejudice in other walks of life, have led to that sort of social protest and revolt we call crime, then we must look for remedy in the sane reform of these wrong social conditions, and not in intimidation, savagery, or legalized slavery of men.
>
> (1901/2002, p. 88)

By this time, as reviewed earlier, Du Bois had already made significant statements on crime, pointing to discrimination, segregation, lynching, and the attitudes of the courts as explanations for African American criminality (1899). It would be some time, however, before the formal articulation of conflict theory and a little longer before race discrimination was incorporated as a central component (Unnever et al. 2009).

Besides the early work of Du Bois, other early scholarship also made the connection among discrimination, unemployment, and crime in the African American community (see, for examples, Waring 1905; Work 1900), all of which directly speak to conflict theory. As with the previous theories reviewed, much of the early race-related literature pertaining to conflict theory focused on African Americans. In the first decade of the twentieth century, Newsom (1906) argued that crime among African Americans was the product of "barbarous and inhumane treatment and oppression of the Negro," which was simply

> outward manifestation . . . of inward fear of ultimate social intermingling and intermarriage between the races due, first, to the Negro's ever-increasing intelligence, refinement and amassment of wealth; second, to the impression held by many unsophisticated whites that the Negro, in

insisting on his civil and political rights, is really trying to force social equality.

(p. 495)

Also employing a conflict analysis, Wright (1910) suggested that when analyzing crime, one needs to pay attention to the types of offenses. In the article, he compared the impact of crap shooting, which was heavily prosecuted, to bank officials or politicians who defraud their company or constituents. Wright argued that if an observer simply looked at the number of arrests related to crap shooting and compared them to the number of arrests for fraud:

> [The dependence on] mere statistics of arrest and convictions would be misleading; for this last criminal may have operated systematically for years, ruining many people; debauching society as well as corrupting finance, causing public confidence to decrease with harm to himself, his own family and many other families. The injury done by . . . forty crap-shooters is not to be compared with that of the bank defalcator, except in statistics.

(p. 140)

Wright continued by noting the difficulties in comparing the crime of African Americans to those of the larger community, especially when "Negroes . . . had to prove their innocence and not their prosecutors prove their guilt" (p. 140). After mentioning the well-documented differences in arrest patterns for whites and African Americans, he notes that poverty is a factor in crime. In his words, "The crimes of the poor are generally their vices, which affect them more than they affect the other parts of the community. The vices of the well-to-do, on the other hand, are seldom called criminal, unless they become of great social concern" (p. 141). Making the connection among race, poverty, and crime, Wright noted that "Negroes of the great Northern cities, being largely among the poor, must be affected by the differences which poverty makes in these matters" (p. 140).

The next two decades continued to see scholars tackle race and crime by incorporating analyses that turned to discrimination in society and the justice system to explain criminality in the African American community (Grimke 1915; Thompson 1926a, 1926b, 1926c; Wilder 1927;

Work 1913). Towards the end of the 1920s, eminent criminologist Thorsten Sellin also addressed the issue of crime in the African American community. In his work, Sellin (1928) noted the dubious reliability of criminal statistics and also the race discrimination encountered by African Americans in the assorted criminal justice agencies. Pointing specifically to higher arrest and conviction rates for African Americans, he also showed that the discrimination did not end there, but continued on with African Americans receiving heavier sentences than whites (pp. 59–63).

Throughout the 1930s, Sellin and other scholars continued to make strong statements on the role of race prejudice in the justice system (Cantor 1931; Sellin 1930, 1935). In a 1935 article, Sellin examined sentence lengths for instances involving determinate and indeterminate sentences involving African American, Native whites, and foreign-born whites. His results showed that, in instances where determinate sentencing was used, foreign-born whites received the most severe sentences. But, when he examined indeterminate sentences, African Americans had the longest sentences in every category except for homicide (p. 216). Seeking to explain these findings, Sellin opined:

> It may be said, of course, that the statistics presented hide a number of possible variables, such as differences among these races and nativity groups in such factors as recidivism, aggravating circumstances, etc., which might produce differences in the length of sentences attributable to no prejudice on the part of the judge. While these factors may play a role, they are probably not responsible for the great and relatively constant variations observed. These we must largely attribute to the human equation in judicial administration and as evidence that equality before the law is a social fiction.
>
> (p. 217)

When Hill (1936) examined the over-representation of African Americans in Richmond, he concluded that the "white dominant group" bore considerable responsibility for the situation. He noted that, while whites brought African Americans here for one reason—"to work," after nearly 300 years of doing this, the white power structure no longer required their labor. As a consequence, Hill (1936) described the situation that materialized in Richmond:

The city studiously keeps Negroes off its payroll. The Negro is the true Southern Gentleman today in Richmond, for he has nothing to do. His garbage is hauled away by white men; his trash also. White policemen watch over him while he sleeps at night—house on fire, white men risk their lives to put it out for him; white chemists keep his water pure—sick? White city physician and nurse rush to his bedside. If he decides to marry, white clerks are there to fix him up. A Southern Gentleman for true.

(p. 177)

Hill continued by noting the dire conditions in the places where these unemployed African Americans were forced to reside. Moreover, he argued that in places where such conditions were "found the world over," crime was the result.

While the 1940s brought more conflict-oriented research on race and crime (see Abraham 1948; Blanshard 1942), two articles published during the decade provided some of the more important contributions. Early in the decade, Johnson (1941), whose work was discussed in Chapter 4, provided a conflict analysis of African American crime. After suggesting that culture conflict theory was not an appropriate explanation for crime among African Americans, he noted the importance of the race of the victim in the administration of justice. The significance given to white lives (in the form of victims) speaks to the caste system that Johnson suggested existed in the 1940s. Conversely, as was also noted in Chapter 4, black lives were devalued and many intraracial offenses in their community were minimally punished or not punished at all. Such a system mirrors the power differentials found in conflict-oriented perspectives. Johnson, like scholars before him, also pointed to the prevalence of race prejudice throughout the American justice system (pp. 97–102). Moreover, he argued that such prejudice was so strong that it was present even during the defining of crimes (pp. 95–6).

Later in the decade, McKeown (1948), building on the earlier work of noted sociologist William F. Ogburn (1935), directly tested the relationship among poverty, race, and crime. Using data on 91 cities with populations over 100,000, he examined the relationship between what he termed "crimes of the proletariat" (e.g. rape, murder, robbery, assault, burglary, and larceny) and several indices of community economic prosperity taken from the World Almanac and the Census Bureau (McKeown 1948, p. 480). His research found a direct relationship between poverty and crime among African Americans, but found no such relationship among the foreign-born (p. 481).

Towards the end of the 1950s, Dobbins and Bass (1958) sought to determine the relationship among race, unemployment, and prison admissions in Louisiana. Based on prison admissions and unemployment data for 14 years (1941–54), the authors found that unemployment was more strongly related to the criminality of *whites*, not African Americans. To explain this serendipitous finding, they posited that, first, African Americans committed more personal crimes than property crimes. Such an offending pattern would go against the notion that unemployment would be strongly related to prison admissions. Second, they indicated that, due to the significant wage gap between whites and African Americans, the difference between the compensation for unemployment among white workers and African American workers was much larger. As such, an unemployed white worker "might be more likely to resort to criminal means in order to reestablish his income" (Dobbins and Bass 1958, p. 524).

Originally formulated by criminologist Thorsten Sellin in the late 1930s, culture conflict theory, according to Williams and McShane (2014), is heavily based on the work of Chicago School products Louis Wirth and Edwin Sutherland (the latter of the two was to have collaborated with Sellin). Given the numerous dimensions of the theory, Brown et al. (2004) have suggested that it could easily be presented in chapters devoted to subcultural theory, strain theory, and social disorganization (pp. 345–6). Even so, it remains a conflict approach and is presented here as a part of that tradition.

Culture Conflict Theory

Even before Thorsten Sellin officially formulated culture conflict theory in 1938, as noted in Chapter 3, scholars had begun to consider the role of "racial heterogeneity" in the etiology of crime and delinquency (see Elliot 1926). As presented by Sellin, the theory, which clearly has linkages to social disorganization theory, has several basic ideas. A central idea of the theory relates to the rules or norms within a culture. Sellin (1938) suggested that over a period of time, certain behavior becomes so accepted within a culture that "the violation of [it] arouses a group reaction. These rules or norms may be called *conduct norms*" (p. 28; emphasis in original).

Sellin's (1938) theory states that all societies have conduct norms, which vary from one culture to the next and could result in violations in one society not being violations in another (pp. 29–30). Within each society, those in power can control the definitions of conduct norms and hence determine what behaviors become crimes. This leaves the potential for culture conflict. In general, Sellin pointed to three ways conflicts between various cultural codes arise: (1) when the codes clash on the border of contiguous cultural areas; (2) when, as may be the case with legal norms, the law of one cultural group is extended to cover the territory of another; or (3) when members of one cultural group migrate to another (p. 63).

Summarizing these ideas, Sellin (1938) formulated two types of culture conflicts. Of the first type, called primary conflicts, he noted:

> [If] the immigrant's conduct norms are different from those of the American community and if these differences are not due to his economic status, but to his *cultural origin* then we speak of a conflict of norms drawn from different cultural system or areas. Such conflicts may be regarded as *primary* culture conflicts.
>
> (p. 104; emphases in original)

Sellin described secondary conflicts as "conflicts of norms which grow out of the process of social differentiation which characterize the evolution of our own culture" (p. 105). As an example of the applicability of his perspective, Sellin used Native Americans as an illustrative population:

> We need only to recall the effect on the American Indian of the culture conflict induced by our policy of acculturation by guile and force. In this instance, it was not merely contact with the white man's culture, his religion, his business methods, and his liquor, which weakened tribal mores. In addition, the Indian became subject to the white man's law and this brought conflicts as well, as has always been the case when legal norms have been imposed upon a group previously ignorant of them.
>
> (p. 64)

The theory clearly had relevance for Native Americans and the various ethnic immigrants and Negro migrants who were arriving en masse to American cities during the early part of the twentieth century (Fox and Volakakis 1956; Wood 1947). In the late 1970s, building on the culture conflict perspective, Peter Blau (1977) articulated the hypothesis that inequality and heterogeneity contribute to the creation of interpersonal conflict within social structures. Blau and Blau (1982) examined the significance of these concepts in the etiology of crime and found that "racial socioeconomic inequalities are a major source of much criminal violence" (p. 126). However, the racial heterogeneity portion of the theory was only minimally supported.

Lee (1995) examined culture conflict and crime in Alaskan villages. Based on comparative data on eight Yupiit Nation villages and eight non-Nation villages, Lee explored the following proposition: "that colonization (invasion, dominance, and succession) results in conflict (disorder/crime) related to the imposition of laws (social control) associated with the dominant group" (p. 181). Essentially, Lee wanted to find out whether crime was less prevalent in villages that maintained their traditional values. Moreover, Lee was interested in finding out whether those villages that enforce alcohol laws have higher or lower alcohol-related incidents. On the first point, Lee (1995) found that "the rates for felonies and misdemeanors are lower in Nation villages with the exception of liquor violation, drunk in public, minor in possession, and protective custody" (p. 184). On the second point, the results were mixed; however, one thing was clear: the formal laws were "not keep[ing] the villagers from drinking or acting out while drunk" (p. 186). Overall, the study found support for culture conflict theory.

While criminologists have generally neglected culture conflict theory, they have, however, borrowed some ideas from the theory and formulated related theories, such as strain/anomie theory (Chapter 3) and subcultural theory (Chapter 4). Another significant conflict perspective was the articulation of group conflict theory by George Vold. His theory and its relevance to race and crime are reviewed next.

Vold's Group Conflict Theory

In 1958, George Vold, in his well-known text, *Theoretical Criminology* (1958), formulated group conflict theory (pp. 203–19). The theory, which draws on the concept of collective behavior (Turner and Killian 1987), posits that people are always involved in groups, and as a result, they are essentially a product of their group interactions. Within society, Vold argues, group interaction leads to a persistent

> flow of collective action that provides opportunities for a continuous possibility of shifting positions, of gaining or losing status, with the consequent need to maintain an alert defense of one's position, and also always with the ever-present and appealing chance of improving one's status relationship.
>
> (p. 204)

Because of this, Vold (1958) further asserts that the by-product of such a process is the "continuous struggle to maintain, or to defend, the place of one's group in the interaction of groups" (p. 204). According to the group conflict perspective, such a struggle is necessary for the continuance of society. Moreover, group conflict occurs when one group's interest and purposes overlap with those of another group (p. 205). The end result is competition between groups, which can lead one group to feel the threat of replacement by another group. When this situation (or group crisis, as Vold describes it) occurs, group loyalty reaches extreme heights, which results in members doing whatever is necessary to show their devotion to the group (pp. 206–7). In the end, Vold (1958) noted:

> The logical outcome of group conflict should [be] either, on the one hand, conquest and victory for one side with the utter defeat and destruction or subjugation for the other side; or, on the other hand, something less conclusive and decisive, a stalemate of compromise and withdrawal to terminate the conflict with no final settlement of the issues involved.
>
> (p. 207)

To demonstrate the applicability of his theory, Vold provided illustrative examples of the theory to minority group behavior and political situations. In his section on minority group behavior, he argues that group conflict theory can be applied to minority groups within society. While he does not mention race in this section, he does use juvenile gangs—who, at the time, were considered to be heavily populated by racial and ethnic minorities—as an illustrative minority group that has conflicts with the dominant majority. He writes:

> The juvenile gang . . . is nearly always a "minority group," out of sympa-
> thy with and is more or less in direct opposition to the rules and regu-
> lations of the dominant majority; that is, the established world of adult
> values and power. The police ordinarily represent the power and values
> of the adult world, while the gang seeks to operate to get the benefits and
> advantages not permitted it under the adult code.
>
> (Vold 1958, p. 211)

In his section on the political nature of criminal behavior, Vold speaks more directly to how crime can arise from group conflict between those seeking "to change, or to upset the caste system of racial segregation in various parts of the world, notably in the United States and in the Union of South Africa" (p. 217) and those seeking to maintain the status quo. In evaluating his theory, Vold suggested that there were many situations in which group conflict would lead to crime because it ". . . is the normal, natural response of normal natural human beings struggling in understandably normal and natural situations for the maintenance of the way of life to which they stand committed" (1958, p. 218). On the heels of Vold's work, the 1960s would see the rise of conflict theory as one of the leading criminological perspectives.

Conflict Theory: The Developmental Years (1964–75)

In the 1960s, Marvin Wolfgang, Sellin's distinguished protégé, produced an important work that reviewed the literature on race and crime, focusing heavily on African Americans and the American justice system (Wolfgang 1964). His work, which provided one of the most comprehensive treatments of the subject up to that point, revealed a criminal justice system fraught with discrimination. Joining other scholars in the belief that eliminating discrimination in all aspects of American society was critical for reducing crime in the African American community, Wolfgang was optimistic that once "knowledge replac[ed] misconceptions about race and crime," things were destined to improve (p. 63). Unfortunately, less than a decade later, when he addressed the subject again with Bernard Cohen, things had not progressed (see Wolfgang and Cohen 1970).

In the same year as Wolfgang's important work, William Chambliss (1964) published his well-known conflict analysis on the law of vagrancy. While it mirrored the earlier analysis of the convict-lease system by Du Bois (Gabbidon 1999, 2007), his analysis set in motion a series of publications by scholars now commonly associated with the further development of conflict theory. These scholars produced their seminal works in the late 1960s and early 1970s, and many of their works directly speak to race and crime.

The development of conflict theory over the last 40 years is often credited to the writings of William Chambliss (1964, 1969), Hubert Blalock (1967), Austin Turk (1969b), and Richard Quinney (1970). Many of these writings were class-based analyses that suggested that capitalism, class structure, and the manipulation of laws were significant contributors to crime and, as such, in line with Bonger's perspective (reviewed earlier) that changing the structure of society would go a long way toward eliminating crime.

Minority-Group Threat

During the 1960s, pioneering sociological methodologist and statistician Hubert Blalock presented one of the first conflict perspectives that focused on racial minorities (1967). A student of Guy Johnson, whose work was reviewed earlier in Chapter 4, Blalock set out specifically to create a theory of minority-group relations that included "[a major] emphasis . . . on status factors, competition, and power relationships" (p. vii). Referred to as "minority-group threat" or "power-threat" theory, Blalock's perspective encompassed several areas: (1) competition and discrimination; (2) power and discrimination; and (3) minority percentage and discrimination (p. 30).

Competition in jobs is an important part of the threat, which often results in concern by the majority group. According to Blalock (1967), power represents another threat and comes in the form of the following resources: ". . . money, property, prestige, authority, and natural and supernatural resources. Also included are physical strength and the ability to bear arms, voting rights, and various rights achieved by formal education, apprenticeship, or membership in certain organizations (e.g. the right to practice law or union membership)" (p. 113). Moreover, the percentage of minorities is also of concern to majority group members. Of this concern, Blalock wrote:

The larger the relative size of the minority . . . the more minority individuals there should be in direct or potential competition with a given individual in the dominant group. As the minority percentage increases, therefore, we would expect to find increasing discriminatory behavior.

(p. 148)

He also noted, though, that if the discrimination by the dominant group was effective, an increase in the minority percentage would not result in any real competition.

Each of these areas provided the avenues through which Blalock believed whites might be threatened by a minority group. Once whites became threatened, they responded with discrimination. Such discrimination was aimed at stunting the development and growth of the minority population. As such, the majority would accomplish this by, as Allen Liska and Steven Messner (1999) correctly assert, "restricting economic and educational opportunities and restricting political rights (disenfranchisement), which in turn reduce minority resources, and by geographical segregation, which reduces the power associated with minority size" (p. 186). In addition, Blalock (1967) adds that, in those instances, where there is much competition, the dominant group might also resort to overt racial violence (p. 150). In addition, theorists have also suggested that the majority population will use their power to increase the level of policing to control minority groups who are considered a threat (Jackson 1989; Jackson and Boyd 2005). In the past two decades, the theory has had renewed interest, which has produced additional empirical tests. Many recent tests of the theory have been supportive (D'Alessio et al. 2005; Eitle and Monahan 2009; Jacobs and Tope 2008; Keen and Jacobs 2009; King and Wheelock 2007; Parker et al. 2005); there have, however, been some recent tests that have not been supportive (see Leiber, Peck, and Rodriguez 2013; Ousey and Lee 2008). Whereas in the past minority-group threat theory has been applied to blacks, in recent years, research has pointed to Latinos emerging as the new threat (Chiricos et al. 2001; Eitle and Taylor 2008). It is likely that future research in this area will increasingly apply the theory to Latinos.

Chambliss's Sociology of Law Conflict Analysis

Chambliss's seminal sociology of law analysis of the laws of vagrancy in fourteenth-century England provided a clear portrait of how the law could be strategically manipulated to fit the needs of the powerful. While there is no linkage to race and crime, the analysis suggests, as Du Bois's earlier analysis revealed, that poor people or those with little power in society, such as most racial minorities, are susceptible to the "whims" of the powerful, including lawmakers. Chambliss did, however, briefly address race in the introduction to his pioneering volume, *Crime and the Legal Process* (1969):

> The urban Negro, probably more than any other single group, represents a large segment of contemporary American society that shares a value system and a "view of the world" quite at variance with the prevailing middle-class morality. Since this group alone represents some twenty million Americans, it is certainly a significant social fact that the legal system is expected to force a set of values upon this group which is incompatible with their own version of American culture.
>
> (p. 11)

Chambliss (1969) also suggested that the plight of African Americans was consistent with that of "Mexican-American immigrants (of even more recent immigration than the Negro) and large groups of Japanese, Chinese, Southern 'hillbillies,' and Puerto Ricans as well" (p. 11). He continued that America was not as pluralistic as other nations, noting that

> the attempt by the dominant middle class to impose their version of morality on the lower classes generally and on . . . [minority] groups specifically is a source of considerable strain in the legal institution. Thus with the historical emergence of the middle class as the dominant group, we have inherited a source of legal changes and also a source of inherent conflicts which are played out in the arena of the law.
>
> (p. 11)

Austin Turk's *Criminality and Legal Order*

In his book *Criminality and Legal Order*, Turk (1969b) presented his "theory of criminalization." Turk's theory examines the cultural and social differences between authorities and subjects that lead to conflict and eventually to crime. While he argued that cultural differences by themselves do not result in crime, he noted the following four situations in which conflict was likely (p. 55):

- There may be close agreement between the cultural norms announced by authorities and their actual behavior patterns, and similarly high congruence between the way in which subjects who possess the attribute or commit the act evaluate it and their social norms.
- There may be little or no agreement between authorities' verbal and behavioral norms and between those of subjects.
- Authorities' talk and behavior may be highly congruent, while there is little if any agreement between the words and actions of subjects.
- The attribute or act as described in the announced norm may have considerable behavioral import for subjects, though the announced cultural norm has little foundation in the social norms of the authorities.

If conflict did ensue, Turk presented the conditions in which those in opposition to the norm will become criminal and the conditions under which they will be pursued and arrested. On the first point, Turk noted that, depending on the

> significance of the legal norm for authorities, both in regard to congruence of cultural and social norms and in regard to the relative priority of the norm over other norms, the greater the probability that violators will be assigned criminal status.
>
> (p. 64)

Moreover, if there are repeated violations of even the most insignificant norm, the authorities will most likely feel compelled to take action. So which authorities did Turk see as being responsible for determining who becomes criminal and who gets pursued? In short, the police or first-line enforcers as he refers to them are the ones responsible for who receives the most attention. He aptly argued that "higher level enforcers" such as the prosecutors, judges, and even governors "are limited in their ability to get at the target population directly" (p. 65). Describing the power of the police, he wrote that some offenses, such as suburban poker parties, will occur with impunity, while the police "stay on the lookout for cards and craps in Negro slums" (p. 65).

In a similar vein, speaking about the relative power of the authorities in the justice system, Turk writes about the "nightstick law" and "assembly line justice" to which powerless people were subjected. With an eerie contemporary resonance, Turk notes that the enforcers are not concerned about potential investigative errors involving the powerless of a society; in fact, he predicted that there would be "a higher frequency of 'miscarriage[s] of justice'" involving the powerless (p. 70). Given that racial minorities would be heavily represented among the powerless, the theory had, and continues to have, clear implications for understanding the nature of race and crime in America and in similar countries.

After fully articulating his theory, Turk turned his attention to crime trends, where he applied his perspective to the findings. When he examined national arrest data, he found some differences by age, sex, and ethnicity. For example, Turk found that young, nonwhite males were the ones most likely to engage in property and fraud offenses. To explain this, he wrote that their "lack of social acceptance and skills imply lesser opportunity to defraud, resulting in relatively low criminality rates for the adult offenses of forgery, fraud, and embezzlement" (p. 127). However, he was quick to caution readers regarding these figures, writing that if there were more complete figures on white-collar offenses, older white males would be more significantly represented.

Nonwhites were also more prominent in statistics for drug- and alcohol-related offenses, for which Turk argued that white youths were protected by the authorities while nonwhite youths were not (p. 134). For offenses such as disorderly conduct, vagrancy, and suspicion, Turk found that nonwhites had considerably higher rates than whites. Given their low status in American society, he argued that it was surprising that more nonwhites were not represented in the arrests for these offenses. In short, in Turk's view, the numbers provided evidence that nonwhites had, to a large extent, accepted the prevailing legal order (p. 142).

Quinney's *The Social Reality of Crime*

With the formulation of his social reality of crime perspective, Richard Quinney (1970) presented another early classic in the conflict theory tradition. Quinney's theory was based on the following six propositions (pp. 15–25):

- Proposition 1 (definition of crime): Crime is a definition of human conduct that is created by authorized agents in a politically organized society.
- Proposition 2 (formulation of criminal definitions): Criminal definitions describe behaviors that conflict with the interests of the segments of society that have the power to shape public policy.
- Proposition 3 (application of criminal definitions): Criminal definitions are applied by the segments of society that have the power to shape the enforcement and administration of criminal law.
- Proposition 4 (development of behavior patterns in relation to criminal definitions): Behavior patterns are structured in segmentally organized society in relation to criminal definitions, and within this context persons engage in actions that have relative probabilities of being defined as criminal.
- Proposition 5 (construction of criminal conceptions): Conceptions of crime are constructed and diffused in the segments of society by various means of communication.
- Proposition 6 (the social reality of crime): The social reality of crime is constructed by the formulation and application of criminal definitions, the development of behavior patterns related to criminal definitions, and the construction of criminal conceptions.

Quinney's theory is clearly related to the previously discussed labeling and conflict-oriented work of the 1950s and 1960s. His theory proposes that not only do the powerful have the ability to construct the law that defines what will become criminal, but once some acts and the designated actors (typically lower-class persons) are labeled criminal, the information is then disseminated through society by "various means of communication" (e.g. the news media). Quinney's work was representative of others that appeared during the early 1970s (see Chambliss and Seidman 1971). In his work, Quinney (1970) does allude to the role of race, crime, and conflict theory. In his section on the application of criminal definitions, he discussed the racial context of arrests. There he drew on the scholarly literature to note that

> selective enforcement according to racial factors results in part from long-held prejudices of individual policemen. But also important is the fact that the Negro tends to fit the stereotype that police have of the

criminal. Through the use of certain cues, a probabilistic model of law violation, and their past experiences, the police are more likely to arrest the Negro than the white man in a similar offense situation. . . . With such conceptions of events and offenders, a differential in law enforcement according to the racial context of the situation is to be expected.

(p. 130)

Turning his attention to the courts, in the same chapter, he noted that "Negroes, in comparison to whites, are convicted with lesser evidence and sentenced to more severe punishments" (p. 142). Quinney also acknowledged the stark differences in who received the death penalty, and concluded that while African Americans were disproportionately represented in violence statistics, there was generally a greater willingness to execute lower-class racial and ethnic minorities than whites (p. 186).

Later in the text, Quinney (1970) specifically discussed the behavior patterns of each racial or ethnic group. More specifically, he focused on African Americans and persons of other ethnic groups and nationalities. A review of the statistics led him to conclude that where one is in the ethnic-racial social structure matters (p. 221). In Quinney's words:

Each group . . . develops its own behavior patterns in reference to its position in the ethnic-racial structure of society. While the behavior patterns consequently differ from one position to another, their criminality is determined not by the nature of the behavior itself but by the fact that persons in other positions, through the use of legal resources of the state, define the behavior as criminal.

(1970, p. 222)

This context provided the impetus for Quinney's perspective on why African Americans were so involved in crime:

. . . especially among Negroes, a person's behavior may be shaped by the reaction to the position he has been assigned. Much of the behavior of Negroes represents a reaction to subordination, economic insecurity, denial of employment opportunities, restricted participation, and discrimination.

(1970, p. 222)

Using a case study of a small Michigan town, Green (1970) set out to test the racial dimensions of conflict theories such as Quinney's and did find support for the role of socioeconomic status in crime. However, he also found that "the effect of socioeconomic status on arrest rates . . . appear[s] to operate independently of race" (p. 490). Such findings served as the precursor to the race/class debates of the next three decades (see, most notably, Wilson 1978).

Conflict Theory: 1970s–90s

In addition to the aforementioned scholars, in his classic work *Crime and Privilege* (1975), Barry Krisberg, while articulating a critical perspective (referred to then as "new criminology"), clearly added the dimension of race to the theory by integrating the history of criminal justice practices used to control oppressed groups and also highlighting the prison writings of George Jackson, Angela Davis, and other high-profile African American prisoners of the early 1970s. Notably, building on the work of Blauner (1972), Krisberg devoted a whole section of the work to race privilege, which in recent years has been translated into the notion of "white privilege" (see McIntosh 2002).

This notion of white privilege within criminal justice translates into more focus on "crimes in the streets," as opposed to "crimes in the suites." Such actions criminalize the actions of other races and poor whites, while minimizing or looking past the crimes of whites in power. Over the years, in multiple editions of his classic text, *The Rich Get Richer, and the Poor Get Prison* (2007), Jeffrey Reiman has spoken of this in terms of white-collar crimes, environmental crimes, and other corporate crimes that kill thousands of people, who are primarily poor and racial minorities, but rarely result in anyone being severely punished.

In addition to the wave of seminal publications on conflict theory reviewed in the previous section, more such publications flowed well into the 1970s (see Quinney 1977; Spitzer 1975; Taylor et al. 1975). Many of these publications were more Marxist (also referred to as radical criminology) in orientation (for an overview of these perspectives, see Bohm 1982; Lynch et al. 2006), and were based on the belief that crime resulted from a class struggle within society.

In general, Marxists argued that within capitalist societies class struggles between the proletariat (working class) and the bourgeoisie (the
wealthy and powerful) explained the etiology of crime. Essentially, those
in the bourgeoisie controlled most of society's modes of production (e.g.
land) and the resultant wealth and power. Because they are unwilling to
share their prosperity, the result is a surplus of workers who are unemployed. The Marxists argued that crime could be expected from these
ranks (Quinney 1977). Crime, to some Marxists, was defined in terms
of "imperialism, racism, capitalism, and other systems of exploitation
which contribute to human misery and deprive people of their human
potentiality" (Platt 1975, p. 103, as quoted in Bohm 1982, p. 571).

Following this second wave of publications, the conflict perspective became a common theoretical orientation used to contextualize
empirical studies on race and crime. At this same time in the early and
mid-1980s, additional literature began to appear showing that there
was a measure of discrimination in justice systems in the United States
(Blumstein 1982; Christianson 1981; Petersilia 1983; Peterson and
Hagan 1984) and in other parts of the world (Bird 1987; Gordon 1983;
Hanks and Keon-Chen 1984).

During this period, Hawkins (1987) further expanded the conflict
model by examining it in terms of race, crime, and punishment. He
emphasized the need to consider race discrimination in conflict theory
(p. 723). According to Hawkins, at the time, some other considerations usually lacking in conflict theory included victim characteristics,
region, and accounting for race-appropriate behaviors. While the first
two characteristics are self-explanatory, for the latter, Hawkins noted
that anomalies found in some studies do not take into account behaviors that are generally committed by one race that, when committed by
another, result in a punishment that seems out of line.

Finally, Hawkins also suggested that too often conflict theorists do
not consider the previously reviewed power threat approach of Blalock
(1967). As noted previously, the perspective argues that once a majority
population sees a minority group encroaching on spheres traditionally
reserved for majority group members, they respond in a number of ways,
including additional social control (Hawkins 1987, pp. 735–6). To his
credit, Hawkins's modifications of the theory have been supported and
have also served as the theoretical foundation for major publications

analyzing race, ethnicity, and crime (most notably, see Walker, Spohn, and DeLone 2011).

Around the same time of Hawkins's important research, William Wilbanks published his controversial work, *The Myth of a Racist Criminal Justice System* (1987). In contrast to conflict theorists, who argue that discrimination represents a significant factor when seeking to explain why minorities are over-represented in the criminal justice system, Wilbanks argued that, while he believed there was some discrimination in the criminal justice system (using the analogy of having a few bad apples in a barrel), contrary to what was being espoused in much of the race and crime literature:

> I do not believe that *the system* is characterized by racial prejudice or discrimination against blacks; that is, prejudice and discrimination are not "systematic." Individual cases appear to reflect racial prejudice and discrimination by the offender, the victim, the police, the prosecutor, the judge, or prison or parole officials. But conceding individual cases of bias is far different from conceding pervasive racial discrimination.
>
> (pp. 5–6; emphasis in original)

Wilbanks's perspective became known as the "no discrimination thesis" (NDT).

Wilbanks's book and its perspective initiated a series of debates between Wilbanks and Coramae Richey Mann. In contrast to Wilbanks's position, Mann (1990) felt that "the racism in the criminal justice system has become institutionalized in the same way that it has in other organizational segments of the nation such as education, politics, religion, and the economic structure; and the barrel *is* rotten" (p. 16; emphasis in the original).

Mann's perspective became known as the "discrimination thesis" (DT). While the debates became heated, the two had brought to the fore an issue that lay below the surface for many years. In the early 1990s, Mann responded with her highly acclaimed *Unequal Justice: A Question of Justice* (1993). While the debate cooled after the publication of her book, the level of discrimination in criminal justice systems continues to be a central focus of scholars (Lynch et al. 2008). Although Wilbanks never produced the second edition he planned to write (1987, p. x), other scholars have recently continued in his tradition (see, for example, Beaver, DeLisi, Wright, Boutwell, Barnes, and Vaughn 2013; DiLulio 1996; Delisi and Regoli 1999; MacDonald 2003, 2008).

Currently, scholars continue to use conflict theory and the discrimination disparity continuum created by Walker and his colleagues (see Figure 6.1) to contextualize studies on race and crime. Too numerous to review here, studies testing the veracity of conflict theory's ability to account for the disproportionate representation of racial minorities in justice systems span all areas of the criminal justice system (Gabbidon and Taylor Greene 2013).

Contemporary Conflict Perspectives on Race and Crime

Wacquant's Deadly Symbiosis

In the early 2000s, sociologist Loïc Wacquant presented his "Deadly Symbiosis" perspective aimed at explaining the hyper-incarceration of blacks. It provides a compelling analysis of what he believes is the meshing of elements of the prison into ghetto life in black American communities and how prisons have taken the character of the ghettos after the mid-1970s (Wacquant 2000, 2001, 2008a, 2009a). On the whole, his perspective on race and penality across the globe has strands of both labeling and conflict perspectives. In the American context, Wacquant (2001) argues that there have been four "peculiar institutions" whose

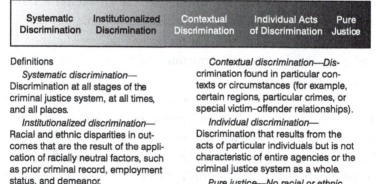

Figure 6.1 The discrimination–disparity continuum. (From S. Walker, C. Spohn, and M. Delone, *The Color of Justice: Race, Ethnicity, and Crime in America*, Wadsworth, a division of Thomson Learning, 2003. With permission.)

effects have been to define, confine, and control African Americans (p. 98). As outlined in Table 6.1, the institutions he outlines include: *Slavery* (1619–865); *Jim Crow* (south, 1865–965); *Ghetto* (north, 1915–68); and *Hyperghetto + Prison* (1968 to present). In Table 6.1, he outlines the form of labor in each period, the nature of the economy, and the way in which blacks were controlled in each period.

During the first three "peculiar institutions," Wacquant (2001) argues that there were two joined yet discordant purposes:

> to recruit, organize, and extract labor out of African Americans, on one hand; and to demarcate and ultimately seclude them from so that they would not "contaminate" the surrounding white society that viewed them as irrevocably inferior and vile . . .
>
> (p. 99)

In the fourth period, he describes in detail how the ghetto became more like a prison. He points to the important role of class and racial segregation, the loss of positive economic function (most notably the loss of manufacturing jobs), the replacement of communal institutions such as local stores, black associations, and churches, with the rise and increasing use of welfare programs, public housing, failing public schools, and the massive increase of agents of the criminal justice system (police officers, probation officers, parole agents, and snitches) (Wacquant 2001, pp. 106–7). Wacquant also discusses how the ghetto "lost its capacity to buffer its residents from external forces . . . it has

Table 6.1 The four 'peculiar institutions' and their basis

Peculiar Institution	Form of Labor	Core of Economy	Dominant Social Type
Slavery (1619–865)	unfree fixed labor	plantation	slave
Jim Crow (South, 1865–965)	free fixed labor	agrarian and extractive	sharecropper
Ghetto (North, 1915–68)	free mobile labor	segmented industrial manufacturing	menial worker
Hyperghetto + Prison (1968–)	fixed surplus labor	polarized postindustrial services	welfare recipient & criminal

devolved into a one-dimensional machinery for naked relegation, a human warehouse wherein are discarded those segments of urban society deemed disreputable, derelict, and dangerous" (p. 107). In addition, he argues that the lives of inner-city residents have become depacified, with residents having fewer networks, and the informalization of survival strategies has resulted in an inner city in which:

> fear and danger [are prevalent] in public spaces; interpersonal relations are riven with suspicion and distrust, feeding mutual avoidance and retraction into one's private defended space; resort[ing] to violence is the prevalent means for upholding respect, regulating encounters, and controlling territory; and relations with official authorities are suffused with animosity and diffidence—patterns familiar to students of social order in contemporary US prisons.
>
> (p. 107)

To further cement his analysis, Wacquant provides two examples. First, he refers to the "prisonization" of residences or homes such as public housing, retirement homes, homeless shelters, etc. In the hyperghetto, many of these places have taken on the character of prisons with fences, bars, identification checks, random searches, curfews, and electronic monitoring (Wacquant 2001). Next, Wacquant uses a similar analysis regarding the prisonization of inner-city public schools where schools typically resemble fortresses, with wired fencing, steel doors, metal detectors, cameras, and armed guards. Of inner-city schools, he writes: ". . . it appears that the main purpose of these school [sic] is simply to 'neutralize' youth considered unworthy and unruly by holding them under lock for the day so that, at minimum, they do not engage in street crime" (p. 108). He continues by powerfully noting that the environment that is present in schools "habituates the children of the hyperghetto to the demeanor, tactics, and interactive style of the correctional officers many of them are bound to encounter shortly after their school days are over" (Wacquant 2001, p. 108). On the flip side, Wacquant also shows how the prison has also become like a ghetto. He first points to the racial division and disadvantage that now pervades every facet of the prison experience as well as the post-release period (see also Wacquant 2005); among other things, he also observed that the "code of the streets" now supersedes the long-standing "convict code."

Throughout this discussion he makes clear that the character of ghettos and prisons have "meshed."

In closing, Wacquant has clearly provided scholars with a unique and critical framework for understanding the mass incarceration of racial/ ethnic minorities across the various periods of American history. Notably, he has also written about conditions (at various stages) similar to those in the United States and other countries including Brazil (Wacquant 2008b), France (Wacquant 2007), and Britain (Wacquant 2009b).

Comparative Conflict Theory

Hagan et al. (2005) formulated the comparative conflict theory of perceived criminal injustice. The theory posits that during one's adolescent years perceptions of injustice are developed (Shedd and Hagan 2006). The theory also postulates that there are differences in the intensity of the perceptions of injustice between African Americans and Latinos. Here, it is felt that the perceptions of African Americans will be more intense than those of Latinos. One caveat noted here by the theorists is that the difference in the level of intensity will converge when African Americans and Latinos have had similar experiences with the police. At the heart of the theory is the belief that the opinions of racial and ethnic minorities on criminal injustice "vary across groups based on their relative access to power, social subordination, and exposure to harsh crime control methods used against them" (Buckler et al. 2008, p. 37; see also Bobo and Johnson 2004).

Tests of comparative conflict theory have been relatively supportive of the so-called "gradient effect" with blacks perceiving the most injustice, followed by Hispanics, then whites (Buckler and Unnever 2008; Buckler et al. 2008; Gabbidon and Jordan 2013; Hagan et al. 2005). The "differential sensitivity" part of the thesis has not been supported. Thus, in the most recent studies, Hispanics who had negative encounters with the police did not perceive more injustice than blacks (Buckler and Unnever 2008; Buckler et al. 2008).

Genocide and Conflict Theory

In 2005, John Hagan, Wenona Rymond-Richmond, and Patricia Parker took the conflict theory, race, and crime literature in a new direction, with their analysis of genocide in the African region of Darfur, Sudan.

Moving away from the application of conflict theory to the North American and European contexts, these authors, like others before (for an early pioneering text on crime causation in Africa, see Clifford 1974), have added to what Clifford referred to as "African criminology" or the study of crime in Africa. While such research has traditionally been contextualized using the colonial model (see Chapter 8), Hagan and his colleagues argue that conflict theory can explain genocide in Africa and other parts of the world.

Listed as one of *Parade Magazine's* 2013 worst dictators (http://parade.condenast.com/175305/parade/top-10-worst-dictators/#omar-a l-bashir-3/), Omar al-Bashir of Sudan has ruled over a country where estimates suggest that somewhere between 180,000 and 400,000 Africans from the Darfur region of Sudan have been killed. Hagan and his colleagues (2005) drew on conflict theory to explain what they consider genocide or what they refer to as "the crime of crimes." Using survey data collected from a U.S.-funded study of the Darfurians in refugee camps in Chad, they sought to determine whether the actions of the Sudanese government constituted genocide. The data from 501 respondents described countless incidents of state-sanctioned killing and rape. The data also revealed that the violence and rapes were targeted at African—not Arab—villages (p. 544). In general the data supported the authors' thesis that "the Arab-dominated government advanced its interest in its power and control of Sudan by empowering local Arabs and destroying and dislocating local African groups, using racist ideology as a divisive and destructive motivating means to accomplish this goal" (pp. 549–50).

After finding support for their thesis and declaring the events in Darfur as constituting genocide, Hagan et al. (2005) close their research noting the inattention that such incidents have received from criminologists around the world. Their powerful indictment of the discipline is worth quoting in full: "Modern criminology possesses the theory and methods to document, describe, analyze and explain 'the crime of crimes' and other important violations of international criminal law. The denial and neglect of these crimes in modern criminology itself needs explanation" (p. 556). In addition to the work of Hagan and colleagues (see also Hagan and Rymond-Richmond 2009), other scholars have also started to explore genocide as an important criminological topic (Ducey

2008; Hinton 2005; Moon 2011; Mullins and Rothe 2007; Rafter 2008; Rafter and Walklate 2012; Winterdyk 2009).

Critical Race Theory/Criminology

Another conflict perspective that originated in legal circles is critical race theory (CRT). Prominent legal scholars Derrick Bell and Richard Delgado have been at the forefront of shaping the perspective (Crenshaw et al. 1995). The theory has two goals. First, it aims to determine how the law is used to maintain white supremacy and continue to oppress people of color. Second, it aims to counter or stop the use of the law (e.g. crack cocaine vs. powder cocaine) and criminal justice practices (e.g. racial profiling) to oppress people of color (Russell 1999). Delgado and Stefanic (2001) have also presented the tenets of CRT. First, racism is ever present in American society and is, thus, a daily occurrence in American society. The second tenet is referred to as "interest convergence," or the notion that whites benefit (materially and in other ways) from racism, so they "have little incentive to eradicate it" (Delgado and Stefancic 2001, p. 7). Third, critical race theorists believe race to be socially constructed, manufactured classifications. Here, critical race theorists are particularly concerned about the racialization of groups. Specifically, they express concern about "the ways the dominant society racializes different minority groups at different times, in response to shifting needs such as the labor market" (Delgado and Stefancic 2001, p. 8). Critical race theorists also believe that, because of their distinct histories and experiences, racial and ethnic minorities have a "unique voice of color" perspective to offer society.

Glover (2009) has expanded critical race theory to criminology by articulating what she refers to as "critical race criminology." She argues that critical race criminology "places race at the fore of social analyses" (p. 2). Further, she writes that

> Critical race criminology specifically addresses traditional and contemporary examinations of race in criminology and contests the way the discipline produces and represents race by focusing on and indeed validating experiential knowledge via the social narrative of marginalized communities.
>
> (p. 2)

After articulating the theory, rather than focusing on traffic stop data, Glover (2009) instead applies the theory to *victims* of profiling. In short, her analysis using critical race criminology as its foundations argues that the victims of racial profiling should become the center of analysis. Her qualitative interviews with victims of racial profiling reveals the importance of shifting the emphases away from quantitative stop data to in-depth study of the impact of racial profiling on the lives of racial and ethnic minorities (see also Brunson 2007; Higgins and Gabbidon 2009). In addition to racial profiling, scholars have argued that critical race theory can also be applied to private prisons in America (Hallett 2006), the intersection of race and gender during the slave-era when black women were openly raped by white slave masters (Tellis et al. 2010), and the lynching of black men (Tellis et al. 2010). Ross (2010) has also recently argued that critical race theory has relevance in criminology.

There have been a few persistent criticisms of critical race theory. First, because much of the work is based on storytelling and personal narratives, which moves away from "objective" or "value-free" analyses, some critics have concluded that the perspective is unscientific. Also, according to K. Russell (1999), some have argued that "CRT amounts to academic whining about women and minorities . . ." (p. 183). Even with these criticisms, the perspective has become a standard legal theory, especially among women and minority legal scholars.

General Criticism of Conflict Theory

Along with Hawkins's concern about the oversimplification of the theory, a few other shortcomings have been noted with conflict theory. Bohm (2001) notes that the perspective does not take into account individual differences. That is, not all people who are oppressed or discriminated against will respond the same way. In addition, it has been suggested that, while conflict theory might explain property crimes, it does not provide an appropriate explanation for "predatory crimes" (Moyer 2001, p. 215). Others have suggested that, in some of its forms, the theory is not testable. A final criticism of the theory is that the theory calls for the creation of a socialist society, which has been referred to as unrealistic and utopian (Moyer 2001, p. 214).

Conclusion

As early as the late nineteenth century, scholars such as W. E. B. Du Bois used concepts now associated with conflict theory (e.g. unemployment, race discrimination, etc.) to explain crime among racial/ethnic minorities. Later, other prominent criminologists, such as Sellin, Bonger, Vold, and Wolfgang, were also among those whose works connected conflict theory, race, and crime. In the last 40 years, because of the works of Chambliss, Quinney, Turk, Blalock, and Hawkins, conflict theory has continued to be used to contextualize disparities in the criminal justice system. With the recent development of "Deadly Symbiosis," comparative conflict theory and critical race theory, the conflict perspective has continued to have relevance for contextualizing race, ethnicity, and crime. Furthermore, with the work of Hagan and his colleagues, conflict theory is now being applied to genocidal activities. Therefore, even with its numerous shortcomings, the theory has remained current and will likely remain one of the most popular theoretical frameworks among race and crime scholars.

7

SOCIAL CONTROL PERSPECTIVES
ON RACE AND CRIME

According to Imogene Moyer, the term "social control" was first used in a series of articles published in the late 1800s in the *American Journal of Sociology* (2001, p. 131). The author of those articles was noted sociologist Edward A. Ross. Shortly after the publication of the articles, Ross published the book *Social Control: A Survey of the Foundations of Order* (1901), which was one of the first books on social control. In his work, Ross had very little to say about blacks or other racial minorities, but the few comments he made were quite telling.

Suggesting ways to "uplift" blacks, Ross wrote:

> It is now recognized that not churches alone will lift the black race; not schools; not contact with the whites; not even industry. But all of these cooperating can do it. The growth of higher wants, coupled with the training to new skills, is the best lever for raising the idle, quarrelling, sensual Afro-American.
>
> (p. 336)

He continued by suggesting ways that the "backward" members of the black race could succeed, saying that "infecting" them with "a high estimate of cleanliness, neatness, family privacy, domestic comfort, and literacy is quite as truly a moralizing agency as dread of future punishment or love of an ethical God" (p. 336). Some of the themes presented in this early articulation of race and social control theory sound eerily similar to the sorts of things that some conservative adherents to social control theory currently espouse (e.g. morality, literacy/intelligence, and crime, etc.).

French sociologist Emile Durkheim is also credited with formulating one of the first social control perspectives. In his work, *The Rules of Sociological Method* (1895), Durkheim noted that crime was a normal aspect of all societies. No society has ever existed without its presence. In Durkheim's view, there were reasons for the existence of crime. First, he felt crime was necessary for social change. For example, at some juncture, protest over some social issues might result in arrest, but in the long run such "criminal" activities might result in a change in social policy. He also felt that, on occasion, the common concern about crime brought communities together (Martin et al. 1990, p. 287).

At times, though, Durkheim felt crime was a result of the breakdown of societal norms, which resulted in what he referred to as anomie or a breakdown of norms (see Chapter 3). It is notable that in his pioneering work *Suicide* (1897/1951), in which he used suicide rates as a proxy for the level of anomie within a society, Durkheim felt a need to include a chapter on race (see Durkheim 1897/1951, Chapter 2). His apprehensions towards distinguishing groups by race would fit easily in some modern day texts. On the topic of race, he wrote that "the sociologist must be very careful in searching for the influence of races on any social phenomenon. For to solve such problems the different races and their distinctions from each other must be known" (p. 85). He continued by noting that race was used more simply to describe a group of people and the categorization was more in line with nationality. Throughout the chapter, Durkheim argued that the difference in suicide rates between European "races" was not a product of heredity but of one's upbringing and environment.

Modern day social control theorists aim "to explain factors keeping people from committing criminal or delinquent behavior" (Williams and McShane 2014, p. 161). The theory has linkages to the classical school, Durkheim's anomie perspective, social disorganization theory, and psychological approaches (Moyer 2001, pp. 133–8). Following the work of Ross and Durkheim on social control, scholars unanimously agree that Albert Reiss, Walter Reckless, Simon

Dinitz, Ellen Murray, Greshem Sykes, and David Matza provided some of the earliest social control perspectives. Later, the work of Travis Hirschi served as the instigator of contemporary social control theory and also as the foundation for the "general theory of crime," which is currently the most popular iteration of social control theory (Gottfredson and Hirschi 1990). This chapter begins with a review of some of the work of the social control theorists writing in the 1950s and 1960s.

Social Control Perspectives: 1950s and 1960s

Reiss's Social Control Perspective

Reiss's (1951) early perspective examined the role of personal and social control in the etiology of delinquency. His perspective defined personal control as "the ability of the individual to refrain from meeting needs in ways which conflict with the norms and rules of the community" (p. 196). He defined social control as "the ability of social groups or institutions to make norms or rules effective" (p. 196). This early paper sought to determine which personal and social controls were related to delinquent recidivism.

Using an all-white sample, the author found that significant predictors in controlling the recidivist behavior of juveniles included the role of primary groups, community and institutional controls, and personal controls. Reiss described primary groups as those that should meet the needs of children and also ensure that they internalize the appropriate norms and rules. Community and institutional controls speak to the nature of the community in which juveniles reside. If the juvenile lives in a community that is not characterized by social disorganization (overcrowding, lack of recreational facilities, poor housing, etc.), then community and institutional controls will prevail (p. 201). In addition, Reiss (1951) noted the significant role of schools in controlling behavior:

> A major set of institutions which exercise control over the person are those providing formal education. Within the school, the child is provided with a set of learning experiences which are presided over by adult authority. Such experiences generally take place within a framework of controlling behavior in conformity with conventional norms.
>
> (p. 201)

Finally, Reiss suggests that those who conform to norms have the following characteristics:

(a) mature ego ideals or non-delinquent social roles, i.e. internalized controls of social groups governing behavior in conformity with non-delinquent group expectations, and (b) appropriate and flexible rational controls over behavior which permits conscious guidance of action in accord with non-delinquent expectations.

(p. 203)

Reiss's social control theory, as suggested earlier, clearly integrated a wide range of criminological perspectives.

Reckless and Dinitz's Social Control Perspective

The 1950s saw a wave of publications that employed the social control perspective. Of note, though, is the work of Ohio State University professors Walter Reckless and Simon Dinitz (in conjunction with several of their graduate students). During the period, they produced a series of publications that contributed to the development of the theory (Reckless et al. 1956, 1957a, 1957b; Dinitz et al. 1957). These articles examined two questions: (1) What insulates an early teenage boy against delinquency? (2) Is it possible to identify certain components that enable young adolescent boys to develop or maintain nondelinquent habits and patterns of behavior in the growing-up process? (Reckless et al. 1956, p. 744).

In their first attempt to examine these questions, Reckless and his colleagues examined white delinquency among 125 "good" boys. The results of their examination suggested that "insulation" or protection from delinquency is achieved when the boys internalize nondelinquent values. However, the research did not locate the source of these values, especially in high-delinquency areas. The researchers, however, surmised that it might have come from parents, family members, priests, or teachers (Reckless et al. 1956, p. 746). In addition, they noted that "playing the part of the good boy and remaining a good boy bring maximum satisfactions (of acceptance) to the boy himself" (p. 746).

During this period, Reckless and his colleagues also published a second wave of studies related to social control theory. In this series of articles, the authors again examined two samples of white youth. One group was considered "insulated" or "good" boys in comparison to delinquent subjects. The authors found that the two groups were fairly comparable. However, two notable differences include a lower percentage of "insulated" delinquents from broken homes. In addition, the "insulated" group had better self-concepts (Dinitz et al. 1957; Dinitz et al. 1958; Dinitz et al. 1962; Reckless, Dinitz and Kay 1957).

Sykes and Matza's Techniques of Neutralization

In 1957, Sykes and Matza outlined another social control perspective. Their "techniques of neutralization" perspective is based on the premise that, while juvenile delinquents adhere to societal norms most of the time, they will, at times, commit delinquency or violate social norms if they can provide justifications or rationalizations for their actions. Such rationalizations, according to Sykes and Matza, often "precede deviant behavior and make deviant behavior possible" (p. 666). The authors refer to the justifications used to engage in deviant behavior as "techniques of neutralization" (p. 667).

In their paper, they outline five techniques. First, they discuss the denial of responsibility. Here, the authors argue that juveniles falling under this technique will blame their behavior on "forces outside the individual and beyond his control such as unloving parents, bad companions, or a slum neighborhood" (Sykes and Matza 1957, p. 667). Denial of injury is the second technique of neutralization. This technique occurs when a youth suggests that his or her behavior has not really harmed anyone. For example, in this view, vandalism is simply "mischief," while stealing a car is simply just "borrowing." The third technique of neutralization is the denial of the victim. By minimizing the status of the targeted victim, adherents to this technique wonder what the big "fuss" is about when people express concern about attacks against "undesirables" or other deserving targets. So who constituted such targeted populations? The authors provided the following comments to illustrate who and what were fair game:

> Attacks on homosexuals or suspected homosexuals, attacks on members of minority groups who are said to have gotten "out of place," vandalism as revenge on an unfair teacher or school official, thefts from a "crooked" store owner—all may be hurts inflicted on a transgressor, in the eyes of the delinquent.
>
> (p. 668)

The last two techniques of neutralization include condemnation of the condemners and the appeal to the higher loyalties. With the former, the authors suggested that delinquents would justify their behavior by taking the attention off their behavior and focusing on the persons "condemning" them. In such a scenario, the youth will suggest that those who are the condemners are "hypocrites, deviants in disguise, or impelled by personal spite" (p. 668). The youths will also argue that persons in authority have it in for them; as such, they are likely to view such persons with cynicism. Illustrative of this are the following views that might prevail among the youth: "Police it may be said, are corrupt, stupid, and brutal. Teachers always show favoritism and parents always 'take it out' on their children" (p. 668). The last technique of neutralization is the "appeal to higher loyalties." This justification rests on the belief that the deviant or delinquent behavior is acceptable because it represents activity that, though in violation of societal norms, serves some higher purpose. Such a higher purpose might involve not "squealing" on a friend or gang member.

In sum, these five techniques of neutralization provided key concepts that moved the social control perspective forward. In regard to its relevance for explaining racial differences in crime and justice, the authors did not directly test the perspective. However, it is obvious that some of the neutralizations could apply to all races. Moreover, it is clear the perspective has particular relevance for explaining certain types of crimes perpetrated against racial minorities. For example, considering the historical period when the perspective was written, the denial of victim neutralization could have easily been applied to hate crimes perpetrated against racial minorities during the civil rights era. Sadly, while nearly five decades have passed since the formulation of their perspective, this technique of neutralization likely remains applicable to such crimes today (Gerstenfeld 2010).

Reckless's Containment Theory

In 1961, as the culmination of his earlier research, Reckless presented his containment theory, outlining his perspective in the first paragraph of his seminal article. He noted that "containment theory is an explanation of conforming behavior as well as deviancy" (p. 42). The theory has two key elements: inner and outer containment. According to Reckless,

Inner containment consists mainly of self-components, such as self-control, good self-concept, ego strength, well-developed superego, high frustration tolerance, high resistance to diversions, high sense of responsibility, goal orientation, ability to find substitute satisfactions, tension-reducing rationalizations, and so on.

(pp. 44–5)

Outer containment refers to those institutions that serve as a buffer "to hold [one] within bounds" (p. 45). Such things include family members and teachers, who reinforce accepted societal norms.

While much of the research used to formulate containment theory and early social control perspectives focused exclusively on white males, it is apparent from the components of the theory that they likely have relevance for racial and ethnic minorities. By the end of the 1960s, the social control perspective was further refined with the work of Travis Hirschi (1969). His important work, which is reviewed next, provided one of the first attempts to apply social control theory to a racially mixed sample.

Travis Hirschi's *Causes of Delinquency*

Published in 1969, Hirschi's *Causes of Delinquency* formally laid out what is now known as control theory. At the core of the theory is the question: "Why *do* men obey the rules of society?" (p. 10). Drawing on the earlier social control literature, the perspective argues that people conform to the rules when they have a strong bond or connection to society. Therefore, when such bonds are weakened, individuals are likely to engage in delinquent behavior.

Outlining his theory, Hirschi articulated four key bonds. One's attachment to society was the first bond. According to Hirschi, if someone is attached to others (e.g. spouse, friends, family, etc.), he or she is less likely to engage in deviant acts (pp. 18–19). The second critical bond was commitment. Here, Hirschi surmised that those individuals who were committed to conventional activities (e.g. education and occupational careers) were more likely to consider the ramifications of their actions and thus less likely to engage in delinquency. Involvement was the third bond. Relying on the old adage "idle hands are the devil's workshop," Hirschi argued that being active or involved in community activities kept youth busy with conventional activities and away from illicit ones (pp. 21–3). Hirschi's final bond was belief. This bond was based on the premise that there is "a common value system within the society or group" (p. 23). When this bond to the societal value system is broken, as with the other bonds, there is an increased likelihood of an individual engaging in deviant behavior.

After discussing the foundations of his perspective, Hirschi provided a test of the theory. Based on data from California schools, he combined data from school records, self-report surveys, and police records to determine the level of support for his theory. The research resulted in a sample with several thousand students. Of these students, after excluding females, about 41 percent were black and the remaining participants were white (pp. 35–7). Hirschi, like theorists before him, realized that black Americans were different from white Americans. However, even though he noted that "Negroes occupy a highly disadvantageous position in the opportunity structure; the Negro's stake in conformity to conventional expectations is decidedly small; Negro 'culture' is lower-class in character; Negro family life produces faulty ego and superego development" (p. 65), Hirschi believed a closer look at certain variables could account for the differences in delinquency between black and white youth.

Based on his data, Hirschi found that 42 percent of blacks and 18 percent of whites had criminal records two years prior to the study (p. 75). When he examined other data, he found less distinct differences between blacks and whites. For example, 42 percent of blacks and 35 percent of whites had been picked up by the police, and "49 percent of the Negro and 44 percent of the white boys report having committed one or more delinquent acts during the preceding year." Even after considering official data and self-reports, Hirschi could not account for the large differences between black and white youth. Seeking to explain this, he wrote:

> [The difference] . . . does not result from interdepartmental differences in defining and recording cases by the police, it cannot result from "errors" in data collection such as those that may explain the unusually low rate of delinquency among white boys in the two schools. Although the official delinquency rate among Negro boys is partially accounted

for by differences in actual delinquency activity (the self-report difference between Negro and white boys persist[s] when the controls used
in the case of official delinquency are applied), the discrepancy in the
strength of the relation between these two measures of delinquency and
race remain[s] to be explained.

(1969, pp. 77–8)

To further explain these differences, Hirschi first turned to the official
reaction hypothesis (labeling theory), noting that "the police do patrol
more heavily in Negro areas; the police do think that Negroes are unu-
sually likely to commit criminal acts . . ." (p. 79). However, on the same
page where he asserts these potential explanations, Hirschi stated that
"there is no reason to believe that the causes of crime among Negroes are
different from those among whites" (p. 79). From there, he argued that
because of their unfavorable attitudes towards the police, the actions of
blacks are more likely to result in more formal action (recording of the
offenses) than the informal resolution of trivial matters. Finally, Hirschi
concluded his discussion of racial differences in delinquency by pointing to verbal achievement scores, which, in his interpretation of the
data, almost completely removed race from the equation. He argued
that, irrespective of race, those students who scored poorly on such tests
were more likely to engage in delinquent activity.

Thus, since blacks often scored lower than whites on these tests, it
was concluded that "differences in academic achievement go a long way
toward explaining Negro-white differences in delinquent activity" (p.
80). Even though he noted that some of the differences in delinquency
between black and white youth were "exaggerated by differential police
activity," Hirschi was quick to qualify such a conclusion by adding,
"This may not mean that the police are biased against Negroes in the
traditional meaning of the term, but it most assuredly means that there
is a Negro-white differential that cannot be removed by statistical analysis" (p. 81). In the remainder of Hirschi's work, he sparingly references
the role of race and principally focuses on the findings related to the
explanatory power of the bonds postulated in his theory.

In more recent years, Unnever et al. (2009) have reexamined Hirschi's
original data and noted that he neglected to examine several measures
related to racial discrimination. Their reanalysis provided a new angle

on Hirschi's data. Of their initial results including the measures for racial discrimination, the authors wrote:

> even when controls are introduced, perceived racial discrimination significantly predicts greater involvement in delinquency. African American youths who report that they were treated badly because of their race were significantly more likely to engage in criminal behavior *after controlling for the strength of their social bonds.*
>
> (p. 393; emphasis added)

In fact, the authors note that the predictive power of racial discrimination is only surpassed by one bond, involvement (pp. 393–4). Several other findings also speak to the significance of race in Hirschi's dataset. First, those African Americans that had the least amount of respect for the Richmond police were more likely to engage in delinquency. Second, there were several school-related findings of significance. African Americans who were "doing well in school and respected school authority . . . [were] less likely to offend" (p. 402). Those African Americans who perceived racial discrimination and did not devote significant time to homework were more likely to offend. Further, African Americans who felt there was discrimination in schools were more likely to offend. The parent-child bond was also a significant predictor of delinquency. Here, those African Americans who were attached to their parents were less likely to offend.

Unnever et al. (2009) make note of the "criminological road that was not taken" by Hirschi. They believe that, because Hirschi failed to analyze racial discrimination in his study (which they conclude was not because of Hirschi's own racial bias), it "impoverished our understanding of crime" (p. 378). Even so, Hirschi's theory remains one of the most popular theories in criminology. It has generated an abundance of scholarship investigating the validity of Hirschi's bonds. Some of this literature is reviewed next.

Social Control Theory, Race, and Crime

In the late 1980s, Matsueda and Heimer (1987, p. 287) provided a test of the role of race, family structure, and delinquency. In the opening of their article they noted that there was little empirical research examining the race and delinquency relationship. They surmised that there were three reasons for the dearth of research in the area. First, they noted that the subject was "politically sensitive and controversial" (p. 826). Second, they noted that most scholars had attributed racial differences in crime and delinquency to "racial bias in the criminal justice system" (p. 826). Third, they argued that, over the years, there had been difficulty in reliably measuring racial disparities.

Given this situation, the authors attempted to examine the strength of differential association and social control theory in explaining race, family structure, and delinquency. Using the same dataset as Hirschi (the Richmond Youth Project), the authors, who employed more advanced statistical techniques than Hirschi, found more support for differential association than social control theory. For example, they noted that "the most striking difference [by race] is that the total effects of broken homes on delinquency [are] much larger for blacks than nonblacks" (p. 836). They also found the nature of one's neighborhood to be a key factor. More specifically, "Blacks from broken homes who also live in troubled neighborhoods are more likely than those residing in trouble-free neighborhoods to associate with delinquents, learn an excess of definitions favorable to delinquency, and, consequently, violate the law" (p. 836).

At the same time that Matsueda and Heimer were writing, Stephen Cernkovich and Peggy Giordano also published a series of articles testing the viability of social control theory to explain racial differences in delinquency. The first article, which was not a direct test of the role of race in social control theory, examined the nature of family relationships and delinquency (1987). Using survey data from 942 interviews, the authors secured a sample that was 50 percent black. They aimed to test the association between family interactions or the strength of one's family attachment and delinquency. The research revealed that "internal family dynamics are considerably more important than family structure in affecting delinquency" (p. 316). While males tended to engage in more delinquency than females in all family situations, the researchers also found that "blacks are considerably more delinquent than whites in mother-only homes" (p. 313). Overall, though, the authors concluded that their model explained female delinquency better than male delinquency, and the model also explained white male delinquency better than nonwhite male delinquency (p. 315).

Five years after their initial study, the authors used the same dataset to directly test the role of school bonding in delinquency among black and white youth (Cernkovich and Giordano 1992, p. 267). The research made use of several scales to examine the level of school attachment, attachment to teachers, school commitment, perceived risk of arrest, school involvement, parental communication, and perceived opportunity (pp. 269–72). The initial results found no significant differences between black and white males. The results by racial composition of school were quite interesting. They found that

> blacks in mixed-race school environments report greater school involvement than whites in mixed schools and whites in predominantly white schools; blacks attending predominantly white schools also report significantly higher levels of involvement in school than do whites in mixed-race environments.
>
> (p. 275)

The results also showed that "blacks attending predominantly white schools are more likely than blacks attending mostly black schools to believe that arrest will negatively affect their future educational and occupational opportunities" (p. 275). As for the role of school bonding on delinquency, the research revealed very few significant differences. One curious finding was that those black males who were involved in sports and other activities were involved in higher levels of delinquency. The authors sought to explain this with the supposition that "extracurricular activities might detract from the more academic dimensions of school bonding, which in turn, are more important inhibitors of delinquent involvement" (p. 278); however, additional analyses did not support their contention. Overall, the results supported Hirschi's assertion that his theory is race neutral. That is, the tenet of his perspective related to school bonding was applicable to all races.

Rodriguez and Weisburd (1991) used an integrated model of social control theory developed by Elliott et al. (1985) to explain delinquency among Puerto Rican youth. The model incorporates aspects of strain theory, social learning theory (e.g. criminal behavior is learned), and social control theory (see Figure 7.1). Using a sample of 1,077 Puerto Rican males from the South Bronx, the authors replicated the work of Elliott and his colleagues, whose research was based on a national

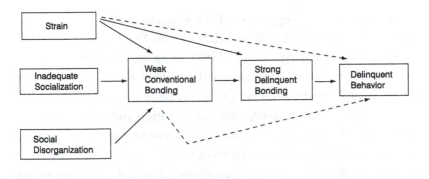

Figure 7.1 The Integrated Social Control Model (From O. Rodriguez and D. Weisburd, "The Integrated Social Control Model and Ethnicity: The Case of Puerto Rican American Delinquency," *Criminal Justice and Behaviour*, 18(4): 464–79. With permission.)

sample. The key elements of emphasis in this research were the role of family bonding and cultural factors. In short, the authors believed that, because of the strong family influence in Puerto Rican families, peer involvement leading to delinquency would be less than in the other families. The following summary of the results confirmed the authors' hypotheses: "Family involvement has more direct influences on delinquency for Puerto Rican Americans than for the general population. In turn, the role of peers is much less important for Puerto Rican Americans" (pp. 477–8).

Using the same dataset as Rodriguez and Weisburd, Sommers et al. (1993) also found that familial values serve as a mediating factor in delinquency among Puerto Rican males. Besides the role of the family, the authors also examined the role of acculturation among the youth. What they found was that, in some instances, the level of acculturation of Puerto Rican youth did have an impact on deviant behavior. Of this relationship, the authors wrote:

> Youth with high levels of acculturation had low family involvement but high involvement with peers and exposure to delinquent peers. Thus the risk of delinquency increases as acculturation leads to alienation and isolation from a supportive Puerto Rican community and efforts to achieve status as a minority in a discriminatory Anglo environment are frustrated.
>
> (pp. 53–4)

The research was supportive of the important role of sociocultural factors when considering delinquency among Puerto Rican youth. In contrast to these findings, Pabon (1998), using the same dataset, argued that employing family solidarity and familism as sociocultural constructs is problematic because "[it] might be that the Hispanic population is quite heterogeneous, reflecting historical and cultural diversity as well as wide variations in terms of employment, income, educational attainment, health status, utilization of health and social services, origin within current U.S. borders or conditions of arrival, and generational status" (p. 952). Because of these considerations, Pabon argued that the results of research using such constructs should be viewed with caution.

After 2000, several authors sought to determine the applicability of social control theory to Asian Americans (Go and Le 2005; Jang 2002; Chang and Le 2005). As with the prior analyses of the theory, Jang (2002) investigated whether the theory could explain the differences in deviance (school misbehavior) among a sample of Asian and non-Asian Americans. In line with the research on Hispanics, the theoretical foundation of the research rested on the belief that Asian Americans are more attached to their families. More specifically, Jang hypothesized that Asians would be less likely to engage in deviant acts than other groups because they were more

> *attached* to conventional institutions of informal social control and their authority figures (i.e. family/parents and school/teachers), *committed* to conventional goals (e.g. academic achievement), *involved* in conventional activities (e.g. schoolwork), socialized to hold conventional *belief* (e.g. respect for authority), and associated with conventional friends.
>
> (p. 650; emphases in original)

The results of the self-report research found that Asian Americans did report lower deviance than other groups. Jang contextualized this finding by noting that the various racial/ethnic groups had varying family backgrounds and levels of school bonding. For example, the Asian American youth were more likely to emanate from families with higher incomes and two-parent families (p. 671). In agreement with previous research, the study found school bonding variables to be significant predictors of deviance. On the other hand, family bonding did not explain the differences in deviance between Asian Americans and other racial/ethnic groups. Jang concluded the article noting that, regardless of cultural differences, the theory held up pretty well under common situations related to social control theory (e.g. socializing with peers uninterested in education, associating with peers who believe it is acceptable to violate social norms, etc.).

Drawing on tenets of social control theory, recent research has examined the role of Native American adolescent social networks (Rees, Freng, and Winfree 2014). Rees et al. (2014) sought to better understand Native American peer social networks in comparison to white peer social networks in school settings and found significant differences. As the authors note: "Compared to American Indian youth, school-based friendships of Whites are much more conducive to network flows of information, friendship support and influence" (p. 419). The authors further assert that "on average, Native American youth are less connected within their schools, and this may well serve as a protective factor at least in the sense of school friendships advocating delinquent behavior" (p. 419). The researchers also note the detrimental impacts (e.g. social rejection, exclusion, and explicit ostracism) of Native Americans being isolated in school settings.

Criticisms of Social Control Theory

Over the years, social control theory has received several criticisms. First, because the original formulation of the theory did not consider more serious offending, some have suggested that the theory is more appropriate for explaining minor offending. Second, some scholars criticized the theory because it was not originally applied to females. However, since these initial criticisms, the theory has been successfully applied to female offending (Brown et al. 2004, p. 364). Third, the theory also has been criticized because the origin and nature of the social bonds are never clearly articulated. Finally, initial tests of Hirschi's theory did not stand up to longitudinal tests (p. 365).

Even with these criticisms, Hirschi's theory remains one of the most cited and researched perspectives among criminologists. In 1990, Hirschi collaborated with Michael Gottfredson to publish *A General Theory of Crime*, which presented a revised version of social control theory. The core tenets of the perspective are reviewed next. In addition, several studies that have applied the theory to racially diverse samples are reviewed.

Gottfredson and Hirschi *A General Theory of Crime*

Gottfredson and Hirschi's (1990) revised social control theory was based on the core concept of self-control. In its simplest form, the theory posits that "people who lack self-control will tend to be impulsive, insensitive, physical (as opposed to mental), risk-taking, short-sighted, and nonverbal, and they will tend therefore to engage in criminal and analogous acts" (p. 90). So what did the authors consider the causes of low self-control? To locate such causes, they returned to the roots of social control theory. First, in their view, the leading cause of low self-control was "ineffective child-rearing" (p. 97). To ensure a child learns self-control, Gottfredson and Hirschi (1990) point to a three-pronged approach: "someone must (1) monitor the child's behavior; (2) recognize deviant behavior when it occurs; and (3) punish such behavior" (p. 97).

Other key elements of the theory include parental criminality, family size, single-parent families, and the working mother. Such additional elements argue that if parents have low self-control and have been involved in criminal activity, they are not likely to socialize their children appropriately (pp. 100–2). In addition, as one's family size increases, it is more likely that the children will become delinquent (pp. 102–3). In short, the increased number of children reduces one's capacity to consistently follow the three-pronged approach to teach children self-control. Moreover, in line with the literature reviewed throughout this book, the authors, for obvious reasons, suggested that single-parent households headed by females are also important considerations. Finally, the authors argue that the increased presence of women in the workforce also plays a role in the nature and level of supervision provided to children.

In addition to the family, Gottfredson and Hirschi (1990) argue that schools represent an institution that can also teach self-control. They point to four key reasons why the schools are able to do so. They note that teachers have ample time to monitor the behavior of children. As such, like parents, they are able to recognize deviant and disruptive behavior. Moreover, school administrators, like parents in the home environment, have a vested interest in "maintaining order and discipline" (p. 105). Furthermore, like parents at home, "the school in theory has the authority and the means to punish lapses in self-control"

(p. 105). While the authors do consider other important considerations, such as the stability of criminal behavior over time and the role of personality in criminal offending, the focus here is on how the theory explains racial differences in offending.

The authors do devote attention to race and culture in two chapters. The first discussion commences in the chapter where they discuss other variables that are usually control variables in empirical research (e.g. age, gender, and race). The second discussion occurs in the chapter on "culture and crime." In the first chapter, the authors make note of the differences in offending among blacks and other groups. After noting the differences, they show the weaknesses of traditional approaches (strain and subcultural approaches) in explaining such differences. Holding firm to their "general theory," the authors wrote:

> There are differences among racial and ethnic groups . . . in levels of direct supervision by family, and thus there is a "crime" component to racial differences in crime rates, but . . . differences in self-control probably far outweigh differences in supervision in accounting for racial or ethnic variations. Given the potentially large differences among racial groups in the United States in the elements of child-rearing . . . (monitoring, recognizing, and correcting evidence of antisocial behavior), it seems to us that research on racial differences should focus on differential child-rearing practices and abandon the fruitless effort to ascribe such differences to culture or strain.
>
> (p. 153)

In their later discussion of culture and crime, the authors simply reiterate that, contrary to conventional wisdom, their "general theory of crime" holds true across cultures (pp. 169–79).

So what have scholars made of the claim that the "general theory of crime" is universal? Well, until fairly recently, the theory was not applied to diverse samples with the aim of testing whether the perspective could explain racial and ethnic differences in deviance (Pratt and Cullen 2000, p. 943). However, some early tests of the theory with diverse samples were generally supportive (Longshore 1998; Longshore and Turner 1998). In 2000, more articles that directly sought to test whether Gottfredson and Hirschi's theory was applicable across race and ethnic lines began to appear in the literature. Some of this literature continued to find support for aspects of the theory in areas or samples having diverse populations (see Hay 2001; Lynam et al. 2000). Another body of literature that examined the question of race/ethnicity more directly did not find support for the race-neutral aspect of the theory (Higgins and Ricketts 2005; Kirchner and Higgins 2014; Lynskey et al. 2000).

Vazsonyi and Crosswhite (2004) conducted direct tests of the cross-cultural validity of the general theory of crime. The researchers used an African American sample comprising low-income public school students (n = 661) and a control sample of white students from a small city to determine the validity of the theory in explaining differences by race and gender. In line with previous tests of the theory, "self-control was consistently predictive of deviance . . . In addition, low self-control was predictive of a variety of deviant behaviors in both males and females" (pp. 425–6). While there were some differences by gender, on the whole, there was considerable support for the basic explanatory power of the theory, irrespective of race and gender (see also Church et al. 2009; Delisi and Vaughn 2008; Lieber et al. 2009; Stewart et al. 2004; Burt et al. 2006).

Criticisms of *A General Theory of Crime*

Though the race and self-control literature is still emerging (as evidenced by this review), the results on the theory have been mixed; most tests of the theory found support for its core tenets. In general, though, the theory has not been without its critics. Moyer (2001), for example, argued that the authors' discussion of rape was woefully misleading and lacking. Specifically, she suggested that in their explication of the foundations of their theory, they understated the seriousness and prevalence of rape and family violence (pp. 154–5). Others believe that, as evidenced by some of the literature reviewed here, race and class should be given more attention in the general theory (see Lilly et al. 2002). Finally, it has also been suggested that the theory engages in "mother blaming." Of this concern, Moyer wrote: "The authors mentioned that delinquents are more likely to come from single-parent and female-headed households. They did not place any blame for delinquency on the father who leaves the home and does not provide adequate guidance for his children" (p. 155). These criticisms have not, however, stopped researchers from continuing to test the validity of the theory.

Race and Life-Course Criminology

Shortly after the publication of *A General Theory of Crime*, Sampson and Laub (1993) presented their life-course criminological perspective, which incorporated several core aspects of social control theory. Their award-winning work, *Crime in the Making: Pathways and Turning Points through Life* (1993), in contrast to the work of Gottfredson and Hirschi (1990), argued for a longitudinal examination of the etiology of criminal behavior. The theory, which builds on the work of Glen Elder (1985), examines how changes over the lifespan exert an impact on whether someone initially engages in crime or not, continues to commit crime (becomes a recidivist), or desists from crime.

At the heart of the life-course perspective are two core concepts. The first is a trajectory, which Sampson and Laub (1993) define as "a pathway or line of development over the life span, such as work life, marriage, parenthood, self-esteem, or criminal behavior. Trajectories refer to long-term patterns of behavior and are marked by a sequence of events" (p. 8).

The second core concept is transitions, which are "marked by life events (such as first job or marriage) that are embedded in trajectories and evolve over short time spans" (p. 8). According to Sampson and Laub, "The interlocking nature of trajectories and transitions may generate *turning points* or a change in the life course" (p. 8; emphasis in original). So how does this perspective relate to criminology?

Throughout their work, Sampson and Laub (1993) provided a reanalysis of data from the classic work of Sheldon and Eleanor Glueck (1950). In doing so, they relied heavily on the social control perspective in which they considered social bonds to schools, peers, and family, etc. In addition, though, because they take a "developmental" approach to the etiology of crime causation, they also examined the role of adult social bonds such as job stability, commitment to conventional educational and occupational goals, and one's marital attachment. Each of these bonds was found to be "significantly and substantially related to adult antisocial behavior, regardless of childhood delinquency" (p. 148). Overall, there was considerable support for their life-course perspective.

Given that their sample was all white, the authors were limited to what they could say regarding the role of race in the life-course perspective. Nevertheless, similar to Gottfredson and Hirschi (1990), Sampson and Laub (1993) also imply the universality of their perspective in the following passage:

> . . . the Glueck data allow us to discuss crime in a "deracialized" and, we hope, depoliticized context. In this regard we believe that the causes of crime across the life course are rooted not in race, and not simply in drugs, gangs and guns—today's policy obsessions—but rather in structural disadvantage, weakened informal social bonds to family, school, and work, and the disruption of social relations between individuals and institutions that provide social capital.
>
> (pp. 254–5)

This pronouncement argued that the life-course perspective was race neutral. Notably, in their follow-up to their pioneering research, nothing more is said on the matter (see Laub and Sampson 2003). As such, very few researchers have attempted to determine whether race does, in fact, have no role over the life-course.

Interestingly, in the same year as the publication of Sampson and Laub's work, Delbert Elliott, in his presidential address to the American Society of Criminology, presented results of his research that had direct implications for the question of race and the life-course (1994). Focusing on serious violent offenders, Elliott's address laid out the then present state of violent offenders, which revealed different prevalence rates between blacks and whites. While the rates peaked at nearly the same age (16 for girls and 17 for boys), the significant differences were of serious concern. He also noted the progression of offenses, from minor delinquency to more serious index offenses. As for the relevance of his address for understanding the role of race in life-course criminology, Elliott's data revealed that "nearly twice as many blacks as whites continue their violent careers into their twenties" (p. 14).

Furthermore, Elliott found that "for those living with a spouse or partner, no significant differences are found between blacks' and whites' continuity rates, but this difference continues for those living by themselves or in other arrangements" (p. 14). Such findings bolstered some early support for core aspects of Sampson and Laub's perspective. However, the overall differences by race left their supposition regarding the universality of their perspective open for debate.

Another important investigation on the question of race and the life-course was conducted by Piquero et al. (2002), who put the notion of race neutrality to the test. In their research, Piquero et al. examined two research questions: "(1) Do changes in local life circumstances eliminate the race/crime relationship? and (2) Is the relationship between changes in local life circumstances and changes in criminal activity invariant across race?" (pp. 655–6). To answer these questions, they turned to data on 524 parolees (who were followed over seven years in the 1970s) from the California Youth Authority (CYA). The diverse sample included 254 whites and 270 nonwhites comprising 33 percent African Americans and 16.6 percent Hispanics (p. 659). By examining arrests for violent and nonviolent offenses, the authors sought to determine whether adult social bonds such as full-time employment and marriage differentially affected the diverse sample.

Overall, there was mixed support for the life-course perspective. The findings showed that "even after controlling for stable individual differences, marriage is negatively associated with nonviolent arrests for whites and nonwhites alike. In addition, our results also show that 'traditional' as opposed to 'common-law' marriages have differential effect on criminal activity" (p. 666). In general, the results indicated that, in most instances, traditional marriages inhibited criminal activity while common-law marriages did not. One exception to this was in the case of nonwhites, where it was found that marriage was not "a significant inhibitor of violent arrests" (p. 666). Based on their findings, the authors were left with the conclusion that "race remains an important predictor of violence, even after controlling for changes in local life circumstances" (p. 666).

Piquero and colleagues sought to explain some of these differences with three suppositions. First, they presented the long-standing possibility that nonwhites were "differentially selected for criminal justice processing." Second, they suggested that race may, in fact, be a "social construct" that "can change over the life course and/or serve as a proxy for social events or negative 'turning points'" (p. 666). Put another way, because of their exposure to disadvantages in so many aspects of their lives, nonwhites are more likely to encounter situations where they are more likely to engage in crime. Because of this, the authors argue for the reformulation of the life-course perspective. In their words: "Perhaps another way to incorporate race into the life-course perspective would be to build on the life-course ideas and language by arguing that race, and the differential levels of disadvantage faced by racial groups, serves as a 'breaking point' in life events" (p. 667).

Finally, Piquero and his collaborators argue that the race effect could be a product of the types of crimes that are typically examined in such research. Here, building on arguments presented by others, the authors point to the possible existence of

> "caste segregation" [that] leads to the commission of street crimes among nonwhites and suite crimes among whites. In sum, race relations may have strong implications for the ability of individuals to build social capital and thus race may be the place where life events diverge.
>
> (p. 667)

Notably, some of the authors' suppositions explaining the potential role of race in the life-course have been discussed in previous chapters, but have not yet been applied to the life-course model.

A Note on Race, Crime, and Conservative Criminology

Moral Poverty and Super-Predators

On the heels of the Ronald Reagan presidency, conservatism swept the nation. This conservative movement had a variety of core ideas that were central to its platform. One such idea was the declining morality in America. Persons such as William Bennett, the former secretary of education and "drug czar," started to argue that something needed to be done about the breakdown of families and societal mores. During the 1990s, Bennett teamed with John Dilulio and John Walters to publish the book, *Body Count: Moral Poverty . . . and How to Win America's War against Crime and Drugs* (1996). By teaming with Dilulio, who had already established himself as one of the leading conservative thinkers, the authors produced the conservative treatise on crime and justice.

Their arguments center on ideas clearly linked to social control theory. In *Body Count*, the authors define their core concept—moral poverty—as

> the poverty of being without loving, caring, capable, responsible adults who teach the young right from wrong. It is the poverty of being without

parents, guardians, relatives, friends, teachers, coaches, clergy, and others who *habituate* (to use a good Aristotelian word) children to feel joy at others' joy; pain at others' pain; satisfaction when you do right; remorse when you do wrong.

(pp. 13–14, emphasis in original)

After presenting a plethora of statistics, Dilulio and Walters argue that as a result of the presence of moral poverty in America, there was a rising prevalence of "super-predators" within society. Building on Dilulio's earlier work (1994, 1995a, 1995b, 1996), the authors describe "super-predators" as youth who commit deadly violent crimes (particularly drug- and gang-related offenses). The authors note that, unlike in previous generations, "[super-predators] do not fear the stigma of arrest, the pains of imprisonment, or the pangs of conscience" (p. 27). They place the locus of such predators in inner-city communities and predicted that such youth were likely to start showing up in suburban and rural areas as well. The focus on inner cities leads to a discussion of racial disparities in the justice system, which they chalk up to "differences in social circumstances and socializing influences" (p. 46). They wrote that "the disproportionate number of black children who commit crimes is largely traceable to the disproportionate number of black children who grow up without two parents, and who suffer abuse and neglect" (p. 46).

The discussion of moral poverty and "super-predators" was clearly directed at inner-city minority youth (particularly Hispanics and blacks). Such youth were felt to have the greatest risk of becoming "super-predators." The fallout from Dilulio's earlier work and the publication of *Body Count* produced nationwide fear of an epidemic of youth violence; especially among minority youth. However, it is widely believed that the claims made in the conservative treatises of the 1990s were overstated (Greve 2006; Haberman 2014; Hayden 2005; Shultz 2006). Even so, conservative thinkers of the 1990s, using tenets of social control theory, succeeded in instilling a level of fear in American society regarding violent crime among minority youth that has yet to subside. This period also spurred policies that supported mass incarceration. Yet, in a strange twist, scholars have observed that conservatives are now among the chorus of voices that are seeking to drastically change the mass incarceration practices of the past (Dagan and Teles 2014).

Abortion, Race, and Crime

In 2005, conservative commentator William Bennett entered the spotlight again with comments on his morning show linking abortion, race, and crime. Bennett suggested that "If your sole purpose was to reduce crime . . . you could abort every black baby in this country, and your crime rate would go down" (Bennett as quoted in Tapper 2005, p. 1). He continued by adding "That would be an impossible, ridiculous and morally reprehensible thing to do, but your crime rate would go down" (Bennett as quoted in Tapper 2005, p. 1). His comments set off a firestorm of criticism accusing Bennett of being racist. Nonetheless, Bennett's comments rested on research that had been presented at a conference in the late 1990s and that had produced a controversial article by Donohoe and Levitt (2001). The authors presented the thesis that the crime drop in the 1990s could be largely attributed to the legalization of abortion in 1973.

There are two primary aspects of their theory. First, the authors argue that abortion reduces the pool of individuals who would later engage in crime. Second, the theory relates to race and crime in that, in their view, abortion is not random. According to Donohoe and Levitt's thesis, those likely to have abortions include unwed mothers, teenagers, and blacks. Further, because of the challenges often faced by these parents, if they did not abort the pregnancy, their offspring would likely be at high risk for criminal activity. Their thesis received national attention in the same year as Bennett's comments with the publication of the national best-seller, *Freakonomics*, that was authored by Levitt and Dubner (2005), and included a chapter on the abortion and crime thesis. On the whole, while there have been supporters of the thesis (Barro 1999), the majority of the tests and replications of the theory in America (see Chamlin et al. 2008; Foote and Goetz 2006; Hay and Evans 2006) and in England and Wales (Kahne et al. 2008) have not found support. In fact, one of the earliest studies criticizing their research found that legalizing abortion actually increased murder rates a few percentage points (Lott and Whitley 2001). Nonetheless, despite these criticisms, Donohue and Levitt (2004, 2006) continued to defend their thesis.

Conclusion

This chapter introduced the long history of social control perspectives. The theory has its roots on American and European shores. From the very beginning, the perspective has sought ways to explain what aspects of society keep people from engaging in crime and deviant behavior. While doing so, over time, creators of the perspective have addressed racial and ethnic differences in offending and victimization. In recent years, the perspective has been presented as race neutral, but tests of the theory have suggested otherwise. It was also discussed that, during the 1990s and 2000s, much of the conservative rhetoric was based on ideologies rooted in the social control perspective. In sum, the chapter provided evidence that the social control perspective has and continues to have some relevance for understanding race, ethnicity, crime, and justice.

8
COLONIAL PERSPECTIVES
ON RACE AND CRIME

As noted in the preface, the colonial perspective is likely the least recognized and examined criminological theory. Thus, while colonization is an age-old practice, theorists have overlooked the explanatory power of colonial-based perspectives to explain the etiology of crime and violence in colonial and postcolonial societies. The perspective has particular relevance for countries where populations have or continue to be dominated by colonial practices or regimes. The chapter begins with a general overview of the perspective, which draws heavily on Becky Tatum's 1994 pioneering articulation of the theory. The chapter continues with an examination of the few available empirical tests of colonial-based perspectives. The next part of the chapter is devoted to the review of Biko Agozino's 2003 counter-colonial criminological perspective, which has put criminology on notice regarding the clear relevance of the colonial model for understanding the emergence of Western criminology and its use to perpetuate racist crime-related colonial doctrines. The chapter closes with a review of Saleh-Hanna's analysis of colonialism and the Nigerian criminal justice system. As with previous chapters, this one includes some general weaknesses of the colonial perspective.

The Colonial Model: An Introduction

The colonial model has its foundations in the work of psychiatrist and activist Frantz Fanon (1963, 1967a, 1967b). While Fanon used the model to examine the relations between blacks and whites in colonial settings, Robert Blauner (1969) and Robert Staples (1974; 1975; 1976a, pp. 218–22; 1976b) leaned heavily on intellectuals of the Black Power Movement, such as Stokely Carmichael and Charles Hamilton (1967), and were among the first to substantively apply the theory to crime.

Applying the perspective to the conditions of African Americans, Blauner (1969) provided the following definition of colonialism:

> Colonialism traditionally refers to the establishment of domination over a geographically external political unit, most of them inhabited by people of a different race and culture, where this domination is political and economic, and the colony exists subordinated and dependent on the mother country. Typically the colonizers exploit the land, the raw materials, the labor, and other resources of the colonized nation; in addition a formal recognition is given to the difference in power, autonomy, and political status, and various agencies are set up to maintain this subordination.
>
> (p. 395)

Moore (1970), Barrera (1979), and more recently, Urbina and Smith (2007) have applied the perspective to Mexican Americans, while Blauner (1972) has also generally applied the model to Native Americans (see also Banks 2007). In the 1987 work *Gringo Justice*, Mirande Alfredo reviewed the historical treatment of Mexican Americans by the criminal justice system and formulated a theory of "gringo justice," integrating the colonial model and conflict theory (1987, pp. 216–36). Becky Tatum (1994, 2000a), outlining a more recent version of the colonial perspective, separated the colonization process into four phases.

Becky Tatum's Articulation of the Colonial Model

The first phase is the forced entry into another country. This typically involves "a small minority of outsiders" whose aim is to economically exploit the resources of the colonized. During the second phase of colonization, the "colonial society" is formally established. Tatum (1994) suggests that such a society is formed on the basis of cultural imposition, cultural disintegration, and cultural recreation (p. 35). Cultural imposition is the process whereby the colonizer's culture begins to supersede that of the colonized. Cultural disintegration occurs when the colonizer purposely "constrains, transforms, or destroys the indigenous values, orientations, and ways of life" (p. 35). Further, the colonizer begins to portray the colonized as lacking morals and representing the "quintessence of evil." In its worst manifestation, Tatum notes that "zoological terms are used to describe the native. The colonizer speaks of the native's reptilian motions, the stink of the native quarters, those children that seem to belong to no one, and that laziness stretched out in the sun" (p. 35). Because of distaste for the culture of the colonized, the colonizer negatively portrays the culture and history of the colonized, while at the same time reshaping native history to emphasize the history of the colonizer.

When the colonizer dominates governmental institutions, the colonial process has reached phase three. This is when the society is based on a simple dichotomy: the colonized and the colonizers. By dominating the political institutions of society, the colonizer is able to use power to control "agents of the state." All articulations of the theory note the important role that agents of the state (or "internal military agents" as they are called by Staples) play in maintaining order in a colonial society (for an excellent discussion of the role of police in British colonial Africa, see Killingray 1986; for a similar analysis of the police in Guyana, see Mars 2002). Recent research has continued to examine the role of the justice system and its agents in controlling the colonized (see Greenburg and Agozino 2012; Shalhoub-Kevorkian 2014; Pavlich 2014; Wilson, Parks, and Mastrofski 2011).

Writing during the tail end of the turbulent 1960s, Blauner (1969) described the role of the police in the lives of black Americans:

> The police are the most crucial institution maintaining the colonized status of black Americans . . . Police are key agents in the power equation as well as the drama of dehumanization. In the final analysis they do the dirty work for the larger system by restricting the striking back of black rebels to skirmishes inside the ghetto, thus deflecting energies and attacks from the communities and institutions of the larger power structure.
>
> (pp. 404–5)

The final phase of colonization is the creation of a caste system based on racism (Tatum 1994, p. 36). The colonizer uses racism as the tool of choice to create a race-based hierarchy within society. As a consequence, all political, social, and economic institutions operate based on the newly instituted racial stratification, which is typically rooted in white supremacy. Even with the race-based stratification, the colonizers also "recognize a social class hierarchy among the colonized" (p. 37). Here, Tatum argued that the colonial society affects the colonized in different ways. More specifically, the middle-class natives are less likely to feel the brunt of the colonial regime. Even so, in all instances, the colonized—regardless of class—are worse off than their colonizers.

As a consequence of these four phases, the theory posits that there are psychological consequences for the colonized. Specifically, Tatum noted that alienation is the key psychological product of one's exposure to colonialism. Alienation is defined as "a feeling of psychological deprivation arising from the belief that one is not a part of society and that the values of a nation are not congruent with the individual's own orientation" (1994, p. 38). Drawing on Fanon's conception of alienation, Tatum provided the following five types of alienation: "self-alienation, alienation against significant others (or one's racial group), alienation against the general others, cultural alienation, and alienation against the creative social praxis" (p. 38). These varying forms of alienation produce a variety of emotions and subsequent actions such as self-hate (Wilson 1990), the disdain of American society (Cox 1976, pp. 268–71), and frustration-aggression (Pouissant 1972, 1983); some of these contribute to the level of violence in the black community (Clark 1965; Grier and Cobb 1968; Jeff 1981).

The perspective also suggests that the resulting violence can manifest itself in two ways. First, there could be "vertical violence," where the colonized lash out against their colonizer. Second, the more likely scenario is that "horizontal violence" will occur. In such violence, the colonized, unwilling to challenge their oppressor, take out their anger on their own people (typically in the form of intraracial violence). Those who do not turn to violence often concede to the oppressor's power by attempting to assimilate, but as postulated by the theory, they do this fully aware that they can assimilate only so much in the colonial society.

While African Americans were not colonized in a sense that Native Americans or Mexican Americans were, according to Tatum, internal colonialism, which best explains the situation of African Americans, occurs "when foreign control of a state or territory is eliminated and the control and exploitation of subordinate groups passes to the dominant group within the newly created society" (1994, p. 41), producing many of the same characteristics of the more traditional colonization process. The formulation of internal colonialism (see Carmichael and Hamilton 1967; and more recently, Hawkins 2011) is the conception of the theory that characterizes the literature related to the colonial perspective, race, and crime. Using African American history as her backdrop, Tatum (1994, pp. 42–7) outlined the economic, political, and social subordination that has characterized their American experience. In doing so, she also continued to show the utility of the perspective for understanding race and crime. The next section of this chapter examines a variety of empirical assessments of the colonial perspective.

Scholarship Examining the Utility of the Colonial Perspective

Though researchers have been studying crime in colonial and post-colonial societies for some time, it is only within the last three decades that the colonial model has been used to contextualize such studies. Thus, while early studies speak of tenets related to the colonial model, the actual scholarship never mentions the perspective (see, for example, Blackwell 1971). Roy Austin (1983) was one of the first to test the theory empirically. After noting the similarities between the colonial model and the more traditional subculture of violence perspective, Austin noted that the perspective had been neglected and that such neglect was "unwarranted." Even so, he noted that certain portions of Fanon's conception of the theory were not in line with subcultural theories. More specifically, he wrote:

> [Fanon's] statements on the place of oppression and exploitation in the genesis of excessive violence are far more explicit and condemnatory than those of subcultural theorists. Moreover, his arguments favoring the violent overthrow of repressive regimes certainly exceed the implications for change generally drawn from subcultural and most other mainstream social scientific analyses.
>
> (p. 95)

From his review of the theory, Austin argued that reducing violence in colonial society is not predicated on the "cathartic letting of blood of the colonizer," but would also be affected by a reduction in the "impediments to the achievements of conventional values" (p. 96). To test this supposition, he examined data from before and after the decolonization of the Caribbean island of St. Vincent. The island did not formally become independent until 1969, but the decolonization process had been ongoing since the early 1950s, when voting rights were extended to all adults (p. 96).

Taking advantage of the gradual nature of the decolonization process in St. Vincent, Austin sought to determine whether crime and imprisonment rates declined during this period. His analysis revealed that rates of violence did, in fact, decrease during the decolonization period (p. 97). While he did not find similar support for the model in the case of murder and manslaughter, he did note that this could have been the product of the increasing availability of lethal weapons during the 1960s (p. 97). Austin concluded his analysis noting that the colonial perspective is a viable perspective for contextualizing violence among minority groups in industrialized societies.

Four years later, Austin (1987) returned to the colonial perspective. For this test of the perspective, he examined whether economic progress for American blacks in the 1960s and 1970s, combined with cultural changes (in the form of the Black Power Movement), contributed to a decline in criminal violence in the black community. Using various economic indicators and data from the Uniform Crime Reports, Austin found support for the notion that the economic progress and the internalization of positive self-esteem from the Black Power Movement was associated with lower levels of violence among blacks.

In a pioneering study of Native American homicides and suicides, Ronet Bachman (1992) formulated a theoretical model that considered internal colonialism. In her model, she argued that "no model explaining any phenomenon with regard to American Indians would be complete without acknowledgment of the colonization process to which our government has subjected this population" (p. 36). In her model, internal colonialism is an antecedent variable and, as she put it, "was perhaps the catalyst that caused these other deleterious conditions to develop" (p. 77). As shown in Figure 8.1, Bachman's model begins with internal

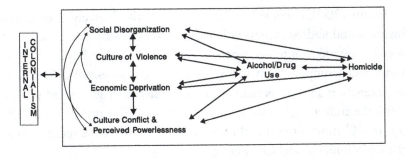

Figure 8.1 Theoretical model for American Indian homicide. (From R. Bachman, *Death and Violence on the Reservation*, Westport, CT: Greenwood Publishing Group, 1992. With permission.)

colonialism, but then incorporates more traditional perspectives such as social disorganization, culture of violence, economic deprivation, and culture conflict and perceived helplessness. Though Bachman's work was an empirical assessment of her theory (involving interviews and data from official sources), she did not include a test of the role of internal colonialism.

One of the most comprehensive tests of colonial theory was conducted by Tatum (2000b). Building on her original conception of the theory (see Figure 8.2), she formulated several propositions related to the model that examined the connections among race, class, and oppression; how race and class are associated with the availability of social support; and issues related to alienation (pp. 27–8). More specifically, she formulated the following five propositions:

1. Race, social class, and the interaction of these two variables are associated with the structural and perceived oppression.
2. Race, social class, and the interaction of these two variables are associated with the availability of social support systems in a youth's environment.
3. Social support systems influence the association between perceived oppression and alienation.
4. Alienation is positively associated with crime and violence.
5. Alienation is inversely associated with assimilation.

These propositions reflect her addition of the concept of social support as a mediating factor in the response to alienation.

Tatum (2000a) defined social support as the "perceived or actual instrumental and/or expressive provisions supplied by the community, social networks, confiding partners, or formal agencies" (p. 163). She views social support from these various entities as essential in reducing alienation and subsequent crime and violence in adolescent youths. With the addition of social support to her model, Tatum (2000a; 2000b, pp. 16–30) moved towards the development of what she referred to as the neocolonial model (see Figure 8.3).

Relying on survey data from African American, Mexican American, and white juniors and seniors at two high schools in a major southwestern urban area, Tatum tested her propositions. Her survey instrument included measures for structural oppression, perceived oppression, alienation, social support, class, assimilation, and crime. Using multivariate analyses, in the area of perceived oppression, Tatum's results did find that, as expected, "African American youths show higher levels of perceived social oppression than both white and Mexican American youth"

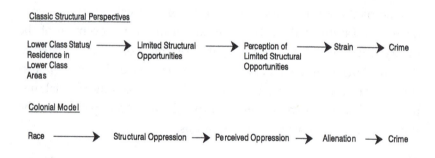

Figure 8.2 Tatum's colonial model. (From B. L. Tatum, *Crime, Violence, and Minority Youths*, Aldershot: Ashgate Publishing Ltd, 2000. With permission.)

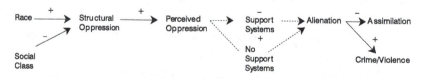

Figure 8.3 Tatum's neocolonial model. (From B. L. Tatum, *Crime, Violence, and Minority Youths*, Aldershot: Ashgate Publishing Ltd, 2000. With permission.)

(p. 67). In addition, her results did not find any significant differences regarding the levels of social support by race and class. Results concerning alienation, though significant, were not in the expected direction. While it was expected that African Americans would have the highest levels of alienation, Tatum's results showed that Mexican Americans had higher levels. Also, there were no variations in alienation by class. Summarizing her overall findings, Tatum (2000b) wrote:

> As an explanation of minority crime, the neocolonial model appears to be more effective in explaining the delinquency of African American youths. This holds true even when different types of delinquency are analyzed. Although the variables in the causal model are applicable to Mexican Americans, to explain Mexican American delinquency, other characteristics of their colonization or collective experiences need to be incorporated into the analysis.
>
> (p. 97)

Even with the limited support for her model, Tatum noted the importance of perceived oppression and alienation in understanding delinquency. In short, she argues that the neocolonial model offers a new way of examining delinquency among racial and ethnic minorities. As such, she recommends that researchers continue to test and refine the perspective.

The colonial model clearly has applicability for racial groups who have been subjected to colonization (most notably, Native Americans, African Americans, and Mexican Americans). While the empirical tests have been mixed, there need to be additional direct tests of the theory. Tatum (1994) has also noted several additional concerns with the theory. First, as reflected in other structural models, she noted that two people can be exposed to the same oppression yet respond differently; in such instances, the model does not account for the different adaptations. Second, as with conflict theory, the model is difficult to test. Another weakness of the model is that it does not adequately address class issues (pp. 48–50).

Within the last decade, the colonial perspective has been rejuvenated with the work of Biko Agozino. Theoretical in nature, Agozino's work has sought to contextualize the development of criminology in Western countries and its impact on non-Western societies—particularly those in countries that have been colonized. Some of his important work is reviewed in the next section.

Agozino's *Counter-Colonial Criminology*

Nearly two decades ago, Patrick Ecobor Igbinova (1989) published a commentary on criminology in Africa in which he noted the impediments to the study of criminology there. Of the state of criminology in Africa, he opined: "Criminology—the science of crime—is poorly established in African countries and criminological research has received scant attention. Consequently, research findings on crime and criminality are not widely disseminated; access to relevant international journals is rare" (p. v). After stating this reality, he noted that the limited development of criminology in African countries was a product of several things. First, the social sciences, in general, were under-represented in African universities. Second, African countries were dealing with other problems that were prioritized over criminology. Third, criminology, as in other countries, had not gone through "the stage of academic acceptance" (p. vii). Finally and most significantly for the present discussion, "pioneer researchers in African criminology have been Europeans rather than Africans. Indeed, the few African experts in pure criminology . . . received their training, mostly in the United States and Britain" (p. vii).

Reviewing Igbinova's commentary represents a good starting point for a discussion of Agozino's important counter-colonial perspective. Very early in the development of his work, Agozino has been concerned with what he refers to as the decolonization of criminology. One aspect of this decolonization involves removing the limitations Western thinkers and others have placed on what is criminological literature. For example, he would likely quibble with Igbinova's assessment regarding his identification of the pioneering researchers of African criminology. More than a decade ago, he noted the radical criminological themes in African literature (Agozino 1995) and, more recently, the relevance of the lyrics and activities of musicians such as Peter Tosh (Agozino 2003, pp. 214–27). This sort of thinking has been a staple of Agozino's work.

Another aspect of this decolonization process is the decolonization of victimization, which he defines as "an end to the marginalization, exploitation, and oppression in the criminal justice system and in society on which victimization is based" (Agozino 1997, p. 171). His attempt to decolonize criminology includes doing so at the theoretical level, in hopes of changing the way in which justice systems operate, and in the general thinking emanating from the discipline. For example, in his view, justice involves more than just the so-called punishment of offenders (POO) perspective, where the concern is punishing criminals. It also involves dealing with concerns related to the punishment of the innocent (POTI), which receives limited interest from criminologists and justice system officials (Agozino 1997).

All of these ideas come together in his work, *Counter-Colonial Criminology: A Critique of Imperialist Reason* (2003). At its most basic level, Agozino's general thesis is that "criminology is concentrated in former colonizing countries, and virtually absent in the former colonized countries, because criminology is a social science that served colonialism more directly than many other social sciences" (p. 1). More specifically, Agozino's work is focused on

> how imperialism used criminological knowledge and how it can be seen as a criminological project—imprisonment with or without walls, a widening of the net of incarceration, and how the close kinship between the two fields of knowledge and power, criminology and imperialism, served both.
>
> (p. 6)

So how does Agozino support this contention? In short, he takes the discipline of criminology to task for excluding the role of colonization in countries (particularly black countries). He does so in a systematic fashion by addressing the shortcomings of several major criminological perspectives. Beginning with the leader of the classical school, Cesare Beccaria, Agozino takes issue with some of the key events leading up to the rise of the school, which was based on the notion of offenders having "free will" and the belief that, in justice systems, the "punishment should fit the crime." Drawing on Piers Beirne's well-regarded work on the origins of criminology (Beirne 1993), he noticed that Beirne traced the history of the classical school to a Frenchman who was wrongly executed in 1761 for the murder of his son (who had really committed suicide). Not long after the outrage following this incident, Beccaria published his classic treatise on crime and punishment.

The stir surrounding the wrongful execution and later publication of Beccaria's treatise led Agozino to the conclusion that "the execution of a single innocent Frenchman counts for more in the conventional history of criminology than the genocidal transatlantic slavery in which millions of Africans were destroyed or the genocide of Native Americans and Aboriginal Australians by European *conquistadors*" (Agozino 2003, p. 14; emphasis in original). In essence, Agozino asks a good question: given the height of the slave trade during this era, why has no one considered the savagery and brutality (a form of punishment) of millions of innocent people (mostly Africans) worthy of criminological analysis? He continues on this theme, asking poignant questions about why criminologists have also ignored the nature of colonial regimes, which have, over the past few centuries, conducted massive amounts of white-collar crime that left many African countries in considerable debt (pp. 31–2).

Moving to the labeling perspective, Agozino (2003) described that the fact that leaders such as Nkrumah, Castro, Mandela, and others, who were

> formally defined as criminals or terrorist[s] [were] redefined as heroes and political leaders around the world, must have forced some criminologists to question the positivistic assumption that there is a clear line dividing normality and pathology under a mythically consensual collective conscience.
>
> (pp. 40–1)

Therefore, in his analysis, he challenges Durkheim's notion that all mechanical societies have a collective conscience or a "uniformity of the lives, work, and beliefs of their members" (Vold and Bernard 1986, p. 146). In Agozino's view, there is no collective conscience in colonial nations. Therefore, who becomes considered (or labeled) a "criminal or terrorist" is a product of who is running the colonial regime. In his final assessment of the theory, he writes:

> The insights of the labeling perspective are attractive to researchers in the Third World because they expose the hypocrisy of administrative criminology that supports the imprisonment of human rights campaigners and innocent poor people while the powerful criminals get away with murder. The adoption of this perspective should warn scholars that just

because someone ends up in prison it does not necessarily mean that he/
she is a criminal.

(2003, pp. 47–8)

Turning to a critique of conflict theory next, Agozino again noted the
absence of colonialism and imperialism in the scholarship of Marxists.
This was particularly intriguing to him because the work of Marx and
Engels speaks to such concerns. More specifically, he wrote that "Marx
had identified a class, the lumpenproletatiat, a parasitic class . . . whose
crimes paled into insignificance compared to the crimes of colonialism and the crimes necessary for the primitive accumulation of capital"
(2003, p. 51). Even the classic work on the "new criminology" by Taylor
et al. (1973) excludes any discussion of "imperialist crimes and how to
eliminate such crimes" (Agozino 2003, p. 52). Similar to conflict theory,
feminist criminology is also singled out for its lack of attention to the
"crimes of imperialism and the struggles of colonised women and men
against imperialist reason" (p. 64).

These examples of Agozino's thesis point to an important hole in
most "mainstream" criminological perspectives. Since the publication
of his work, he has continued to tackle the issue of decolonization in
criminology (Agozino 2004a, 2005) and imperialist actions (Agozino
2004b). Some of his more recent work has examined what has been
referred to as "gunboat" or "gunslinger" criminology (Agozino 2005;
Onyeozili 2004). This research provides further contextualization of the
continuing conflicts in West Africa. According to Agozino (2005), such
conflicts are the result of

> imperialism in colonial and post-colonial areas. I refer to the kind of
> criminology that grows from this seed bed of conflict as "gun boat" or
> "gunslinger" criminology and suggest that it is not possible to apply the
> techniques of comparative criminology to this region without an under-
> standing of the longstanding transnational practices of imperialism.
>
> (p. 117)

This set of work emphasizes the precolonial history of West African
countries and notes how military force and the criminal justice were the
machineries used by European colonizers to achieve their objectives. In
fact, Agozino's work shows how, in Nigeria, one could trace the origins

of the increasing number of prisons back to the colonization period (p. 127).

From his work on counter-colonial criminology, Agozino appears to suggest two clear implications. First, he argues that the "reparative justice" movement could be used as a model for criminology (Agozino 2004c). This movement is one championed by people of African descent who are seeking reparations for the slave trade and other wrongs. Agozino sees their struggle as intimately tied to the healing process surrounding the transatlantic slave trade and the colonialism that ensued, which, as postulated by Agozino's thesis, revealed the complicity of criminology in this process. In the end, Agozino writes that "criminology is overwhelmingly fixated on how to punish the crimes of the poor more effectively. What the demand for reparations teaches criminologists is that punishment is not always the most effective response to crime" (Agozino 2004c, p. 242).

Second, even with its dubious history, Agozino argues that Third World countries need to develop criminology programs. Why? Because, even though they should formulate criminological perspectives relevant to their own circumstances, Agozino believes that such countries should have a firm grounding in Western criminology since "it was part of the technology with which they were colonized for centuries" (Agozino 2003, p. 12).

So what has been the response to Agozino's ideas? There have been several reviews critiquing his text on counter-colonial criminology. To date, most of the reviews have been overwhelmingly favorable (Capeheart 2006; Flood 2007; McIntosh 2005; Mosley 2005; Onyeozili 2005; Oriola 2006). Zoller and Onwudiwe (2005), for example, "enthusiastically recommend this groundbreaking research in African criminology, and urge all scholars in Africa and the Third World to read the book" (pp. 72–3). Odo (2005) writes that "a very important aspect of this book is to challenge contemporary criminology to 'get real' about [slavery, colonialism, and their continuing legacies]" (p. 74). Odo also recommended that *all* criminologists read the book. He considered the text as one critical to the "sustenance of the discipline" (p. 76). Christian (2006) goes further by stating that "this is a book that deserves to be on all criminological reading lists" (p. 57). Japanese scholar Yoshinobu Nakajima echoes Christian's sentiment by opining that *"Counter-Colonial Criminology* is a book scholars in the field must not ignore" (Nakajima 2004, p. 741). Most of the reviewers see considerable merit in Agozino's thesis and its potential to take criminology in an important new direction. Recently, Kitossa (2012) has applied Agozino's counter-colonial criminology to Canada.

There have, however, been criticisms of Agozino's work. Sen (2004) identified several weaknesses. After acknowledging Agozino's laudable interdisciplinary perspective, Sen writes that "while Agozino's work is undoubtedly an impassioned piece of polemic, it suffers from a lack of an argument of its own, and there are long stretches when the author appears to do little more than review one book after another" (p. 1). In short, Sen does not view Agozino's perspective as anything new. He also takes issue with what he refers to as Agozino's "shallow grounding in the histories of colonialism, including the history of crime and punishment in colonial societies" (p. 1). Finally, he categorizes Agozino's work in the most radical genre of black studies, which he views as a problem because:

> with its presupposition of unhistoricalized and thus stable racial, political and moral identities, it inevitably reproduces colonial categories of identity, behavior and academic discipline. Typical of national responses to colonialism, such critiques can seek to reverse or usurp a set of power relationships, but they cannot deconstruct the basic assumptions that make nation, race, colony, metropole and discipline politically meaningful.
>
> (pp. 1–2)

Christian (2006), though supportive of Agozino's thesis, believes that he does not "'fully' escape the Eurocentric cannon" (p. 57). Thus, while Agozino attempts to distance himself from Western thinkers, Christian is not convinced that he succeeds in doing so. His specific criticism is that, if Western thinking is lacking, then there should be even more discourse from "alternative schools of thought, particularly from the perspective of Africans" (p. 57). Even though he credits Agozino for broaching some of the literature of black American and African scholars, he argues that more of this type of literature needs to be brought to the fore of his perspective.

Saleh-Hanna's Penal Colonialism in Nigeria

Following the work of Agozino, Saleh-Hanna (2008) applied colonial theory to Nigeria. In doing so, she penned the term "penal colonialism" to describe the Nigerian criminal justice system (p. 21). Speaking of penal colonialism in Nigeria, she writes:

> Penal coloniality promotes divisions and stigmas that keep poor populations in fear of each other, thus unable to form a solidarity that can effectively challenge oppressive conditions. These functions of the Nigerian penal system are similar to the functions and roles of the criminal justice system in the West.
>
> (p. 31)

Saleh-Hanna and Ume (2008) traced the development of formal criminal justice systems and the use of prisons in the colonial period. Prior to this period, community sanctions prevailed and "[b]anishment or execution of offenders by the community (today what we use prisons to accomplish) *was always a last option*" (Saleh-Hanna and Ume 2008, p. 57; emphasis in original). The authors discuss the fact that imprisonment was actually "alien to Africa's core values in the administration of justice" (p. 57). They provide support for this suggestion by noting that *"The vast majority of the current prisons in Nigeria were built in the first two decades of colonial rule"* (p. 59; italics in original). Saleh-Hanna and Ume (2008) provide a clear picture about the economic exploitation of Nigeria that had long-standing consequences for the country and the criminal justice system.

In general, Saleh-Hanna's work shows the connection between the British colonial rule in Nigeria and the postcolonial period in which remnants of the colonial past has resulted in large numbers of impoverished Nigerians. In fact, she discussed the criminalization of poverty in which the prisons are populated by poor people. In addition, the dire conditions and brutal treatment occurring in Nigerian prisons are highlighted by narratives by inmates who have served time in these colonial remnants (see Affor 2008a, 2008b; Akporherhe 2008).

Conclusion

This chapter began by providing an introduction and some empirical evaluations of the more traditional internal colonialism perspective. It included an extended discussion of the emerging counter-colonial perspective of Biko Agozino. Saleh-Hanna's more recent application of the colonial model to Nigeria closed out the chapter. Though historically neglected in criminology, colonial perspectives have considerable promise for contextualizing race and crime in precolonial, colonial, and postcolonial societies. Thus, criminologists need to pay greater attention to the impact of imperialism and colonization on the lives of people of color and racial and ethnic minorities around the world.

9
GENDER AND RACE-CENTERED PERSPECTIVES ON RACE AND CRIME

In the last two editions of this text the final chapter was solely devoted to feminist theory. This edition includes much of the same content that appeared in those earlier editions, but the chapter has been expanded to include the race-centered perspective crafted by Unnever and Gabbidon (2011). Both gender and race-centered perspectives share the philosophy that there are unique characteristics of a particular demographic (e.g. females, African Americans, Native Americans, etc.) that require theoretical perspectives solely devoted to that demographic. Scholars who created gender-based (feminist) perspectives have long argued for female-specific theories to explain crime among females. In recent years, Unnever and Gabbidon (2011) have made a similar argument and advanced a theory that is solely devoted to explaining African American offending. The first part of the chapter examines the nature and viability of feminist perspectives that have been used to explain criminality and victimization among racial and ethnic groups.

History of Feminist Theory

Feminist theory is inextricably linked to two early movements in American history and also to the more recent women's movement beginning in the 1970s. The first two movements that served as the foundation for feminist theory were the anti-slavery movement and the "first wave" of the women's rights movement. The anti-slavery movement of the 1800s was championed not only by noted statesman and abolitionist Frederick Douglass and other prominent blacks, but by countless white women who began forming and participating in anti-slavery societies as early as the 1830s (Davis 1983, p. 34).

In fact, it was at an 1840 anti-slavery convention in London that Lucretia Mott and Elizabeth Cady Stanton conceived the idea to hold the first women's rights convention. Even though the actual conference was not held until eight years later in Seneca Falls, New York, the pioneering event produced the Seneca Falls Declaration, which addressed numerous concerns related to the treatment of women. Such concerns related to the limitations placed on women in regard to property rights, educational opportunities, employment opportunities, guardianship rights in the case of divorce, voting rights, and, in general, the notion that women were "civilly dead" when they were married. At the time, these "radical" ideas started the first wave of the American women's movement that culminated in women's suffrage in 1920 (Daly and Chesney-Lind 1988).

It is important to highlight that this early history clearly shows the intersection of race and gender in the movement. Observers of the period argue that, besides Frederick Douglass and Sojourner Truth, who gave her powerful "Ain't I a Woman" speech at an 1851 women's convention in Akron, Ohio, other black women such as Harriet Tubman, the Grimke sisters (Angelina and Sarah), and Ida B. Wells-Barnett were among the important contributors to the movement (hooks 1981; Moyer 2001, p. 245). Given this early history, the further development of the women's movement at the turn of the twentieth century naturally included discussions of race and class. According to Daly and Chesney-Lind (1988), the second wave of the women's (or feminist) movement began "in the mid-1960s in conjunction with the civil rights movement, the new left, and a critical mass of professional women" (p. 497). The second wave of the movement "denounced the domestic or private sphere as oppressive to women and sought to achieve equality with men in the public sphere. In this intellectual context, feminists challenged gender-based laws and legal practices formulated from separate spheres [of] thinking" (p. 509).

Based on more than 150 years of activism surrounding the women's movement, feminist theory has become a mainstay in criminology and other disciplines. Before providing reviews of feminist perspectives on race and crime, the general forms of feminist theory are reviewed. In addition, the chapter reviews some of the early criminological scholarship that examined race and gender. The chapter also examine some of the more recent literature that incorporates feminist analyses of race and crime.

Feminist Theory: An Overview

Feminist theory has its roots in feminism. So, to begin the discussion of feminist theory, a definition of feminism is in order. McCann and Kim (2003) define feminism as "political activism by women on behalf of women" (p. 1). Seeking to elucidate the origination of the term, they found that its origins were in "the French word for woman, 'femme,' with the suffix meaning political position, 'ism,' and [the word] was used in that time to refer to those who defended the cause of women" (p. 1). They also note that the definition of the term has not been "stable or fixed" and has changed over time, which has resulted in considerable debate. Daly and Chesney-Lind (1988) adhere to the definition that "a feminist holds that women suffer discrimination because of their sex, that they have needs which are negated and unsatisfied, and the satisfaction of these needs requires a radical change" (p. 502).

Whichever definition one uses, nearly all of them point to the fact that society is based on "male-centered (or androcentric)" conceptions of the world, which negate the experiences of women and also points to the domination of males over females (Daly and Chesney-Lind 1988, pp. 499–500). Also, regardless of the definition used, three core ideas of feminist theory relate to paternalism, sexism, and chivalry (Williams and McShane 2010). Paternalism is based on the premise that "females need to be protected for their own good" (p. 189). As such, men believe that it is their role to protect them. In the criminal justice arena, this translates into girls being detained more than boys for status offenses. Sexism is based on the notion that men and women are not equal. Therefore, society discriminates against women simply because of their sex. Such a belief manifests itself through the difficulty women face in being hired for certain jobs, receiving equal pay, and, in a criminal justice context, being treated the same by criminal justice officials.

Chivalry is an old concept that relates to the practice of men treating women with courtesy and kindness. In criminal justice research, the concept has been used to explain situations where women are treated differently (more favorably) in sentencing decisions. For example, while a male might receive an extensive sentence for a particular offense, as a result of the "chivalry factor" females might be given a lighter sentence. Moreover, Williams and McShane aptly note that "chivalry is one way in which paternalism can be practiced" (2010, p. 189).

Besides simply having core elements, feminist theory comes in several versions. The focus here is on the following versions: liberal feminism, socialist feminism, radical feminism, and black feminist theory. Liberal feminism is rooted in the belief that gender inequality is a product of "the creation of separate and distinct spheres of influence and traditional attitudes about the appropriate role of men and women in society" (Simpson 1989, p. 607). Those who adhere to this conception of feminist theory believe that simply by eliminating policies that discriminate against women and enacting policies that foster equal rights, society can be transformed (p. 607).

Socialist feminism draws on Marxist theory and espouses that "gender oppression is an obvious feature of capitalist societies" (Simpson 1989, p. 607). Such theorists view the problem in terms of patriarchy and class domination. Thus, in line with Marxist approaches, the only way to eliminate such oppression is to move to a socialist society "that is free of gender and class stratification" (p. 607). Radical feminists see their oppression as being the result of "male aggression and control of women's sexuality" (p. 607). In her work *Intimate Intrusions: Women's Experience of Male Violence* (1985), Elizabeth Stanko described the "ordinary" experiences of violence that oppress women on a daily basis. Such experiences include sexual and physical acts of violence (e.g. rape, domestic assaults, sexual harassment, etc.), which are often accepted as "boys will be boys" (p. 9). Since Stanko linked male violence to gender inequality, she argued that achieving autonomy outside the home is critical to combating such violence and inequality. She also argued that changing societal stereotypes about occupational areas open to women was critical to overcoming gender inequality (pp. 166–8).

Black Feminism

For some time, much of the feminist literature focused on the plight of middle-class white women. But, beginning in the early 1980s, black feminists began to contextualize the nature of their unique experience (for a concise history of black feminist scholarship, see Schiller 2000). Early black feminist scholars such as hooks (1981, 1984) argued that not only was the plight of black females excluded from the feminist literature, but there was also a measure of hostility when black females brought up the question of race. Speaking of her own experience, she wrote:

> In 1981, I enrolled in a graduate class on feminist theory where we were given a course reading list that had writings by white women and men, one black man, but no material by or about black, Native American Indian, Hispanic, or Asian women. When I criticized this oversight, white women directed an anger and hostility at me that was so intense I found it difficult to attend the class.
>
> (1984, p. 12)

When hooks confronted the students about their anger, she was informed that she was the angry one, not them. After the class ended, though, one of the students capitulated that she—not hooks—had been the angry one (1984, p. 13). Continuing her analysis, hooks pointed to the primary issue surrounding the status of black women:

> As a group, black women are in an unusual position in this society, for not only are we collectively at the bottom of the occupational ladder, but our overall social status is lower than that of any other group. Occupying such a position, we bear the brunt of sexist, racist, and classist oppression.
>
> (p. 14)

In the mid-1980s, Patricia Hill Collins also explicated black feminist thought by articulating three significant themes in such writings (1986). First, she pointed out that black feminist thinkers stressed the importance of self-definition and self-valuation. Collins argued that it was essential for black women to define themselves because it allows them to challenge the stereotypical images presented of them. In doing so, they are also concerned about "the credibility and intentions of those possessing the power to define" (p. 517). Self-valuation refers to their efforts to resist their designation as "other." That is, when they value their existence, they are no longer dehumanized, which, according to Collins, is "essential to systems of domination" (p. 518).

Second, Collins notes that black feminists (like hooks) are drawing "attention to the interlocking nature of race, gender, and class oppression" (1986, p. 519). In short, she felt that it was important to highlight this point because, unlike white women, black women were (and remain) subordinate in a number of ways. Finally, Collins noted that black feminist scholars were emphasizing the importance of black women's culture. Collins viewed this as being critical because

> black feminists have not only uncovered previously unexplored areas of the black female experience, but they have also identified concrete areas of social relations where Afro-American women create and pass on self-definitions and self-valuations essential to coping with the simultaneity of oppression they face.
>
> (p. 521)

Throughout the exposition of her perspective, Collins also argued that black females remained outsiders in the academy, but such a status was important to continue to generate important ideas related to black females. In some ways, she viewed the assimilation of black females into the discipline as undesirable because doing so would require them to accept the superiority of white males—something counter to feminism in general. Black feminist scholarship continued to flourish during the 1980s and 1990s (see Collins 1989, 1990; Davis 1983; hooks 1989, 1990, 1993; Lorde 1984), with a diversity of scholarship including some from black feminist lesbians (Lorde 1985).

So how does black feminist theory help contextualize gender, race, and crime? In a pioneering article critiquing feminist criminological theory for excluding issues pertaining to black women, Marcia Rice (1990) described this lack of attention devoted to black women as the other "dark figure of crime" (p. 58). Elaborating on the concept, she wrote that

> the term is used here to refer to the way in which black female offenders have been overshadowed by both black men and white women in the criminological literature. Black female offenders are straddled between

what I call "black criminology". . . which has focused on black men and feminist criminology which is largely concerned with white women.

(p. 58)

After reviewing the relative contribution of "black criminology," Rice continued to note the shortcomings of the available literature. In fact, her review revealed that, in spite of the considerable amount of studies on black men,

> none of these studies included black women or considered issues of particular relevance for them. For example, concern about the high rates of arrest of black people on the streets does not extend to black women who are harassed by the police on suspicion of soliciting. There can be little justification for this neglect: black women make up over 20 per cent of the prison population, but only around 5 per cent of the general population.
>
> (1990, p. 58)

Taking on feminist criminology next, Rice stated that the feminist literature did not take into account the "economic pressures and cultural distinctions" between black and white women (in Britain). In addition, feminist literature considered "women" a homogeneous category, even though there were clear distinctions between white women and black females. She also expressed concern about the way in which black women as a group were portrayed as homogeneous, which did not take into account the differences among the various black ethnic groups such as Afro-American, Afro-Caribbean, and Asian women (p. 63).

Expanding on Rice's arguments, Daly and Stephens (1995) also discuss the "dark figure" of criminology. Early in their analysis, they focus on the issue of what name should be used to describe issues related to black and minority females. Here the authors debate the nature and meaning of specific terms. Second, the authors "compare arguments on race and gender across several bodies of literature: black feminist theory in sociology and literature, feminist and critical race theory in law and black women's scholarship in criminology" (pp. 189–90). Besides summarizing quite a bit of the literature presented earlier in this section, the authors also noted how critical race theorists, black women scholars in criminology (scholars who do not necessarily identify with feminists), and feminist scholars are all speaking a similar language. Finally, they examined the available research "on black women, victimization, crime and justice" (p. 190).

In general, a review of the available information did reveal disparities between white and black females in crime and victimization data. From this discourse some of the key "debates or developments" related to applying black feminist theory to this disparity are revealed. First, the convergence theory is discussed, which was based on the idea that crime trends involving black males and females were becoming similar (or converging) more rapidly than those of white males and females. Such theories, however, had minimal support. Second, there is debate about "whether structural sources of inequality may play an even greater role in black than white women's crime" (Daly and Stephens 1995, p. 203). In their review of the literature, it was found that structural issues affected black females more than white females, while social-psychological processes (e.g. self-esteem) had more of an impact on white females. Third, while the literature pointed to a "victimization-criminalization" connection among all women, it was noted that when poverty and race discrimination are combined, there are even fewer options for survival.

By addressing these areas, the authors aimed to advance the theoretical and research agenda of black feminists or other multi-ethnic feminists. In closing, Daly and Stephens propose that a "community" of diverse scholars be mobilized to "unify ourselves and the scholarship we present. We must work collectively on the problem of exclusion of minority group voices from the field" (1995, p. 206). In forming such a collaboration it was hoped that the "shared experiences of racism, of sexism, of victimization, etc. can matter in the relationships formed between researchers and the subjects of their research" (p. 206).

The next section of the chapter examines some of the early literature focused on gender, race, and crime. Though much of this early literature was not feminist in nature, it provided some early insights into how scholars explained criminality among female racial/ethnic minorities.

Early Scholarship on Race, Gender, and Crime

Much of the earliest literature on race, gender, and crime argued that, for a variety of reasons, racial minorities, including the female members, were more criminal than other racial/ethnic groups. In general, the early literature on gender and crime was rooted in the biological perspective. As noted in Chapter 2, chief among those purveying such doctrines was Lombroso. After reviewing Lombroso's early work on females, Doris Klein (1973) concluded that "Lombroso described female criminality as an inherent tendency produced in individuals that could be regarded as biological atavisms, similar to cranial and facial features, and one could expect a withering away of crime if the atavistic people were prohibited from breeding" (p. 4). Lombroso saw prostitutes as born criminals (whores and "bad women") who were not feminine, while noncriminal females were considered feminine (ladylike and "good women"). When considering the notion of white and nonwhite offenders, Lombroso's approach was implicitly based on a hierarchy of human development that, according to Klein, included white men at the top of the hierarchy and nonwhite women at the bottom (p. 8). Much of his discussion related to criminal traits clearly pointed to those present in darker people and nonwhites (Klein 1973).

One of the earliest direct American criticisms of Lombroso's perspectives came from Frances Kellor, who had a diverse educational background including legal training at Cornell and social science training at the University of Chicago (see Gabbidon 2001). Kellor produced several pioneering studies on American Negroes around the turn of the twentieth century, which pointed to the conditions in the south that accounted for most of the criminality among American Negroes (see Kellor 1901a, 1901b, 1901c, 1901d, 1901e, 1901f, 1901g).

Kellor's mentor, William I. Thomas, an early member of the faculty at the University of Chicago's Department of Sociology, also presented arguments on female criminality (Klein 1973; Mann 1984a). Much of Thomas's early work from his book, *Sex and Society* (1907), reiterated tenets from Lombroso and Ferrero's work (Mann 1984a, p. 57). Both scholars started with biology and sexuality as their foundation. With his next book, *The Unadjusted Girl* (1923), Thomas moved away from the biological approach and started to consider the role of one's social environment and biology (see Mann 1984a, pp. 58–9). Nevertheless, many of the views presented were based on prevailing stereotypical views of women as manipulative, cold, scheming, and vain (Klein 1973, p. 15).

Such stereotypes were also race based. For example, as noted earlier, black women were widely believed to be more "masculine" than white females. An excellent illustration of this can be found in E. A. Hooton's *Crime and the Man* (1939), which was reviewed in Chapter 2. In Chapter 9 of his text, "Negro and Negroid Criminals," Hooton presented the picture observed in Figure 9.1, which was meant to graphically portray the level of rapes by racial/ethnic groups.

In the first illustration, a man representing foreign whites, who had the highest ranking of rape, is shown carrying off a helpless white woman. The second illustration in the figure shows that native whites of foreign parentage had the second highest ranking of rapes, with old Americans having the third highest ranking. The picture used to depict this clearly illustrates that the two men in the picture are having some difficulty controlling the foreign woman because she has her hand around the neck of one assailant while the other struggles to control her. This picture reveals that while the white woman was having some success fighting off the perpetrators, it was likely that they would be successful in their attempt to rape her.

The final illustration was reserved for Negroid and Negroes, who ranked fourth and fifth. Here what we see is a black women clearly "getting the better" of her two black assailants. The picture shows how this black woman can handle herself in the face of this dangerous situation. She is shown kicking one assailant in the face while

Figure 9.1 Illustration of women's response to attempted rape based on racial/ethnic group. (From E. A. Hooton, *Crime and the Man*, Harvard University Press, 1939. With permission.)

simultaneously punching the other. This image aligns with the notion that the most "feminine" women (whites) would be less likely to fight off their attacker; on the other hand, as one progressed to the most masculine (black) women, they would be more capable of fighting off their attacker.

This figure presents the depiction of one of the classic stereotypical views of black women that have developed since their arrival in America. Hooton's figure presents black women as "Amazons" or as being "masculine, domineering, strong, tough, assertive and able to endure hardships no 'lady' was supposedly capable of enduring" (Young 1986, p. 307). Other stereotypical portrayals that have developed over time include the mammy, matriarch, welfare mom, and jezebel or whore (Huey and Lynch 1996, p. 75). The mammy was described as the "dark, fat, jolly, nurturing, faithfully obedient domestic servant who happily serves the white folks" (Huey and Lynch 1996, p. 76). This stereotypical image was felt to render black women less threatening to "elite white male power" (p. 76). In contrast to the mammy, the matriarch was perceived as a "strong black woman" who was seen "as ruling her family with an iron fist and castrating her [man]" (p. 76). The Amazon was one form of the matriarch categorization (Young 1986, p. 307). The welfare mom was another image presented of black women. This image portrayed black women as abusers of the welfare system. As a result of their dependency on the welfare system, they were willing to have additional children—simply to increase their monetary benefits (Huey and Lynch 1996, p. 77).

The final characterization of black females was the jezebel or whore, in which they were viewed as promiscuous, with an insatiable sexual appetite (Young 1986, pp. 309–10; Huey and Lynch 1996, pp. 77–8; for a discussion linking some rap music to this characterization, see Adams and Fuller 2006). Strangely enough, though, this categorization was in direct contradiction to the portrait of black women as Amazons, which must have been put aside because black women have been "desired" by white men as early as the slave era (Fishman 1995a) and into the twenty-first century with the great migration of blacks to northern cities. There they became the rapacious sexual targets of white men who employed them as domestic servants (Davis 1983). Such stereotypical sexual views were also perpetuated by European men when they had their first contacts with Native American women (see Fischer 2002, pp. 55–97). Over the past century, other racial and ethnic females have also been laden with stinging sexual stereotypes. Latinas, for example, have been depicted as "promiscuous and dishonorable women" (Castro 2006, p. 90), while Asian women have been "stereotyped as erotic and exotic, submissive, and a good wife" (Nakayama 2006, p. 105).

Von Hentig and Pollak on Black Women and Crime

Shortly after the publication of Hooton's work, Hans von Hentig (1942) devoted an article solely to crime among colored women (black females). His pioneering work examined the various statistics related to crime, after which he concluded that "the predominance of arrests of colored women is striking" (von Hentig 1942, p. 103). From there, he provided readers with a plethora of statistics that relate to arrests, prison admissions, mortality rates, and a host of other areas that all showed the dire social status of black women in America. Seeking to explain the stark disparities between native white and black women, von Hentig (1942) pointed to several factors.

First, he argued that whites had "intentionally selected and bred a definite physical and mental type of man; he has forced him to become warped, and has driven out mental traits which are indispensable to modern life" (p. 121). After making this point, von Hentig alluded to the fact that, even with their dire circumstances, "the colored woman has been permitted to survive better the disfiguring interferences of the white race. Perhaps she has saved the colored race from destruction by keeping and transmitting the more desirable attributes of her race" (p. 121). One could easily interpret von Hentig's suggestion as pitting black males against black females, thus arguing that while black women had it bad, the "real" problem could be found with black men. The notion that black women were "saving the race" also placed an unfair burden on black women. This again reflects the black Amazon stereotypical view that likely led von Hentig to believe that black females were able to "shoulder" such a burden.

Continuing with his analysis, von Hentig also identified economics as having a central role in the criminality among colored women. Expounding on this point, he pointed to the limited avenues of employment open to colored women, the minimal pay they received, their high levels of unemployment, and the dangerous nature of the occupations in which they were accepted (e.g. slaughter and packing houses, tobacco factories, cotton mills, etc.). It was also argued that the adjustment of blacks to American slavery was still having an impact on their behavior. Finally, von Hentig argued that there was an "incredible" fear of the colored race, even though, in his estimation, they were decreasing in number. Even so, the presence of this exaggerated fear pointed him to the following additional explanation for the acute arrest figures: "From this obscure fear it is but one step to the discriminatory practice of many law-enforcing agencies" (p. 122). In short, he made the connection between fear and the manifestation of that fear in the form of what is now commonly referred to as "racial profiling."

Much like the "androcentric" scholarship pertaining to whites, very little scholarship following von Hentig's work focused on black women or, for that matter, on other racial/ethnic females. For example, Pollak (1950) presented several suppositions as to why females were under-represented in crime figures. First, he argued that the crimes most committed by females were vastly under-reported (e.g. shoplifting, thefts by prostitutes, domestic thefts, abortions, perjury, and disturbance of the peace) (p. 1). In a similar vein, he argued that even if offenses were uncovered involving women, there was less vigilance in prosecuting them. Here, he was clearly arguing that the "chivalry hypothesis" was present. Finally, he argued that because of gender roles (women being primarily housewives), women had "many opportunities to commit crimes in ways and by means which are not available to men and which reduce the public character of many offenses" (p. 3). Using homicide as an example, he noted that women, in contrast to men, were likely to use poison in the commission of the offense; as a result, their crime was not as easily detected (p. 3).

So what did Pollak have to say about minority women? His analysis was limited to black women. After testing a series of suppositions that examined whether their criminality (determined by arrest ratios and prison commitment ratios) was equal to that of white women, closer to that of black men, or surpassed that of white men, Pollak concluded that, while black females were more criminal than white females but less than white males, such data did not take into account the fact that "anti[N]egro bias on the part of white police officers leads to a much larger number of unjustified arrests of [N]egroes than of white persons" (p.116). Further, Pollak argued that the police would be less likely to extend the "chivalry" benefit to black women, which would also have an impact on arrest and prison statistics. In closing his discussion on race, Pollak also posited that "the social position of the [N]egro woman seems to be much freer than that of the white woman. Therefore, it may well be that her ways of committing crimes are more accessible to discovery than those which white women employ" (1950, pp. 118–19). Pollak's work set in motion the consideration of new suppositions regarding black female criminality.

Wolfgang's *Patterns in Criminal Homicide*

In 1958, Marvin Wolfgang published his work, *Patterns in Criminal Homicide* (previously reviewed in Chapter 4). This was significant for two reasons. First, this was one of the few studies to seriously examine race and sex that, in the process, expanded on Pollak's earlier work. In "Race and Sex Differences" (Chapter 3), Wolfgang provided an analysis that revealed black males constituted the largest share of homicide victims and offenders during the four years represented in his data (1948–52), while the remaining racial and gender characteristics of homicides fell in the following order: white males, black females, and white females (p. 32). However, when the raw numbers ($n = 588$ victims and $n = 621$ offenders) were converted to rates per 100,000 population, the order changed to reflect that black females were second only to black males in their rates as victims and offenders of homicide (p. 33). In Chapter 12, "Race and Sex Relationships," Wolfgang examined the nature of the victim-offender relationship. The most significant finding here was that 94 percent of the homicides involved persons of the same race. Thus, most of the homicides were intraracial.

At the end of his treatise, Wolfgang has very little to say about the race and sex dynamics of his research. He does argue that there is likely a subculture of violence among those who engage in such violence. However, he never says whether such a supposition applies to black females; thus, one is left with the feeling that his thesis is gender neutral. He does, however, suggest that "future research should provide for more precise standardization of race and sex than has been the case in past research. Negroes and whites should be compared on the basis of several controlled variables, including socioeconomic status, education, occupation, etc." (1958, p. 330). So while Wolfgang did not find a need to create a gender-specific theory to explain violence among women, it is clear from his suggestion that he understood the complex interplay of race, gender, and crime.

The additional significance of Wolfgang's work relates to the fact that some of the results related to race and sex influenced Freda Adler's (1975) classic work on convergence theory. As a student of Wolfgang, Adler initiated the contemporary era of scholarship related to women and crime; in the process, she also instigated some stirring suppositions regarding black female criminality. The next section of the chapter turns to the contemporary era and begins with a review of Adler's classic, *Sisters in Crime*.

Contemporary Scholarship on Race, Gender, and Crime

Adler's Sisters in Crime

Dedicated to her friend and mentor Marvin Wolfgang, Adler's *Sisters in Crime: The Rise of the New Female Criminal* (1975) not only set the stage for a discussion about the projected trends for white female criminality, but also devoted a chapter to the plight of black women in the American justice system. Adler argues that black women are in fact different from white females; however, her explanation for the differences relates to historical and cultural factors not biology (p. 135). It is her belief that, because they had to take on the role of the breadwinner in black families, black females were more evolved as "women" than white females. Because of this, their crime patterns have "converged" or begun to look more like those of males than females. Describing the process leading to this convergence, Adler wrote:

> Because the black woman is burdened with the problems adherent to the family provider, because she must meet these financial obligations under conditions which afford her little access to conventional means, and because she lives in a time frame of impulsive immediacy, she is more likely than a white woman to turn to the lucrative forms of deviant behavior. Vice offenses, although not special to a particular racial group, are special to particular social situations because they provide ready access to easy money. Because there are too few other places to which she can turn for money, she turns tricks.
>
> (p. 150)

However, for black women, the collateral consequences of engaging in criminal activities were high. Thus, this convergence, according to Adler, resulted in

> the black woman . . . [being] viewed differently and responded to differently by everyone from the arresting officer to the probation officer.
>
> At every juncture stand processes and processors whose programs and attitudes reflect not current truths but ancient myths which have dogged her steps up every rung of the social ladder.
>
> (p. 143)

Moreover, now saddled with arrest records, black women would have an even more difficult time securing a job, and their incarceration would also further diminish their ability to support their families (p. 151). In short, Adler was suggesting that, because of myths related to black women, they were now being targeted for unfair treatment by justice officials and other societal institutions, which resulted in debilitating stays in correctional institutions.

To tie up her thesis, Adler then projected that since white women were starting to enter the work force en masse, it was likely that their crime rates would also converge with those of men. Interestingly, during the same year of Adler's publication, Rita Simon (1975) presented a similar thesis regarding the likely crime trends among women (pp. 1–2); however, her book was fairly silent on the issue of race.

Five years after the publication of *Sisters in Crime*, Vernetta Young (1980) investigated the veracity of Adler's suppositions on black women and crime. Using data from the National Crime Survey (now the National Crime Victimization Survey), Young found little support for Adler's assertions. In only one instance was Adler's thesis supported. More specifically, the notion that the crime patterns for black females were closer to those of white males than white females was minimally supported. Of this, Young wrote, "In multiple-offender victimizations, the pattern for crime for black females was closer to that of white males than to that of white females; however, in lone-offender victimizations, there was very little difference in the patterns of crime for the three groups" (p. 32). While there was little support found for the convergence theory, throughout the 1980s scholars continued to examine race, gender, and crime.

Race, Gender, and Crime: The 1980s

During the 1980s, scholars conducted a variety of studies related to black females. For example, Greene (1981) examined the general status of black women in the criminal justice system and noted that the system was lacking in devising approaches that were female specific. She also pointed to the need to collect more descriptive data on black women arrestees, to examine the effects of childrearing in prison, to examine potential alternatives to incarceration for black women, and to conduct an overall assessment of the needs of black women in the system (p. 60).

Diane Lewis (1981) also provided an early focus on black female criminality. Her examination of the problem led her to outline several models of black female criminality. Building on the work leading up to the 1980s, she argued that six main factors were connected to black female crime. These included: (1) age and other demographic characteristics; (2) economic deprivation; (3) status equality between the sexes; (4) distinctive socialization patterns; (5) racism; and (6) sexism (p. 94). As for age and demographic characteristics, she argued that previous research had found that there were more black females than white females in the "crime prone" ages of 15 to 39.

However, her analysis suggested that other factors were also necessary to explain the trends in black female criminality. Economic deprivation, as noted earlier, was believed to have a considerable impact on the lives of black females who had lower education levels than white females and fewer employment opportunities. Status equality related to convergence theory or the belief that the elevated criminality of black females is based on the fact that, unlike in white families, black women have been engaged in the workforce at heavier levels than white females; therefore, they would be more likely to engage in criminality than white females (for more on this thesis, see following review of Laub and McDermott 1985). Lewis also noted that it had been hypothesized that

> black children are expected to be assertive, nonconforming, independent, nurturing, expressive emotionally and focused in personal relationships, regardless of their sex. Since these traits are specialized according to sex among whites, black women who display them are perceived as more "masculine" (i.e. crime prone) than white women, by the dominant culture.
>
> (p. 99)

Finally, both racism and sexism were believed to play a role in the criminality of black females (Lewis 1981, pp. 99–102).

Four years after Lewis's exposition of the various models on black female criminality, Laub and McDermott (1985) also examined black women. Their analysis focused on serious crime by juveniles. Using the convergence theory as their theoretical base, their general hypothesis was that "the total personal crime rates for black female juvenile offenders would exceed those of white female juveniles, and that this should be especially evident for rates of violent crime" (p. 87). Based on data from the UCR and the NCS, they did find some support for one of Adler's earlier suppositions that, as white women headed into the workforce, there would be a convergence between the offending of black females and white females.

However, the Laub and McDermott data revealed that the convergence was the product of a decrease in offending among black female offenders—not a significant increase in offending among white females (p. 93). The notion that there would be a convergence of offenses between males and females was not supported. Thus, overall, Adler's thesis was only minimally supported. The authors concluded by calling for additional research of black female criminality.

The call, in the early 1980s, by Young, Greene, Lewis, and later by Laub and McDermott for scholars to devote more attention to black females was acted on by a number of scholars. During the remainder of the 1980s, scholars examined a variety of such diverse areas as sentencing issues (Mann 1984b), "gender expectations" (Young 1986), and issues severely impacting inner-city areas (Chilton and Datesman 1987; Covington 1988; Mann 1988; Miller 1986).

Interestingly, some of these studies employed some traditional criminological perspectives such as labeling, differential association, social control theory, and relative deprivation. Some of them revealed that even when portions of these theories were supported, the intersection of race, gender, and crime posed an additional challenge.

Outside the United States, the 1980s also saw other countries faced with challenges regarding race, gender, and crime. In Canada, Hagan (1985) examined the nature of race, gender, and crime involving native Canadians and non-native Canadians. Drawing on the work of Bonger (discussed in Chapter 6), Hagan tested a theory of race, gender, and crime that considered structural factors such as restrictions in labor force participation (p. 130). In general, he outlined the following three hypotheses, which were somewhat informed by the earlier work of Wolfgang (1958):

> (1) Differences between racial minority and majority group crime rates will be greater for women than men; (2) differences between male and female crime rates will be greater within racial majority then minority groups; and (3) the differences between racial minorities and majority group crime rates will increase faster for women than men with age, as will the differences between male and female crime rates for members of racial majority groups.
>
> (Hagan 1985, pp. 130–1)

To test these hypotheses, Hagan analyzed data from Ontario's correctional institutions and Canadian census figures. His analysis showed support for all three hypotheses. Of note, though, is that Hagan reported significant findings regarding non-native women and native women. While they were both found to be affected by their structural position in society, according to Hagan's results, non-native women felt the impact less than native women. Elaborating on this finding, he wrote: "Native women are also restricted from full social and economic participation, but with much higher levels of economic hardship. The consequences of this difference between the structural positions of native and non-native women are reflected in the much higher crime rates of the former" (1985, p. 136).

During the end of the decade, black women in Great Britain were also the subject of concern. Chigwada (1989) described the "double disadvantage" of racial and gender stereotyping that black women (primarily West Indian and West Africans) in Britain were facing. Mirroring the discourse from the United States, her article revealed the disparate treatment reserved for black females in all areas of the British justice system. Her interviews with incarcerated black women revealed that, too often, they felt their initial introduction to criminal justice officials was a product of racist assumptions regarding, among other things, their immigration status. That is, all blacks were presumed to be illegal immigrants. Black women were accorded fewer privileges while incarcerated and felt the conditions of such institutions were appalling, but officials had a lack of concern regarding such conditions.

Like black females in the United States, there were inferences that black females in Britain were receiving longer sentences than other offenders, and that black females paid a penalty when they did not meet the acceptable gender role of the "middle-class" white women (for a similar analysis in the American context, see Young 1986). It was also suggested that black women were criminalized "at a far earlier stage in their 'criminal' careers than other offenders" (p. 104). It was believed that this contributed to other issues pertaining to employability, potential income, and custody issues (pp. 104–5).

In closing, Chigwada (1989) was fairly direct in pointing to the origin of the problem: "The subordination of Black women to white people in this society is largely responsible for the disproportionate numbers of black women in prison. In order to reduce the number of black women who enter prisons each year their criminalization by the police and press must stop" (p. 105). These findings suggest that, during the 1980s, black women around the globe were being discriminated against—a finding that, unfortunately, was unchanged in the 1990s (see Chigwada-Bailey 1997).

Race, Gender, and Crime: 1990s to 2000s

The 1990s saw more researchers around the globe investigating the intersection of race, gender, and crime. Early in the decade, using data from a nationally representative sample of 992 black females and 2,878 white females, Hill and Crawford (1990) examined the value of numerous perspectives to account for criminality among black and white females. Specifically, their research partially examined components of the following theories: "social control, liberation/gender role socialization . . . [differences in crime rates are attributable to the way in which males and females are socialized] . . . , self-esteem, deprivation, strain, urbanism, and maturation" (p. 605). In line with research from earlier decades, their research revealed greater prevalence rates among black females.

Moreover, the research showed that while the theories were weak predictors of criminality, they fit white females better than black females—a finding that the authors suggested was a result of "the empirical neglect of the black female offender [that] has had important consequences for the development of theory" (p. 621). Further, the authors found that "the effects of structural forces on criminal involvement appear to be mediated by social-psychological processes for white, but not for black, women. Rather, the criminality of black women appears to be more directly tied to structural forces" (p. 621). The authors argued, as those before them had, that the nature of black female criminality differed from that of white females; therefore, any valid theory must account for such differences.

Pointing to the shortcomings of previous theories used to explain race, gender, and crime, Simpson (1991) argued for the consideration and development of the following three perspectives: neo-Marxian, power-control, and socialist-feminist theory. Because it takes into account the class position of workers, Simpson argued that neo-Marxism provides a potential foundation for understanding violence among black females. Even so, as with the other theories reviewed next, the theory is silent on the issue of race.

The second theory that she endorsed was power-control theory. Originally formulated by John Hagan, the theory proposes that delinquency is the result of the class and familial structures. In patriarchal homes where males are the primary breadwinner and there is a measure of unequal parenting (with men dominating), male children "are socialized to have a greater taste of risk than females" (Simpson 1991, p. 122). As a consequence of this imbalance, males are more likely than females to engage in delinquency. On the other hand, when things are reversed, with women holding the power and control and female children provided more leeway in their socialization, they "become more risk prone and consequently more delinquent" (p. 122). Lacking from this theory is any indication that it can account for the differences in power-control relationships in black families, which, because of their position in the American social structure, are very different from white families.

The third theory Simpson proposed was socialist feminism. The perspective is based on the notion that patriarchal capitalism explains the differences in offending by class and gender. According to Simpson, "Patriarchal capitalism creates two distinct groups: the powerful (males and capitalists) and the powerless (females and working class).

Opportunities to commit crime vary according to one's structural position" (1991, pp. 124–5). In this structure, Simpson argues, crime among the powerful is simply their domination and control of the powerless.

On the other hand, she argued that crime among the powerless can be viewed as "forms of resistance and accommodation to their structural position" (p. 125). Adapting this perspective to the plight of blacks in general and black females in particular has its obvious weaknesses. The theory does not account for racial oppression and racism, which, along with the other things postulated by the theory, are likely to exert an impact on the nature and type of offending among black women. The theory also does not include a mechanism to account for intragender variations in violent offending among black males and females (p. 125).

To make the previously reviewed theories more applicable for contextualizing violence among black females, Simpson put forth the suggestion that three concepts need to be considered. First, she pointed to power. The dynamics of power relations in black families due to their social and economic status within society must be considered in any theory seeking to understand black female violence. She also notes that, because of racism, patriarchy is experienced differently for black women. She writes: "Although black women recognize their own subordination to men, they keenly feel the racism that keeps black males 'in their place.' Racism changes the features of male privilege and dominance within the black family" (p. 126).

Control was the second significant concept. Here, Simpson wrote that in most families (working and upper class) "control operates through patriarchal structures" (p. 126). However, because of their heavy presence in the underclass, black families, again, have a different experience from that of whites. Thus, unlike whites (members of the privileged group), black females must operate in a racist system that alienates them and leaves them with little reason to be invested in or conform to societal norms. Therefore, they are likely to engage in more crime than white women. The final concept that Simpson argues should be integrated into prospective theories attempting to contextualize violence among black women is culture. In short, Simpson argues that the social milieu that includes the daily reality of violence that black women are raised and exist in for most of their lives should be considered by any prospective theory.

The 1990s also produced articles examining other important areas of concern to race, gender, and crime. Examples of such articles included those focusing on violence (Freedman 1996; Mann 1991, 1993), black female delinquency (Greene 1994), gender and race in the courts (Daly and Tonry 1997), and the effect of the war on drugs on black women (Bush-Baskette 1998; Stewart 1996). There was also an increasing diversification of the literature in the 1990s and 2000s. More research examining racial or ethnic females other than blacks emerged (Schaffner 2008). One area where this was evidenced was domestic violence. Besides its focus on black women (see Potter 2008; Richie 1996), the domestic violence/battering literature began to see more scholarship on Asian Americans (Bui and Morash 1999; Huisman 1996) and Hispanics (Hazen and Soriano 2007; West et al. 1998; Zara and Adler 2008). The decade also saw additional attention being paid to female gangs involving Latinas (Portillos, Jurik, and Zatz 1996) and Pacific Islander/Asians (Joe and Chesney-Lind 1995). However, this literature became more abundant from 2000 onward when researchers began to see changes in the nature of female participation in gangs, particularly among people of Hispanic descent (Sule 2005; Valdez and Flores 2005).

Another significant body of literature that emerged during the 1990s was James Messerschmidt's work on masculinities and crime. Since his perspective had important implications for gender, race, and crime, it is reviewed next.

Messerschmidt's *Masculinities and Crime*

In his work *Masculinities and Crime: Critique and Reconceptualization of Theory* (1993), Messerschmidt presents the argument that discussions of gender in feminist theory were inadequate because they did not address masculinity or "maleness." In arguing for the incorporation of masculinity into feminist theory, he argued that masculinity is constructed depending on one's situation. Therefore, the way one behaves as a male or "doing gender" is based on a whole host of situations, which result in what he refers to as "structured actions" (see Figure 9.2). Detailing this process, he writes:

> Although masculinity is always individual and personal, specific forms of masculinity are available, encouraged, and permitted, depending upon

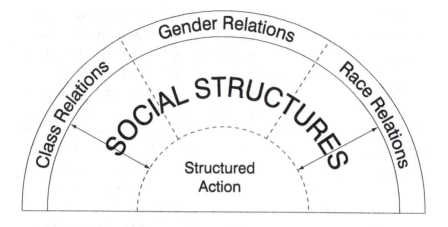

Figure 9.2 Social relations, social structures, and structured action. (From J. W. Messerschmidt, *Crime as Structured Action: Gender, Race, Class and Crime in the Making*, Thousand Oaks, CA: SAGE Publications, 1997, p. 5.)

one's class, race, and sexual preference. Masculinity must be viewed as structured action—what men do under specific constraints and varying degrees of power.

(p. 81)

A specific form of masculinity that Messerschmidt considers is hegemonic masculinity. This form of masculinity "is defined through work in the paid-labor market, the subordination of women, heterosexism, and the driven and uncontrollable sexuality of men . . . hegemonic masculinity emphasizes practices toward authority, control, competitive individualism, independence, aggressiveness, and the capacity for violence" (p. 82).

To illustrate the basic premise of his thesis, Messerschmidt examines how various categories of males "do gender." Therefore, while he examines how white, middle-class boys and white, working-class boys "do gender," he also devotes attention to how lower-working class, racial-minority boys "do gender." He points out that, in general, most white boys acquire their masculinity through sports and academic success. However, white, working-class boys see school as an "emasculating" force.

Fighting is also another way they construct their masculinity. For lower-working-class racial-minority boys, the construction of their masculinity is based around struggle. Unlike white youth, particularly the more affluent ones, black youth do not have access to resources "to sustain a masculine identity. For many of these youth (although far from all), life is neither the workplace nor the school; it is the street" (p. 102). In their lives, since school is not viewed as a place where they will get ahead, they construct their masculinity in school through physical violence (p. 104).

Outside school, Messerschmidt proposed that black youth expressed their masculinity in the form of serious property crime (most notably, in the form of robbery) and group violence (see also Staples 1982; hooks 2004). For the latter offense, he used the 1989 Central Park jogger case where the notion of "wilding" was constructed as an "ideal type" of group violence (in the form of a group or gang rape) (pp. 114–17). But in recent years, this case has been revealed as both a media fabrication and another instance of criminal *injustice*, with several innocent black youth wrongly convicted of participating in the group rape (Burns 2012; Cohen 2003). Thus, one is left wondering what other example Messerschmidt might have used to argue that such activity was, because of social structural issues, race-specific—especially considering that all racial and ethnic groups engage in some form of group violence (e.g. gang activity). In recent years, Messerschmidt has also considered how his theory applies to lynchers, hustlers, girls in gangs, and persons he described as "murderous managers" at NASA (see Messerschmidt 1997, 2013).

Two final areas of consideration include the recent push towards the creation of black feminist criminology and the general limitations of the feminist and gender, race, and crime literature.

Black Feminist Criminology

While the most recent literature on gender, race, and crime continues to tackle important issues such as the portrayal of African American women in the news (Meyers 2004), the experience of young black females in inner-city communities (Miller 2008), and the processing of racial and ethnic women in the United States and abroad (Chigwada-Bailey 2003; Farrant 2009; Young and Adams-Fuller 2006), the work of Hillary Potter seeks to formally integrate feminist theory with criminology. Similarly to the previously discussed work of Daly and Stephens (1995), Potter's black feminist criminology (BFC) theory is based on the integration of black feminist theory and critical race theory (see Chapter 6). More specifically, she argues that BFC is different from other feminist perspectives because it takes into account: "(a) social structural oppression, (b) the black community and culture, (c) intimate and familial relations, and (d) the black woman as an individual" (2006, pp. 110–11). In short, in contrast to mainstream feminist theories, she argues that the BFC perspective places black women at the center of analyses.

Using intimate partner abuse as an illustration of the utility of BFC, Potter shows how traditional feminist theory falls short in explaining such abuse against black women (and other minorities). She discusses how because black women usually have "limited access to adequate education and employment as consequences of racism, sexism, and classism," they are often at a disadvantage. This disadvantage translates into "poor responses by social service professionals and crime-processing agents to black women's interpersonal victimization" (p. 114). Continuing with the battering example, Potter discussed how BFC would also consider the nature of the black community and black culture. Here she notes that community factors such as black women tending to be more egalitarian and independent and the elevated levels of violence would be accounted for in a BFC.

Culturally, BFC would also consider "The role of religion and spirituality in African American women's experience with abuse" (2006, p. 116). Familial and intimate relationships would also be viewed through a different lens with BFC. On this point, Potter writes that the theory would take into account the unique nature of black families. For example, the inclusion of discussions about the embeddedness of extended family members and other mothers (another woman in the black community who helps rear a child) in the child-rearing role would also inform researchers on the nature of the dependency of battered black women on such familial networks. BFC would also be sensitive to interracial and lesbian relationships (pp. 116–17) and battering connected to such relationships. Finally, Potter argues that BFC would also consider black women as individuals, which means that

> although examined as individuals, the life of the black woman is strongly connected to her location, status, and role in the social structure, the

black community, and interpersonal relationships. Within this category, issues such as mental health, sexual health, and sexuality are addressed. Inclusion of this precept allows a personal yet comprehensive view of battered women.

(p. 117)

It is interesting that Potter, like feminists before her who argued that their theory was a "general feminist theory," argues that her perspective "may also do well in explaining the onset of and responses to abuse in the lives of other women of color, white women, and even marginalized men" (p. 120). While the jury is out on such claims and though BFC is still in its infancy stage, one sees the potential for Potter's perspective to make feminist criminological theory more relevant, at a minimum, for black women. This alone is a considerable step in the right direction.

General Criticisms of Feminist Theory

As was seen by this review, there have been a number of criticisms of feminist theory. First, early on there was very little discussion of class and race issues. Second, the convergence theory proposed that the women's liberation movement would change the nature of offenses among women. Based on the literature reviewed, this claim was not supported. It has also been argued that feminist perspectives have not "adequately accounted for historical changes in patriarchy and its various forms" (Beirne and Messerschmidt 2006, p. 407). Recently, Wright and Boisvert (2009) have added that "Feminist . . . 'perspectives,' . . . have pushed criminology even further from strict scientific reasoning, and their advocates have trumpeted this with adulation" (p. 1232). Finally, as was noted by Messerschmidt, feminist theory has not taken into account the role of masculinities or "maleness" in female victimization. Criticisms aside, it is clear that the development of feminist theory has, in general, been critical to the furtherance of the study of female issues within criminology and criminal justice.

Race-Centered Theories: A Theory of African American Offending

It is likely that many of the readers of this text are wondering why a section on race-centered criminological perspectives appears in a chapter that also discusses feminist theory. This is a good question. In short, the two theories share the same underlying philosophy. As mentioned in the introduction to the chapter, the discipline is filled with theories that purport to be general theories that explain all criminal behavior regardless of clear differences. In other words, as you have read in the eight preceding chapters, some theorists argue that their perspectives can explain all types of crime committed by all groups. The strongest example of this is the general theory of crime that was discussed in Chapter 7. In contrast, race-centered criminological perspectives depart from the "general theory" ideology. Instead, race-centered perspectives argue that theories should be race specific. The rationale for such perspectives is that no group has had the same experience as other groups and theories need to address these differences— something that general theories don't see as being relevant. Recently, Unnever and Gabbidon (2011) have presented a race-centered criminological theory that focuses on African American offending. It represents one of the few attempts to provide a comprehensive theory to explain African American offending. A summary of the theory is presented below.

A Theory of African American Offending

In their book, *A Theory of African American Offending, Race, Racism, and Crime*, Unnever and Gabbidon (2011) argue that, given the sordid historical treatment of blacks in America, the discipline should have a theory solely devoted to explaining their offending. Recognizing that there has been an abundance of fine scholarship that examines racial discrimination occurring in the American criminal justice system, Unnever and Gabbidon decided to venture into the vastly understudied area of explaining African American offending. In other words, scholars have aptly been fixated on discrimination in the justice system but have neglected investigating the reasons for the high rates of serious crimes committed by African Americans. Moreover, they have also neglected the nuances of African American offending such as differences by ethnic group, gender, color, etc. Unnever and Gabbidon believe any theory devoted to explaining African American offending needs to account for these within-group distinctions. Even so, they do not totally discount the value of general theories—they simply believe that such theories can be complementary to an overall race-centered perspective.

Unnever and Gabbidon begin their theory with the premise that many African Americans share a similar worldview that has been informed by their collective historical memories of their treatment during the slavery era, the Jim Crow era, and currently through their lived experiences in a country where racial injustices remain a reality that is experienced either personally or vicariously. They assert that African American offending—in part—can be explained by perceptions of, and experiences with, perceptions of criminal injustice. In their words, the authors write: "We posit that the belief that the criminal justice system is racist heightens the tendency for African Americans to perceive criminal justice injustices and to react to them with shame, anger, hostility, and defiance" (p. 173). The authors continue by stating: ". . . we hypothesize that these emotive responses substantially undermine the potential of the law to restrain offending behavior. That is, it is difficult for African Americans to believe that they should obey the law when they see it as a racist means to disrespect, harass, humiliate, bully, and unfairly imprison them" (p. 173).

Another core aspect of their theory relates to the role of racial discrimination in offending. Drawing on the extant public opinion survey research on racial discrimination, they find that studies consistently show that nearly all African Americans perceive that they have already or will encounter racial discrimination at some point in their lives. Here, the authors state that encountering racial discrimination increases the probability of African American offending in two ways. First, they believe that experiencing racial discrimination will hinder African Americans from bonding with white-dominated social institutions such as schools. In particular, incorporating aspects of social control theory, the authors note that the more toxic school environments tend to be for African Americans, the weaker their attachment and commitment to schools—which can result in increased offending. On this point, the authors assert: ". . . it is difficult for African Americans to build strong ties with institutions that disrespect them and unfairly discriminate against them because of their race" (p. 177).

Unnever and Gabbidon also argue that negative stereotypes represent another form of racial discrimination that potentially increases the likelihood that African Americans will offend. The authors identify three pathways in which pejorative stereotypes can increase the likelihood of African American offending. First, drawing on the secondary deviance concept of labeling theory, the authors argue that, at times, African Americans will internalize the negative depictions that are often portrayed throughout American society and imitate them. More specifically, Unnever and Gabbidon hypothesize that "[some] African Americans, especially young Black men, internalize and act out the pejorative gendered racialized stereotype that African American males are remorseless superpredators" (p. 179). Second, the authors believe that pejorative stereotypes negatively impact African Americans in the same way as racial discrimination. As such the authors posit that "... pejorative stereotypes of African Americans—particularly when there is chronic exposure—are debilitating. That is, they deplete ego resources as African Americans are continually confronted with negative stereotypes that 'put them down.' We assert that the negative emotions that arise can oscillate between depression-humiliation and anger—defiance" (p. 179). Finally, the authors state that, similar to their discussion on offending tied to racial discrimination, encountering negative stereotypes increases the likelihood of African American offending because it also diminishes bonds with white-dominated social institutions.

The authors aptly address the concern that since their theory relies heavily on encountering race discrimination and negative racial stereotypes that there is the potential to over-predict offending among African Americans. In other words, if nearly every African American experiences some form of racial discrimination, the logical conclusion by some might be that all African Americans will become offenders. The authors flip this thinking by devoting attention to the following question: why do so many African Americans encounter racial discrimination but do not offend? They provide two concrete answers to the question. First, they argue that a key aspect of offending that is tied to experiences with racial injustices in the degree of exposure. More specifically, the authors argue that

the degree of exposure to racial injustices should be measured across multiple dimensions including, but not limited to: age of onset (i.e., at what age did the individual first encounter racial injustice); who committed the racial injustice (e.g., was it a person in authority such as a school teacher or a police officer), the frequency of exposure (i.e., how often was the individual exposed; was it daily, weekly, or monthly), and the duration of the exposure (i.e., did it persist across the person's life course). We further posit that scholars should assess the degree to which the individual is embedded in networks that both sensitize and reinforce perceptions of racial injustices.

(p. 183)

Another factor that Unnever and Gabbidon believe distinguishes those African Americans that are more likely to offend than those who don't resort to offending is racial socialization practices (Burt et al. 2012). Psychologist Chase Lesane-Brown of Vanderbilt University has defined the racial socialization process as "[those] specific verbal and non-verbal messages transmitted to younger generations for the development of values, attitudes, behaviors, and beliefs regarding the meaning and significance of race and racial stratification, intergroup and intragroup interactions, and personal and group identity" (Lesane-Brown 2006, p. 400). Unnever and Gabbidon believe that it is through this process—that two-thirds of African American families practice—that ". . . parents proactively attempt to prepare their children for encounters with criminal justice injustices, racial discrimination, and the invidious consequences of being depreciately stereotyped" (p. 183). The authors discuss several types of racial socialization practices but generally suggest that if African American neglect to racially socialize their children ". . . [it] puts them at greater risk for experiencing the deleterious consequences of racial injustices that are related to offending (e.g., anger-hostility-defiance-depression and weak social bonds)." Unnever and Gabbidon believe that in the absence of parents racially socializing their children this will construct their racial identity from peers and street culture. The authors also believe that African Americans whose parents ". . . overly emphasize the mistrust of whites and encourage their children to become overly defiant in the presence of racism are likely to develop stigma sensitivity and stigma consciousness . . . researchers have found that these heightened states of sensitivities may cause African Americans to have less self-control, a factor that is unequivocally related to offending" (p. 185). A schematic presentation of the entire theory is presented in Figure 9.3.

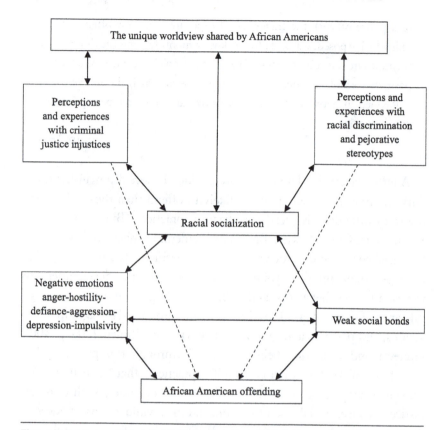

Figure 9.3 A theory of African American offending. (From James D. Unnever and Shaun L. Gabbidon, *A Theory of African American Offending: Race, Racism, and Crime*, New York: Routledge, 2011, p. 188. Reprinted with permission from Taylor & Francis.)

In addition to the basic foundations outlined in their theory, Unnever and Gabbidon also provide insights into the nuances of differences in African Americans offending tied to within-group characteristics such as gender, place, and ethnicity. In terms of gender, the authors posit that "... gender differences in offending are related to gender disparities in the degree to which African American males and females encounters criminal justice injustices, racial discrimination, and racial injustices" (p. 192; emphasis in original). Since African American males are more likely to encounter these despicable practices, they are more susceptible than African Americans females to the deleterious consequences of them—including offending. The authors also suggest that the differences in racial socialization practices between African American males and females account for differences in offending. I provide a couple of relevant examples here. Relying on the abundant psychological literature, the authors point to the fact that "African American parents are more likely to socialize their daughters with a greater sense of pride than their sons. The research shows that a strong positive racial identity decreases the likelihood of offending and enhances academic commitment and performance" (p. 193). The authors also point to the positive racial socialization that occurs in churches—attended by African American females more than African American males—as another reason for lower offending among African American females.

Unnever and Gabbidon readily recognized—as demonstrated in more than a century of community studies beginning with Du Bois's *The Philadelphia Negro* (1899)—the disadvantaged places where African Americans live and the role of place and its influence on offending. The authors devote considerable attention to the contribution of segregation and neighborhood disadvantage to African American offending. Finally, the authors also mention the difference in offending across the ethnic spectrum of black Americans. Unnever and Gabbidon believe that a central part of the difference in offending among the various black ethnic groups is tied to their level of acceptance of the worldview of native black Americans. In particular, the authors believe that "... less offending should occur among first generation foreign-born blacks who have immigrated to the United States" (p. 202). Moreover, once the immigrants embrace the worldview held by native-born black Americans, they hypothesize that "second generation blacks will approach the same level of offending as native-born African Americans, everything else being equal" (p. 203).

On the whole, the response to Unnever and Gabbidon's theory has been generally positive (Arnold 2014; Bonnet 2012; Hawkins 2014; Lee 2012; Polizzi 2013). Moreover, the limited tests of the theory have found support for its basic tenets (Unnever 2014), as well as its nuances tied to the differing worldviews of native-born black Americans and foreign-born blacks (Unnever and Gabbidon 2014). Even so, there have been some criticisms of their work. Kindle (2012) argues that Unnever and Gabbidon's premise that African Americans have a worldview that is the product of a unique experience in America is questionable because groups such as Native Americans have also experienced a similar trauma in the United States. He also expresses concerns that even though the authors discuss the importance of place and gender to understanding African American offending—they exclude it from the final presentation of the model. In addition, he writes that "I am equally concerned that there was no mention of male African American lifespan development during adolescence and young adulthood because African American offending is so heavily concentrated within these age groups" (p. 188).

In closing, while this section provided a brief introduction to the race-centered perspective of Unnever and Gabbidon, it is likely that in years to come there will not only be additional tests of their theory—there will be the continuing realization that general theories alone are not the answer to understanding the complexities of crime as they relate to African Americans or other racial/ethnic groups.

Conclusion

This chapter first examined feminist perspectives on race, gender, and crime. Beginning with the "first wave" of the feminist movement, scholars and activists have sought to address issues pertaining to women. Early theoretical perspectives related to women pointed to biological differences to explain offending and victimization trends among males and females. Over time, though, scholars began to look to additional factors such as patriarchy, chivalry, paternalism, socialization, race, class, and masculinity. With the development of each of these factors, feminist theory has advanced the capacity to contextualize female crime and victimization. Today, feminist theory is considered a staple perspective in criminology. While it is one of the newer criminological perspectives, it has much to offer criminologists examining race, gender, and crime.

After a review of feminist perspectives, the chapter focused on the race-centered perspective proposed by Unnever and Gabbidon (2011). Their perspective provides an alternative approach to general theories. While few tests of the theory have been conducted, the existing ones show promise. In future years, it is likely that additional race-centered perspectives will emerge.

10
CONCLUSION

This book examined numerous criminological perspectives that have been used to explain racial and ethnic disparities in crime and justice. After reviewing a plethora of relevant research studies, a few things have become clear. First, no single theory explains racial disparities in crime and justice "at all places and at all times." Considering the diversity of issues that face people of color and racial and ethnic groups around the world, such an expectation is clearly unrealistic. If nothing more, the review of such scholarship has shown that the generality of a particular theory is difficult to achieve. Thus, scholars need to be careful when making such claims.

Second, most criminological perspectives have been applied to the question of race and crime. That is, nearly every major criminological perspective, in whole or as a part of an integrated approach, has served as the foundation for a study that directly or indirectly examines the role of race in understanding criminality or victimization. Third, as a consequence of the second point, the logical question, then, is: which one best explains the role of race? But while the question is a simple one, the answer is a bit more complex. For example, when a racial or ethnic minority from an impoverished community commits a homicide during a robbery, one criminologist might trace the criminal act to the offender's biology, while another will look to the offender's sociological background, with yet another criminologist turning to the societal social structure, and so on. The key point here is that determining whose approach is right requires taking into account a host of factors that are not readily available or are simply unknown. Nevertheless, I see some promise in many of the criminological perspectives reviewed in the chapters leading up to this conclusion.

I stand firm in the belief that there remains a group of persons in the world who, based on racism and religious and cultural beliefs, despise people of color and racial and ethnic minorities, and see them as the problems of the planet. Consequently, people of color and racial and ethnic minorities will never receive a "fair shake" in a justice system where such people have considerable influence. As for biological perspectives, in my view, unless the human genome project yields a crime gene, the perspective has little to offer. Even so, I am mindful of the potential of some of the biosocial perspectives (Wright and Boisvert 2009), which combine environmental and biological factors, for understanding crime committed by *all* persons—regardless of race or ethnicity.

Social disorganization and strain perspectives, as they have for the past century, continue to show promise for understanding race, crime, and justice. Further, Elijah Anderson's "code of the streets" subcultural perspective has consistently been supported by empirical research. However, scholars should not be seduced by Anderson's perspective and forget the dire structural conditions that produce or contribute to the development of the code of the streets (Wilson 1987). In fact, according to Oliver (2006), these same structural conditions have resulted in the "streets" becoming another societal institution that influences the development of inner-city youth. Such a supposition warrants further investigation by criminologists.

The labeling perspective, in its most recent incarnation, holds considerable promise for understanding the plight of racial and ethnic minorities in criminal justice. Of particular note is the work of scholars whose work examines the role of stereotypes in the media and among criminal justice professionals who, from the research revealed in Chapter 5, clearly make decisions based on cues from their stereotypical views. Simply put, the *serious* criminologist must pay attention to this important scholarship. As in the past, conflict theory remains an important consideration for those seeking to understand race, crime, and justice. It continues to contextualize how the powerful within society dictate, through the control of social systems, which people end up entangled in justice systems.

From the review of social control perspectives, the long-standing claim of the perspective's "generality" was unfounded. In several instances, the perspective was found to be obviously more relevant for whites than for some racial and ethnic minorities (especially blacks). Furthermore, perspectives tied to conservative criminology have also not been supported. Though there was limited empirical support for the colonial model, it provided another potential avenue for contextualizing crime and justice in colonial and postcolonial societies. All scholars examining such societies must consider the role of colonization. Without doing so, they risk the possibility of missing, as Bachman (1992) notes, the key antecedent variable, which likely explains the disproportionate involvement of people of color and racial and ethnic minorities in colonial and postcolonial justice systems around the world.

In a similar vein, Agozino's work on counter-colonial criminology must become a standard in criminology and criminal justice texts and degree-granting programs. Its importance is twofold. First, it has critically assessed the role of Western criminology in imperialism around the globe (see Godfrey and Dunstall 2013). This contention alone warrants additional inquiry by criminologists. Second, for those Third World countries seeking to get into the criminology arena, Agozino's thesis suggests they should take a close look at the "classics" of Western criminology and proceed with caution. Given the limited success of Western criminology on issues pertaining to racial and ethnic minorities in cities and countries around the world, his text puts them on notice to construct a liberating criminology—not imitate one that, he believes, has been a partner in imperialism.

Finally, feminist perspectives have also shown the propensity to help contextualize the influence of gender on justice system outcomes. However, only in recent years has that promise manifested itself in a perspective that is also applicable to racial and ethnic minorities (especially black females). Hillary Potter's recent black feminist criminological perspective represents a pioneering effort that appears to have considerable promise. Likewise, race-centered perspectives hold promise for better understanding crime causation among specific races/ethnicities.

I close with two final comments. First, race, ethnicity, and crime is an important area of study. It moves the study of the role of race and ethnicity to the forefront of criminology. Therefore, scholars need to continue to produce original qualitative and quantitative research that examines this important question. Too often in my review of the literature I came across studies that tested a particular perspective using the same dataset to test the same theory, in the same way, as a previous study. Criminology needs to remain innovative in its approaches. We should take note of the simulations and experimental studies being done by psychologists. It was refreshing to read some of their research studies. To remain a dynamic discipline, criminologists need to take on more qualitative studies that will yield new insights or serve as tests of current perspectives on race, ethnicity, crime, and justice.

Second, it is obvious from recent scholarship that countries and cities around the globe are also struggling with the same race- and ethnicity-based crime and justice issues as the United States (Bucerius and Tonry 2014; Gabbidon 2009; Kalunta-Crumpton 2010; Phillips and Webster 2014). Therefore, it is incumbent upon those of us who study race and crime to open our eyes to the clear similarities in the area across the globe. Notably, while more international scholarship in this area is emerging, much more comparative research on race, ethnicity, crime, and justice needs to be conducted.

PERMISSIONS

The author and publisher are grateful to those who have given permission to reproduce the following extracts from copyright material:

p. 12: From *Criminal Woman, the Prostitute and the Normal Woman*, (1893) edited by Cesare Lombroso and Guglielmo Ferrero, translated and with a new introduction by Nicole Hahn Rafter and Mary Gibson. Copyright © 2004. Durham, NC: Duke University Press.

pp.19, 20, 21, 204: From *Crime and the Man*, by Earnest Albert Hooton, pp. 69, 171, 302, and 306. Copyright © 1939 by the President and Fellows of Harvard College. Copyright renewed 1967 by Mary C. Hooton. Cambridge, MA: Harvard University Press. Reprinted by permission of the publisher.

p. 27: From *Biobehavioral Perspectives on Criminology*, 1st edition, by Diana Fishbein. Copyright © 2001 Wadsworth, a part of Cengage Learning, Inc. Reproduced by permission of www.cengage.com/permissions.

p. 48: From *The Philadelphia Negro: A Social Study*, by W. E. B. Du Bois (1899). Copyright © 1996. Philadelphia, PA: University of Pennsylvania Press.

p. 51: From *The City*, by Robert E. Park, Ernest W. Burgess, and Roderick D. McKenzie. Used by permission of the University of Chicago Press.

p. 53: From *Juvenile Delinquency and Urban Areas*, by Clifford Shaw and Henry D. McKay. Used by permission of the University of Chicago Press.

p. 62: From "Social Structure and Anomie" by Robert K. Merton in *American Sociological Review*, 3: 672–82 (1938).

REFERENCES

Preface

Dawson-Edwards, C. (2008). Review of *Criminological Perspectives on Race and Crime*. *Journal of Criminal Justice Education*, 19: 308–11.

Gabbidon, S. L., and H. Taylor Greene, (2013). *Race and crime, 3rd edition*. Thousand Oaks, CA: SAGE Publications.

Henderson, H. (2008). Review of *Criminological Perspectives on Race and Crime*. Retrieved at *Canadian Journal of Criminology and Criminal Justice*. www.ccja-acjp.ca/en/cjcr200/cjcr264.html.

Knowles, F.E. (2008). Review of *Criminological Perspectives on Race and Crime*. *Choice*, 45: 1060.

Leiber, M.J. (2008). Theories of racial and ethnic bias in juvenile and criminal justice. In *Racial divide: Racial and ethnic bias in the criminal justice system*, eds. M.J. Lynch, E.B. Patterson, and K.K. Childs. Monsey, NY: Criminal Justice Press, 15–38.

Mann, C.R. (1993). *Unequal justice: A question of color*. Bloomington: Indiana University Press.

1   A Brief Introduction to Race, Crime, and Theory

Agnew, R. (2005). *Why do criminals offend? A general theory of crime and delinquency*. Los Angeles: Roxbury Publishing.

Barak, G. (2009). *Criminology: An integrated approach*. Lanham, MD: Rowman & Littlefield.

Bernard, T. J., J.B. Snipes, and A.L. Gerould. (2010). *Vold's theoretical criminology, 6th edition*. Oxford: Oxford University Press.

Bohm, R.M. (2001). *A primer on crime and delinquency theory, 2nd edition*. Belmont, CA: Wadsworth/Thomson Learning.

Bowling, B., and C. Phillips. (2002). *Racism, crime and justice*. London: Longman.

Chan, W., and K. Mirchandani, eds. (2002). *Crimes of colour: Racialization and the criminal justice system in Canada*. Peterborough, Ontario: Broadview Press.

Christie, N. (2004). *A suitable amount of crime*. London: Routledge.

Curran, D.J., and C.M. Renzetti. (2001). *Theories of crime, 2nd edition*. Boston: Allyn & Bacon.

Durkheim, E. (1938/1895). *The rules of sociological method*. New York: Free Press.

Emanuel, W.G. (1992). *People of color in the Bible series: Volume 1*. Schuylkill Haven, PA: Faith of Jesus Center.

Feagin, R.F., and C. Booher Feagin. (2008). *Racial and ethnic relations, 8th edition.* Upper Saddle River, NJ: Prentice Hall.

Frederickson, G.M. (1981). *White supremacy: A comparative study in American and South African history.* Oxford: Oxford University Press.

——. (2002). *Racism: A short history.* Princeton, NJ: Princeton University Press.

Gabbidon, S.L. (2009). *Race, ethnicity, crime and justice: An international dilemma.* Thousand Oaks, CA: SAGE Publications.

Gabbidon, S. L., and H. Taylor Greene. (2013). *Race and crime, 3rd edition.* Thousand Oaks, CA: SAGE Publications.

Glynn, M. (2014). *Blacks men, invisibility and crime: Toward a critical race theory of desistance.* London: Routledge.

Godinet, M.T., and H.O. Vakalhi. (2009). Conceptualizing delinquency among Samoan adolescents: An integrative model. *Journal of Ethnicity in Criminal Justice,* 7: 135–59.

Gossett, T. (1963). *Race: The history of an idea in America.* Dallas: Southern Methodist University Press.

Hawkins, D. F. (2011). Things fall apart: Revisiting race and ethnic differences in criminal violence amidst a crime drop. *Race and Justice,* 1: 3–48.

Higgins, G.E., ed. (2009). *Race, Crime and delinquency: A criminological theory approach.* Upper Saddle River, NJ: Pearson/Prentice Hall.

Jablonski, S. (1997). Ham's vicious race: Slavery and John Milton. *Studies in Literature, 1500–1900,* 37: 173–190.

King James Bible: The new student Bible (with notes by Philip Yancey and Tim Strafford). (1992). Grand Rapids, MI: Zondervan Publishing House.

Marshall, I.H., ed. (1997). *Minorities, migrants, and crime: Diversity and similarity across Europe and America.* Thousand Oaks, CA: SAGE Publications.

Messner, S.F., M.D. Krohn, and A.E. Liska, eds. (1989). *Theoretical integration in the study of deviance and crime: Problems and prospects.* Albany: State University of New York Press.

Miethe, T.D., and R.F. Meier. (1994). *Crime and its social context: Toward an integrated theory of offenders, victims, and situations.* Albany: State University of New York Press.

Mosher, C.J. (1998). *Discrimination and denial: Systemic racism in Ontario's legal and criminal justice systems, 1892–1961.* Toronto: University of Toronto Press.

Robinson, M., and K. Beaver. (2009). *Why crime? An interdisciplinary approach to explaining criminal behavior, 2nd edition.* Durham, NC: Carolina Academic Press.

Rowe, M. (2012). *Race & crime.* London: SAGE Publications.

Saleh-Hanna, V., ed. (2008). *Colonial systems of control: Criminal justice in Nigeria.* Ottawa: University of Ottawa Press.

Sanders E.R. (1969). The Hamitic hypothesis; Its origin and functions in time perspective. *Journal of African History,* 10, 521–32.

Tonry, M. (2011). *Punishing race: A continuing American dilemma.* Oxford: Oxford University Press.

Walker, S., C. Spohn, and M. DeLone. (2011). *The color of justice: Race, ethnicity and crime in America, 5th edition.* Belmont, CA: Wadsworth/Thomson Learning.

Williams, F.P., and M.D. McShane. (2014). *Criminological theory, 6th edition.* Upper Saddle River, NJ: Prentice Hall.

2   Biological Perspectives on Race and Crime

Akins, S., and R. Griffin. (2000). Multiple birth rates and racial type: A research note regarding r/K theory. *Deviant Behavior: An Interdisciplinary Journal,* 21: 15–22.

Armstrong, C.P., and F. Heisler. (1945). Some comparisons of Negro and white delinquent boys. *The Journal of Genetic Psychology,* 67: 81–4.

Barnhart, K.E. (1933). Negro crime and education. *Opportunity*, 11: 364–7.

Beaver, K. M., J. C. Barnes, and B.B. Boutwell. (2015). *Biosocial vs. nurture debate in criminology: On the origins of criminal behavior and criminality.* Thousand Oaks, CA: SAGE.

Beckman, A.S. (1933). A study of the intelligence of colored adolescents of different socio-economic status in typical metropolitan areas. *The Journal of Social Psychology*, 4: 70–91.

Bellair, P. E., T. L. McNulty, and Alex R. Piquero. (2014). Verbal ability and persistent offending: A race-specific test of Moffit's theory. *Justice Quarterly*, DOI: 10.1080/07418825.2014.918166.

Bonger, W.A. (1943). *Race and crime.* New York: Columbia University Press.

Bradley, M. (1978). *The iceman inheritance: Prehistoric sources of Western man's racism, sexism, and aggression.* New York: Kayode Publications.

Burgess, E.W. (1939). Editor's preface. In *Intelligence and crime: A study of the penitentiary and reformatory offenders*, ed. S.H. Tulchin. Chicago: University of Chicago Press, ix.

Carroll, C. (1900). *The Negro a beast.* St. Louis, MO: American Book and Bible House.

Cullen, F.T., P. Gendreau, G.R. Jarjoura, and J.P. Wright. (1997). Crime and the bell curve: Lessons from intelligent criminology. *Crime and Delinquency*, 43: 387–411.

Darwin, C. (1859). *On the origin of species.* London: John Murray.

——. (1871). *The descent of man, and selection in relation to sex.* London: John Murray.

Devlin, B., S.E. Fienberg, D.P. Resnick, and K. Roeder, eds. (1997). *Intelligence, genes, and success: Scientists respond to "The bell curve."* New York: Springer.

Di Leo, O. (2005). It all started in Madrid. In *Cuban counterpoints: The legacy of Fernando Ortiz*, eds. M.A. Font and A.W. Quiroz. New York: Lexington Books, 39–54.

Doll, E.A. (1920). The comparative intelligence of prisoners. *Journal of Criminal Law, Criminology and Police Science*, 11: 191–7.

Donnellan, M.B., X. Ge, and E. Wenk. (2000). Cognitive abilities in adolescence-limited and life-course-persistent criminal offenders. *Journal of Abnormal Psychology*, 109: 396–402.

Du Bois, W.E.B. (1898). *The study of the Negro problems. Annals of the American Academy of Political and Social Science* (Philadelphia) 11 (January, 1898). Reprinted in Aptheker (1982). *Writings in Periodical Literature Edited by Others Vol. 1* (1891–1909). Millwood, NY: Kraus–Thomson Organization Limited, 40–52.

Dugdale, R.L. (1877). *The Jukes: A study in crime, pauperism, disease and heredity.* New York: G.P. Putnam's Sons.

Ellis, L. (1997). Criminal behavior and r/K selection: An extension of gene-based evolutionary theory. *Deviant Behavior*, 8: 148–76.

Ellis, L., and A. Walsh. (1997). Gene-based evolutionary theories in criminology. *Criminology*, 35: 229–75.

——. (2000). *Criminology: A global perspective.* Needham Heights: MA: Allyn & Bacon.

Farrington, D.F. (2002). Foreword. In *Biology and crime*, ed. D. C. Rowe. Los Angeles, CA: Roxbury Publishing Company, ix–xi.

Ferrero, G. (1900). Savages and criminals. *Independent*, 52: 2688–90. Reprinted in *Pioneering perspectives in criminology: The literature of 19th century criminological positivism*, ed. D.M. Horton (2000). Incline Village, NV: Copperhouse Publishing Company, 95–9.

Fishbein, D. (2001). *Biobehavioral perspectives in criminology.* Belmont, CA: Wadsworth/ Thomson Learning.

Fox, V. (1946). Intelligence, race, and age as a selective factor in crime. *Journal of Criminal Law and Criminology*, 37: 141–52.

Fraser, S., ed. (1995). *The bell curve wars: Race, intelligence, and the future of America.* New York: Basic Books.

Gabbidon, S. L. (2009). *Race, ethnicity, crime and justice: An international dilemma.* Thousand Oaks, CA: SAGE Publications.

Gibson, C.L., A.R. Piquero, and S.G. Tibbetts. (2000). Assessing the relationship between maternal cigarette smoking during pregnancy and age at first police contact. *Justice Quarterly*, 17: 519–42.

Gibson, M. (1998). Biology or environment? Race and Southern "deviancy" in the writings of Italian criminologists, 1880–1920. In *Italy's "southern question": Orientalism in one country*, ed. J. Schneider. Oxford: Berg, 99–115.

———. (2002). *Born to crime: Cesare Lombroso and the origins of biological criminology*. Westport, CT: Praeger.

Gibson, M., and N. Rafter. (2004). Editors' introduction. In *Criminal woman, the prostitute, and the normal woman (2004/1893)*, C. Lombroso and F. Guglielmo. Durham, NC: Duke University Press, 3–33.

Goddard, H.H. (1912). *The Kallikak family: A study in the heredity of feebleminded-ness*. New York: The Macmillan Company.

———. (1914). *Feeble-mindedness: Its causes and consequences*. New York: The Macmillan Company.

———. (1922). *Human efficiency and levels of intelligence*. Princeton, NJ: Princeton University Press.

Goode, J. (2005). Corrupting a good mix: Race and crime in late nineteenth- and early twentieth-century Spain. *European History Quarterly*, 35: 241–65.

Gould, S.J. (1996). *The mismeasure of man*. New York: Norton.

Graham, R. (1990). Introduction. In *The idea of race in Latin America, 1870–940*, ed. R. Graham. Austin, TX: University of Texas Press, 1–5.

Hacker, A. (1995). Caste, crime, and precocity. In *The bell curve wars: Race, intelligence, and the future of America*, ed. S. Fraser. New York: Basic Books, 97–108.

Haymes, S.N. (1996). Race, repression, and the politics of crime and punishment in *"The bell curve."* In *Measured lies: The bell curve examined*, eds. J.L. Kincheloe, S.R. Steinberg, and A.D. Gresson, III. New York: St. Martin's Press, 237–49.

Haynie, D.L., H.E. Weiss, and A.R. Piquero. (2008). Race, the economic maturity gap, and criminal offending in young adulthood. *Justice Quarterly*, 25, 595–622.

Helg, A. (1990). Race in Argentina and Cuba, 1880–930: Theory, policies, and popular reaction. In *The idea of race in Latin America, 1870–1940*, ed. R. Graham. Austin, TX: University of Texas Press, 37–69.

Henderson, C.R. (1901). *Introduction to the study of dependents, defective, and delinquent classes*. Boston: D.C. Heath.

Herrnstein, R.J., and C. Murray. (1994). *"The bell curve": Intelligence and class structure in American life*. New York: Free Press.

Hirschi, T., and Hindelang, M. (1977). Intelligence and delinquency: A revisionist review. *American Sociological Review*, 42: 571–87.

Hoffman, F. L. (1896). *Race traits and tendencies of the American Negro*. New York: Macmillan.

Hooton, E.A. (1939a). *Crime and the man*. Cambridge, MA: Harvard University Press.

———. (1939b). *The American criminal: An anthropological study. Volume 1. The native white criminal of native parentage*. Cambridge, MA: Harvard University Press.

Jacoby, R., and N. Glauberman. (1995). *The bell curve debate: History, documents, opinions*. New York: Times Books.

Jeffery, C.R. (1979). Biology and crime: The new neo-Lombrosians. In *Biology and crime*, ed. C.R. Jeffery. Beverly Hills, CA: SAGE Publications, 7–18.

Kellor, F.A. (1901a). The criminal Negro: I. A sociological study. *The Arena*, 25: 59–68.

———. (1901b). The criminal Negro: II. Southern conditions that influence Negro criminality. *The Arena*, 25: 190–7.

———. (1901c). The criminal Negro: III. Some of his characteristics. *The Arena*, 25: 308–16.

———. (1901d). The criminal Negro: IV. Advantages and abuse of southern penal systems. *The Arena*, 25: 419–28.

Kincheloe, J.L., R. Steinberg, and A. D. Gresson, eds. (1996). *Measured lies: The bell curve examined.* New York: St. Martin's Press.

Knepper, P. (2001). *Explaining criminal conduct: Theories and systems in criminology.* Durham, NC: Carolina Academic Press.

Lane, H.A., and P. A. Witty. (1935). The mental ability of delinquent boys. *The Journal of Juvenile Research*, 19: 1–12.

Lanier, M., and S. Henry. (1998). *Essential criminology.* Boulder, CO: Westview.

Lichtenstein, M., and A.W. Brown. (1938). Intelligence and achievement of children in a delinquency area. *The Journal of Juvenile Research*, 22: 1–24.

Lilly, R.J., F.T. Cullen, and R.A. Ball. (2002). *Criminological theory: Context and consequences.* Thousand Oaks, CA: SAGE.

Lombroso, C. (1876/1911). *Criminal man.* New York: G.P. Putnam's Sons.

———. (1911/1968). *Crime: Its causes and remedies.* Montclair, NJ: Patterson Smith.

Lombroso, C., and G. Ferrero. (1893/2004). *Criminal woman, the prostitute, and the normal woman.* (Translated and with a new introduction by N. Hahn Rafter and M. Gibson.) Durham, NC: Duke University Press.

Lynn, R. (2002). Skin color and intelligence in African Americans. *Population and Environment*, 23: 365–75.

Manolakes, L.A. (1997). Cognitive ability, environmental factors, and crime: Predicting frequent criminal activity. In *Intelligence, genes, and success: Scientists respond to "The bell curve,"* eds. B. Devlin, S.E. Fienberg, D.P. Resnick, and K. Roeder. New York: Springer, 235–55.

Marsh, F.H., and J. Katz, eds. (1985). *Biology, crime, and ethics: A study of biological explanations for criminal behavior.* Cincinnati, OH: Anderson Publishing Co.

McClure, W.E. (1933). Intelligence of 600 juvenile delinquents. *The Journal of Juvenile Research*, 17: 35–43.

Merton, R.K., and M.F. Montagu-Ashley. (1940). Crime and the anthropologist. *American Anthropologist*, 42: 384–408.

Moffitt, T.E. (1993). Adolescence-limited and life-course-persistent antisocial behavior: A developmental taxonomy. *Psychological Review*, 100: 674–401.

———. (1994). Natural histories of delinquency. In *Cross-national longitudinal research in human development and criminal behavior*, eds. E.G.M. Weitekamp and H.-J. Kerner. London: Kluwer Academic Publishers, 3–64.

Murchison, C. (1926a). Mental test and other concomitants of some Negro women criminals. *The Pedagogical Seminary and Journal of Genetic Psychology*, 33: 527–30.

———. (1926b). *Criminal intelligence.* Worcester, MA: Clark University Press.

Murchison, C., and H. Burfield. (1925a). Geographical concomitants of Negro criminal intelligence. *The Pedagogical Seminary and Journal of Genetic Psychology*, 32: 26–44.

———. (1925b). Geographical concomitants of Negro criminal intelligence. *The Pedagogical Seminary and Journal of Genetic Psychology*, 32: 239–47.

Murchison, C., and R. Gilbert. (1925a). Some occupational concomitants of Negro men criminals. *The Pedagogical Seminary and Journal of Genetic Psychology*, 32: 648–51.

———. (1925b). Some marital concomitants of Negro men. *The Pedagogical Seminary and Journal of Genetic Psychology*, 32: 652–6.

Murchison, C., and R. Nafe. (1925). Intelligence of Negro recidivists. *The Pedagogical Seminary and Journal of Genetic Psychology*, 32: 248–56.

Murchison, C., and P. Pooler. (1925). Length of sentence and mental test scores of Negro criminals. *The Pedagogical Seminary and Journal of Genetic Psychology*, 32: 657–8.

Neisser, U. et al. (1996). Intelligence: Knowns and unknowns. *American Psychologist*, 51, 77–101.

Onwudiwe, I.D., and M.J. Lynch. (2000). Reopening the debate: A reexamination of the need for a black criminology. *Social Pathology: A Journal of Reviews*, 6: 182–98.

Orovio, C.N., and M.A. Mulero. (2005). Spanish intellectuals and Fernando Ortiz (1900–41). In *Cuban counterpoints: The legacy of Fernando Ortiz*, eds. M.A. Font and A.W. Quiroz. New York: Lexington Books, 9–38.

Piquero, A.R., C.L. Gibson, S.G. Tibbetts, M.G. Turner, and S.H. Katz. (2002). Maternal cigarette smoking during pregnancy and life-course persisting offending. *International Journal of Offender Therapy and Comparative Criminology*, 46: 231–48.

Piquero, A.R., T.E. Moffitt, and B. Lawton. (2005). Race and crime: The contribution of individual, familial, and neighborhood-level risk factors to life-course-persistent offending. In *Our children, their children: Confronting racial and ethnic differences in American juvenile justice*, eds. D.F. Hawkins and K. Kempf-Leonard. Chicago: University of Chicago Press, 202–44.

Piquero, A.R., and N.A. White. (2003). On the relationship between cognitive abilities and life-course-persistent offending among a sample of African Americans: A longitudinal test of Moffit's hypothesis. *Journal of Criminal Justice*, 31: 399–409.

Rafter, N. (2004). Ernest A. Hooton and the biological tradition in American criminology. *Criminology*, 42, 735–71.

——. (2007). Somatotyping, antimodernism, and the production of criminological knowledge. *Criminology*, 45: 805–33.

——. (2008). Criminology's darkest hour: Biocriminology in Nazi Germany. *The Australian and New Zealand Journal of Criminology*, 41: 287–306.

Reid, I. De A. (1957). Race and crime. *Friends Journal*, 3: 772–4.

Roberts, J.V., and T. Gabor. (1990). Lombrosian wine in a new bottle: Research on crime and race. *Canadian Journal of Criminology*, 32: 291–313.

Rowe, D. C. (2002). *Biology and crime*. Los Angeles: Roxbury Publishing Company.

Rowlands, E.B. (1897). Instinctive criminality and social conditions. *Law Quarterly Review*, 13: 59–69. Reprinted in *Pioneering perspectives in criminology: The literature of 19th century criminological positivism*, ed. D.M. Horton. (2000). Incline Village, NV: Copperhouse Publishing Company, 239–50.

Rushton, J.P. (1995). Race and crime: International data for 1989–1990. *Psychological Reports*, 76: 307–12.

——. (1999). *Race, evolution and behavior (special abridged edition)*. New Brunswick, NJ: Transaction.

Rushton, J. P., and D. I. Templer. (2009). National differences in intelligence, crime, income, and skin color. *Intelligence*, 37: 341–6.

Rushton, J.P., and G. Whitney. (2002). Cross-national variation in violent crime rates: Race, r-K theory, and income. *Population and Environment*, 23: 501–11.

Sagarin, E., ed. (1980). *Taboos in criminology*. Beverly Hills, CA: SAGE Publications.

Sheldon, W.H. (1949). *Varieties of delinquent youth: An introduction to constitutional psychiatry*. With the collaboration of Emil M. Hartl and Eugene McDermott. New York: Harper & Brothers.

Skidmore, T. E. (1990). Racial ideas and social policy in Brazil, 1870–1940. In *The idea of race in Latin America, 1870–1940*, ed. R. Graham. Austin, TX: University of Texas Press, 8–36.

Stone, C.P. (1921). A comparative study of the intelligence of 399 inmates of the Indiana reformatory and 653 men of the United States Army. *Journal of Criminal Law, Criminology, and Police Science*, 12: 238–57.

Sutherland, E. H. (1931). Mental deficiency and crime. In *Social attitudes*, ed. K. Young. New York: Henry Holt and Company, 357–75.

Templer, D. I., and J. P. Rushton. (2011). IQ, skin color, crime, HIV/AIDS, and income in 50 U.S. states. *Intelligence*, 39: 437–42.

Tulchin, S. H. (1939). *Intelligence and crime: A study of the penitentiary and reformatory offenders*. Chicago: University of Chicago Press.

Vold, G. B., T. J. Bernard, and J. B. Snipes. (1998). *Theoretical criminology, 4th edition*. Oxford: Oxford University Press.

Walsh, A. (2003). The sex ratio: A biosocial explanation for racial variation in crime rates. In *Biosocial criminology: Challenging environmentalism's supremacy*, eds. A. Walsh and L. Ellis. New York: Nova Publishers, 61–82.

——. (2004). *Race and crime: A biosocial analysis*. New York: Nova Science Publishers.

Watts, F. P. (1941). A comparative clinical study of delinquent and nondelinquent Negro boys. *Journal of Negro Education*, 10: 190–207.

Wilson, E. O. (1975). *Sociobiology: The new synthesis*. Cambridge, MA: Harvard University Press.

Wilson, J. Q., and R. Herrnstein. (1985). *Crime and human nature: The definitive study of the causes of crime*. New York: Simon and Schuster.

Wright, J. P. (2008). Inconvenient truths: Science, race, and crime. In *Biosocial criminology: New directions in theory and research*, eds. A. Walsh and K. M. Beaver. New York: Routledge, 137–53.

Wright, J. P., K. N. Dietrich, M. D. Ris., R. W. Hornung., S. D. Wessel., B. P. Lanphear., M. Ho, and M. N. Rae. (2008). Association of prenatal and childhood lead concentrations with criminal arrests in early adulthood. *PLoS Medicine*, 5: 732–40.

3 Social Disorganization and Strain Perspectives on Race and Crime

Abbott, E., ed. (1931). *National commission on law observance and enforcement. Report on crime and the foreign born (no. 10)*. Washington, DC: Government Printing Office.

Addams, J., ed. (1895). *Hull House maps and papers*. New York: T. Y. Crowell.

Agnew, R. (1992). Foundation for a general strain theory of crime and delinquency. *Criminology*, 30: 47–87.

——. (2001). Building on the foundation of general strain theory: Specifying the types of strain most likely to lead to crime and delinquency. *Journal of Research in Crime and Delinquency*, 38: 319–61.

——. (2006). *Pressured into crime: An overview of general strain theory*. Los Angeles, CA: Roxbury.

Akers, R. L. (2000). *Criminological theories: Introduction, evaluation, and application*. Los Angeles, CA: Roxbury.

Alexander, M. (2010). *The new Jim Crow*. New York: The New Press.

Almgren, G. (2005). The ecological context of interpersonal violence: From culture to efficacy. *Journal of Interpersonal Violence*, 20: 218–24.

Anderson, E. (1996). Introduction to the 1996 edition. In *The Philadelphia Negro: A social study* (1899), W. E. B. Du Bois. Philadelphia: University of Pennsylvania Press, ix–xxxvi.

Bachman, R. (1991). An analysis of American Indian homicide: A test of social disorganization and economic deprivation at the reservation county level. *Journal of Research in Crime and Delinquency*, 28: 456–71.

Bernard, T. J. (1984). Control criticisms of strain theories: An assessment of theoretical and empirical adequacy. *Journal of Research in Crime and Delinquency*, 21: 353–72.

Blitstein, R. (2009). Weathering the storm. *Miller-McCune*, 2: 48–57.

Blumer, M. (1984). *The Chicago school of sociology: Institutionalization, diversity, and the rise of sociological research*. Chicago: University of Chicago Press.

Bohm, R.M. (2001). *A primer on crime and delinquency theory, 2nd edition*. Belmont, CA: Wadsworth/Thomson Learning.

Booth, C. (1889). *Life and labour of the people in London*. London: Macmillan and Co.

Brinton, H.P. (1932). Negroes who run afoul the law. *Social Forces*, 11: 96–101.

Browning, C. (2002). The span of collective efficacy: Extending social disorganization theory to partner violence. *Journal of Marriage and Family*, 64: 833–50.

Burgess, E.W. (1915). Juvenile delinquency in a small city. *The Journal of Criminal Law, Criminology, and Police Science*, 6: 724–8.

——. (1925). The growth of the city: An introduction to a research project. In *The city*, eds. R. Park and E.W. Burgess. Chicago: University of Chicago Press, 47–62.

Bursik, R.J. (2009). The Dead Sea Scrolls and criminological knowledge: 2008 presidential address to the American Society of Criminology. *Criminology*, 47: 5–16.

Bursik, R.J., and H. G. Grasmick. (1993a). *Neighborhoods and crime: The dimensions of effective community control*. New York: Lexington Books.

——. (1993b). Economic deprivation and neighborhood crime rates, 1960–80. *Law & Society Review*, 27: 263–83.

Cancino, J.M., R. Martinez, and J.I. Stowell (2009). The impact of neighborhood context on intergroup robbery: The San Antonio experience. *Annals of the American Academy of Political and Social Sciences*, 623: 12–24.

Cavan, R.S. (1959). Negro family disorganization and juvenile delinquency. *Journal of Negro Education*, 28: 230–9.

Cernkovich, S.A., P. C. Giordano, and J.L. Rudolph. (2000). Race, crime, and the American dream. *Journal of Research in Crime and Delinquency*, 37: 131–70.

Christian, J., and S. S. Thomas. (2009). Examining the intersection of race, gender, and mass imprisonment. *Journal of Ethnicity in Criminal Justice*, 7: 69–84.

Clear, T.R. (2007). *Imprisoning communities: How mass incarceration makes disadvantaged communities worse*. New York: Oxford University Press.

Clear, T.R., D.R. Rose, and J.A. Ryder. (2001). Incarceration and the community: The problem of removing and returning offenders. *Crime and Delinquency*, 47: 335–51.

Clear, T.R., D.R. Rose, E. Waring, and K. Scully. (2003). Coercive mobility and crime: A preliminary examination of concentrated incarceration and social disorganization. *Justice Quarterly*, 20: 33–64.

Cloward, R.A., and L.E. Ohlin. (1960). *Delinquency and opportunity: A theory of delinquent gangs*. New York: Free Press.

Cochrane, H.S. (1949). The delinquent Negro child. *Phylon*, 10: 252–6.

Cole, S., and H. Zuckerman. (1964). Inventory of empirical and theoretical studies of anomie. In *Anomie and deviant behavior*, ed. M.B. Clinard. New York: Free Press, 243–313.

Diggs, M.H. (1940). The problems and needs of Negro youth as revealed by delinquency and crime statistics. *The Journal of Negro Education*, 9: 311–20.

——. (1950). Some problems and needs of Negro children as revealed by comparative delinquency and crime statistics. *The Journal of Negro Education*, 19: 290–7.

Du Bois, W.E.B. (1899/1996). *The Philadelphia Negro: A social study*. Philadelphia, PA: University of Pennsylvania Press.

Ebbe, O.N.I. (1989). Crime and delinquency in metropolitan Lagos: A study of "crime and delinquency area" theory. *Social Forced*, 67: 751–656.

Eitle, D. and R.J. Turner. (2003). Stress exposure, race, and young male adult crime. *Sociological Quarterly*, 44, 243–69.

Elliott, M.A., and F.E. Merrill. (1934). *Social disorganization*. New York: Harper and Brothers Publishers.

Emerick, N. A., T. R. Curry, T. W. Collins, and S. F. Rodriguez. (2014). Homicide and social disorganization on the border: Implications for Latino and immigrant populations. *Social Science Quarterly*, 95: 360–79.

Epps, E.G. (1967). Socioeconomic status, race, level of aspiration and juvenile delinquency: A limited empirical test of Merton's conception of deviance. *Phylon*, 28: 16–27.

Feldmeyer, B. (2009). Immigration and violence: The offsetting effects of immigrant concentration on Latino violence. *Social Science Research*, 38: 717–31.

Felson, R.B. (2008). Barking up the right tree. *The Criminologist*, 33: 1, 3–6.

Felson, R.B., G. Deane., and D.P. Armstrong. (2008). Do theories of crime or violence explain race differences in delinquency? *Social Science Research*, 37: 624–41.

Firmin, A. (1885/2000). *The equality of the human races*. New York: Garland Publishing.

Frazier, E.F. (1932). *The Negro family in Chicago*. Chicago: University of Chicago Press.

——. (1937). Negro Harlem: An ecological study. *American Journal of Sociology*, 43: 72–88.

Gabbidon, S.L. (1999). W.E.B. Du Bois and the "Atlanta school" of social scientific research: 1897–1913. *Journal of Criminal Justice Education*, 10: 21–38.

——. (2001). W.E.B. Du Bois: Pioneering American criminologist. *Journal of Black Studies*, 31: 581–99.

——. (2002). W.E.B. Du Bois and the "Atlanta school" of sociological research: Laying the foundations of American sociological criminology. Paper presented at the annual American Sociological Association meeting held in Chicago, Illinois.

——. (2007). *W.E.B. Du Bois on crime and justice: Laying the foundations of sociological criminology*. Aldershot, UK: Ashgate Publications.

Gabbidon, S. L., and S. A. Peterson. (2006). Living while black: A state-level analysis of the influence of select social stressors on the quality of life among black Americans. *Journal of Black Studies*, 37: 83–102.

Geronimus, A. T., M. Hicken, D. Keene, and J. Bound. (2006). "Weathering" and age patterns of allostatic load scores among blacks and whites in the United States. *American Journal of Public Health*, 96: 826–33.

Geronimus, A. T., and J.P. Thompson. (2004). To denigrate, ignore, or disrupt: Racial inequality in health and the impact of a policy-induced breakdown of African American communities. *Du Bois Review*, 1: 247–79.

Green, D.S., and E.D. Driver. (1976). W.E.B. Du Bois: A case in the sociology of sociological negation. *Phylon*, 37: 308–33.

Grimke, A.H. (1915). *The ultimate criminal*. Washington, DC: American Negro Academy.

Hanson, L. J. (2010). W.E.B. Du Bois. In *Fifty key thinkers in criminology*, eds. K. Hayward, S. Maruna, and J. Mooney. London: Routledge, 53–8.

Hassett-Walker, C. R. (2009). *Black middle class delinquents*. El Paso, TX: LFB Scholarly Publishing, LLC.

Hayner, N. (1933). Delinquency areas in the Puget Sound region. *American Journal of Sociology*, 39: 314–28.

——. (1938). Social factors in Oriental crime. *American Journal of Sociology*, 43: 908–19.

——. (1942). Variability in the criminal behavior of American Indians. *American Journal of Sociology*, 47: 602–13.

Hayward, K., S. Maruna, and J. Mooney, eds. (2009). *Fifty key thinkers in criminology*. London: Routledge.

Hill, M. (1959). The metropolis and juvenile delinquency among Negroes. *The Journal of Negro Education*, 28: 277–85.

Himes, J.S. (1949). Development and status of sociology in Negro colleges. *Journal of Educational Sociology*, 23: 17–32.

Jang, S.J., and B.R. Johnson. (2003). Strain, negative emotions, and deviant coping among African Americans: A test of general strain theory. *Journal of Quantitative Criminology*, 19: 79–105.

——. (2005). Gender, religiosity, and reactions to strain among African Americans. *The Sociological Quarterly*, 46: 323–57.

Jang, S.J. and J.A. Lyons (2006). Strain, social support, and retreatism among African Americans. *Journal of Black Studies*, 37: 251–74.

Jennings, W.G., N.L. Piquero, A.R. Gover, and D.M. Perez. (2009). Gender and general strain theory: A replication of Broidy and Agnew's gender/strain hypothesis among a sample of southwestern Mexican adolescents. *Journal of Criminal Justice*, 37: 404–17.

Jones, N. (2009). W.E.B. Du Bois. In *Encyclopedia of Race and Crime*, eds. H. Taylor Greene and S.L. Gabbidon. Thousand Oaks, CA: SAGE Publications, 242–6.

Kaufman, J.M. (2005). Explaining the race/ethnicity-violence relationship: Neighborhood context and social psychological processes. *Justice Quarterly*, 22: 224–51.

Kaufman, J.M., C.J. Rebellon, S. Thaxton, and R. Agnew. (2008). A general strain theory of racial differences in criminal offending. *The Australian and New Zealand Journal of Criminology*, 41: 421–37.

Kirk, D.S. (2008). The neighborhood context of racial and ethnic disparities in arrest. *Demography*, 45: 55–77.

Kornhauser, R.R. (1978). *Social sources of delinquency: An appraisal of analytic models*. Chicago: University of Chicago Press.

Krivo, L.J., and R.D. Peterson. (1996). *Extremely disadvantaged neighborhoods and urban crime*. Social Forces, 75: 619–50.

——. (2000). The structural context of homicide: Accounting for racial differences in process. *American Sociological Review*, 65: 547–59.

Lanier, C., and L. Huff-Corzine. (2006). American Indian homicide: A county level analysis utilizing social disorganization theory. *Homicide Studies*, 10: 181–94.

Lanier, M.M., and S. Henry. (1998). *Essential criminology*. Boulder, CO: Westview.

Lee, M.T., and R. Martinez. (2002). Social disorganization revisited: Mapping the recent immigration and black homicide relationship in northern Miami. *Sociological Focus*, 35: 363–80.

Lee, M.T., R. Martinez, and R. Rosenfeld. (2001). Does immigration increase homicide? Negative evidence from three border cities. *Sociological Quarterly*, 42: 559–80.

Lewis, D.L. (1993). *W.E.B. Du Bois: Biography of a race*. New York: Henry, Holt, and Company.

Lilly, R.J., F.T. Cullen, and R.A. Ball. (2002). *Criminological theory: Context and consequences*. Thousand Oaks, CA: SAGE.

Lind, A.W. (1930a). Some ecological patterns of community disorganization in Honolulu. *American Journal of Sociology*, 36: 206–20.

——. (1930b). The ghetto and the slum. *Social Forces*, 9: 206–15.

MacDonald, J., J. Hipp, and C. Gill (2013). The effect of immigrant concentration on changes in neighborhood crime rates. *Journal of Quantitative Criminology* 29: 191–215.

Martinez, R. (2000). Immigration and urban violence: The link between immigrant Latinos and types of homicide. *Social Science Quarterly*, 81: 363–74.

———. (2002). *Latino homicide: Immigration, violence, and community*. New York: Routledge.

———. (2003). Moving beyond black and white violence: African American, Haitian, and Latino homicides in Miami. In *Violent crime: Assessing race and ethnic differences*, ed. D.F. Hawkins. New York: Cambridge University Press, 22–43.

Martinez, R., and M.T. Lee. (1998). Immigration and the ethnic distribution of homicide in Miami, 1985–95. *Homicide Studies*, 2: 291–304.

Martinez, R., J. Stowell, and M. T. Lee. (2010). Immigration and crime in an era of transformation: A longitudinal analysis of homicides in San Diego neighborhoods, 1980–2000. *Criminology*, 48: 797–829.

Martinez, R., and A. Valenzuela, eds. (2006). *Immigration and crime: Race, ethnicity, and violence*. New York: New York University Press.

Mauer, M. (2006). *Race to incarcerate (revised edition)*. New York: New Press.

McClusky, C.P. (2002). *Understanding Latino delinquency: The applicability of strain theory by ethnicity*. New York: LFB Scholarly Publishing LLC.

McKeown, J.E. (1948). Poverty, race, and crime. *The Journal of Criminal Law, Criminology and Police Science*, 39: 480–4.

Merton, R.K. (1938). Social structure and anomie. *American Sociological Review*, 3: 672–82.

Miller, J.M., C.J. Schreck, and R. Tewksbury. (2008). *Criminological theory: A brief introduction, 2nd edition*. Boston, MA: Allyn & Bacon.

Miller, K. (1908/1969). *Out of the house of bondage*. New York: Arno Press and the *New York Times*.

Moon, B., K. Hays, and D. Blurton (2009). General strain theory, key strains, and deviance. *Journal of Criminal Justice*, 37: 98–106.

Morenoff, J.D., R.J. Sampson, and S.W. Raudenbush. (2001). Neighborhood inequality, collective efficacy, and the spatial dynamics of urban violence. *Criminology*, 39: 517–60.

Moses, E.R. (1936). Community factors in Negro delinquency. *Journal of Negro Education*, 5: 220–7.

———. (1947). Differentials in crime rates between Negroes and whites, based on comparisons of four socioeconomically equated areas. *American Sociological Review*, 12: 411–20.

Moyer, I.L. (2001). *Criminological theories: Traditional and nontraditional voices and themes*. Thousand Oaks, CA. SAGE Publications.

Murphy, D.S., and M.B. Robinson. (2008). The maximizer: Clarifying Merton's theories of anomie and strain. *Theoretical Criminology*, 12: 501–21.

Ouimet, M. (2000). Aggregation bias in ecological research: How social disorganization and criminal opportunities shape the spatial distribution of Juvenile delinquency in montreal. *Canadian Journal of Criminology*, 42: 135–56.

Parker, K.F., J.M. MacDonald, G.P. Alpert, M.R. Smith, and A.R. Piquero. (2004). A contextual study of racial profiling: Assessing the theoretical rationale for the study of racial profiling at the local level. *American Behavioral Scientist*, 47: 943–62.

Pattillo, M.E. (1998). Sweet mothers and gangbangers: Managing crime in a black middle-class neighborhood. *Social Forces*, 76: 747–74.

Perez, D.M., W.G. Jennings, and A.R. Gover (2008). Specifying general strain theory: An ethnically relevant approach. *Deviant Behavior*, 29: 544–78.

Peterson, R.D., and L.J. Krivo. (1993). Racial segregation and black urban homicide. *Social Forces*, 71: 1001–26.

———. (1999). Racial segregation, the concentration of disadvantage, and black and white homicide victimization. *Sociological Forum*, 14: 465–93.

———. (2005). Macrostructural analyses of race, ethnicity, and violent crime: Recent lessons and new directions for research. *Annual Review of Sociology*, 31: 331–56.

———. (2010). *Divergent social worlds: Neighborhood crime and the racial-spatial divide*. New York: Russell Sage Foundation.

Quetelet, A.Q. (1833/1984). *Research on the propensity for crime at different ages*. Cincinnati, OH: Anderson.

———. (1842). *A treatise on man and the development of his faculties*. Edinburg: William and Robert Chambers.

Rafter, N., ed. (2009). *The origins of criminology: A reader*. New York: Routledge.

Robinson, M., and D. Murphy. (2009). *Greed is good: Maximization and elite deviance in America*. Lanham, MD: Rowman & Littlefield Publishers.

Rocque, M. (2008). Strain, coping mechanisms, and slavery: A general strain theory application. *Crime, Law and Social Change*, 49: 245–69.

Rodriguez, J.J., and S. Belshaw. (2010). General strain theory: A comparative analysis of Latino & white youth. *Southwest Journal of Criminal Justice*, 7: 138–58.

Rose, D.R., and T.R. Clear. (1998). Incarceration, social capital, and crime: Implications for social disorganization theory. *Criminology*, 36: 441–79.

Rukus, J., and B. Warner. (2013). Crime rates and collective efficacy: The role of family friendly planning. *Cities*, 31: 37–46.

Russell, K.K. (1992). Development of a black criminology and the role of the black criminologist. *Justice Quarterly*, 9: 667–83.

Sabol, W.J., C.J. Coulton, and J.E. Korbin. (2004). Building community capacity for violence prevention. *Journal of Interpersonal Violence*, 19: 322–40.

St. Jean, P.K.B. (2007). *Pockets of crime: Broken windows, collective efficacy, and the criminal point of view*. Chicago: University of Chicago Press.

Sampson, R.J. (1987). Urban black violence: The effects of male joblessness and family disruption. *American Journal of Sociology*, 93: 348–82.

———. (2008). Rethinking crime and immigration. *Contexts* 7: 28–33.

———. (2012). *Great American city: Chicago and the enduring neighborhood effect*. Chicago: University of Chicago Press.

Sampson, R.J., and L. Bean. (2006). Cultural mechanisms and killing fields: A revised theory of community-level racial inequality. In *The many colors of crime: Inequalities of race, ethnicity, and crime in America*, eds. R.D. Peterson, L.P. Krivo, and J. Hagan. New York: New York University Press, 8–36.

Sampson, R.J., and W.B. Groves. (1989). Community structure and crime: Testing social-disorganization theory. *American Journal of Sociology*, 94: 774–802.

Sampson, R.J., J.D. Morenoff, and F. Earls. (1999). Beyond social capital: Neighborhood mechanisms and structural sources of collective efficacy for children. *American Sociological Review*, 64: 633–60.

Sampson, R.J., S.W. Raudenbush, and F. Earls. (1997). Neighborhoods and violent crime: A multilevel study of collective efficacy. *Science*, 277: 918–24.

Sampson, R.J., and W.J. Wilson. (1995). Toward a theory of race, crime, and urban inequality. In *Crime and inequality*, eds. J. Hagan and R.D. Peterson. Stanford, CA: Stanford University Press, 37–54.

Shaw, C., and H.D. McKay. (1942). *Juvenile delinquency in urban areas*. Chicago: University of Chicago Press.

Shoemaker, D.J. (1996). *Theories of crime and delinquency: An examination of explanations of delinquent behavior.* Oxford: Oxford University Press.

Simons, R.L., Y.F. Chen, E.A. Stewart, and G.H. Brody. (2003). Incidents of discrimination and risk for delinquency: A longitudinal test of strain theory with an African American sample. *Justice Quarterly,* 20: 827–54.

Sutherland, E.H., and D.R. Cressey. (1960). *Criminology, 6th edition.* New York: J.B. Lippincott Company.

Taft, D.R. (1933). Does immigration increase crime? *Social Forces,* 12: 69–77.

——. (1936). Nationality and crime. *American Sociological Review,* 1: 724–36.

Toby, J. (1957). The differential impact of family disorganization. *American Sociological Review,* 22: 505–12.

Unnever, J.D., F.T. Cullen, S.A. Mathers, T.E. McClure, and M.C. Allison. (2009). Racial discrimination and Hirschi's criminological classic: A chapter in the sociology of knowledge. *Justice Quarterly,* 26: 377–409.

Unnever, J. D., and S. L. Gabbidon. (2011). *A theory of African American offending: Race, racism, and crime.* New York: Routledge.

Velez, M.B. (2009). Contextualizing the immigration and crime effect: An analysis of homicide in Chicago neighborhoods. *Homicide Studies,* 13: 325–35.

von Hentig, H. (1945). The first generation and a half: Notes on the delinquency of the native white of mixed parentage. *American Sociological Review,* 10: 792–8.

Wakefield, S., and C. Wildeman. (2014). *Children of the prison boom: Mass incarceration and the future of American inequality.* Oxford: Oxford University Press.

Walton, I., C. Dawson-Edwards, and G. E. Higgins. (2014). General strain theory and collegiate drinking patterns among African American female students. *American Journal of Criminal Justice,* DOI: 10.1007/s12103–013–9232–4.

Warner, B. (2014). Neighborhood factors related to the likelihood of successful informal social control efforts. *Journal of Criminal Justice,* 42: 421–30.

Wattenberg, W.M. (1954). Factors linked to race among boys in trouble with Detroit Police, 1948. *The Journal of Negro Education,* 23: 186–9.

Wattenberg, W.M., and J.B. Moir. (1957). A phenomenon in search of a cause. *The Journal of Criminal Law, Criminology and Police Science,* 48: 54–8.

Western, B. (2006). *Punishment and inequality in America.* New York: Russell Sage.

Western, B., and C. Wildeman. (2009). The black family and mass incarceration. *Annals of the American Academy of Political and Social Sciences,* 621: 221–42.

Williams, R.W. (2005). W.E.B. Du Bois and his social-scientific research: A review of online texts. *Sociation Today,* 3: 2 (Fall). www.ncsociology.org/ sociationtoday/v32/williams.htm.

——. (2006). The early social science of W.E.B. Du Bois. *Du Bois Review: Social Science Research on Race,* 3: 365–94.

——. (2009). Atlanta University School of Sociological Research. In *Encyclopedia of Race and Crime,* eds. H.T. Greene and S.L. Gabbidon. Thousand Oaks, CA: SAGE Publications, 37–40.

Wilson, W.J. (1987). *The truly disadvantaged.* Chicago: University of Chicago Press.

——. (1996). *When work disappears.* New York: Knopf.

Work, M. (1900). Crime among the Negroes of Chicago. *American Journal of Sociology,* 6: 204–23.

——. (1913). Negro criminality in the south. *Annals of the American Academy of Political and Social Sciences,* 49: 74–80.

Wright, E. (2002a). Using the master's tools: The Atlanta sociological laboratory and American sociology, 1896–924. *Sociological Spectrum*, 22: 15–39.

——. (2002b). Why black people tend to shout! An earnest attempt to explain the sociological negation of the Atlanta sociological laboratory despite its possible unpleasantness. *Sociological Spectrum*, 22: 335–61.

——. (2002c). The Atlanta sociological laboratory 1896–1924: A historical account of the first American school of sociology. *The Western Journal of Black Studies*, 26(3): 165–74.

——. (2005). W.E.B. Du Bois and the Atlanta sociological laboratory. *Sociation Today*, 2: 1–11. www.ncsociology.org/sociationtoday/v31/wright.htm.

——. (2006). W.E.B. Du Bois and the Atlanta University studies on the Negro, revisited. *Journal of African American Studies*, 9: 3–17.

——. (2008). Deferred legacy! The continued marginalization of the Atlanta sociological laboratory. *Sociology Compass* 2: 195–207.

——. (2012). Why, where and how to infuse the Atlanta Sociological Laboratory into the sociology curriculum. *Teaching Sociology*, 40: 257–70.

Wright, R.R. (1912/1969). *The Negro in Pennsylvania: A study in economic history.* New York: Arno Press and the *New York Times*.

Wu, B. (2009). Intimate homicide between Asians and non-Asians: The impact of community context. *Journal of Interpersonal Violence*, 24: 1148–64.

Wyatt, D.W. (1943). Racial handicaps in the Negro delinquent. *Probation*, April: 112–15.

Yabiku, S.T., A. D. Rayle, S. K. Okamoto, F. F. Marsiglia, and S. Kulis. (2007). The effect of neighborhood context on the drug use of American Indian youth in the southwest. *Journal of Ethnicity in Substance Abuse*, 6: 181–204.

4   *Subcultural Perspectives on Race and Crime*

Allredge, E.P. (1942). Why the South leads the nation in murder and manslaughter. *The Quarterly Review*, 2: 123–34.

Anderson, E.A. (1994). The code of the streets. *Atlantic Monthly*, May: 81–94.

——. (1999). *The code of the streets: Decency, violence, and the moral life of the inner city.* New York: Norton.

——. (2002). The ideologically driven critique. *American Journal of Sociology*, 107: 1533–50.

Ball-Rokeach, S.J. (1973). Values and violence: A test of the subculture of violence thesis. *American Sociological Review*, 38: 736–49.

Barnhart, K.E. (1932). Negro homicides in the United States. *Opportunity: Journal of Negro Life*, 10: 212–14, 225.

Baumer, E., J. Horney, R. Felson, and J. Lauristen. (2003). Neighborhood disadvantage and the nature of violence. *Criminology*, 41: 39–71.

Beckley, A.L. (2008). Race, masculinity, and boot camp failure. *Crime, Law and Social Change*, 49: 303–14.

Berg, M.T., E.A. Stewart, C. Schreck, and R.L. Simons. (2012). The victim-offender overlap in context: Examining the role of neighborhood street culture. *Criminology*, 50: 359–90.

Bernard, T.J. (1984). Control criticisms of strain theories: An assessment of theoretical and empirical adequacy. *Journal of Research in Crime and Delinquency*, 21: 353–72.

——. (1990). Angry aggression among the "truly disadvantaged." *Criminology*, 28: 73–95.

Brearley, H.C. (1930). The Negro and homicide. *Social Forces*, 9: 247–53.

——. (1932). *Homicide in the United States.* Chapel Hill, NC: University of North Carolina Press.

Brezina, T., R. Agnew, F.T. Cullen, and J.P. Wright. (2004). The code of the street: A quantitative assessment of Elijah Anderson's subculture of violence thesis and its contribution to youth violence research. *Youth Violence and Juvenile Justice*, 2: 303–28.

Brunson, R.K., and E.A. Stewart. (2006). Young African American women, the street code, and violence: An exploratory analysis. *Journal of Crime and Justice*, 29: 1–19.

Butterfield, F. (1995). *All God's children*. New York: Knopf.

Cao, L., A.T. Adams, and V.J. Jensen. (2000). The empirical status of the black-subculture-of-violence thesis. In *The system in black and white: Exploring the connections between race, crime, and justice*, eds. M.W. Markowitz and D. Jones Brown. Eastport, CT: Praeger Publishers, 47–61.

Cheatwood, D. (1990). Black homicides in Baltimore 1974–1986: Age, gender, and weapon use changes. *Criminal Justice Review*, 15: 192–207.

Chilton, B. (2004). Regional variations in lethal and nonlethal assaults. *Homicide Studies*, 8: 40–56.

Clarke, J.W. (1998). "Without fear or shame": Lynching, capital punishment and the subculture of violence in the American south. *British Journal of Political Science*, 28: 269–89.

Cloward, R.A., and L.E. Ohlin. (1960). *Delinquency and opportunity: A theory of delinquent gangs*. New York: Free Press.

Cohen, A.K. (1955). *Delinquent boys: The culture of the gang*. New York: Free Press.

Covington, J. (2003). The violent black male: Conceptions of race in criminological theories. In *Violent crime: Assessing race and ethnic differences*, eds. D.F. Hawkins. Cambridge: Cambridge University Press, 254–79.

Curtis, L.A. (1975). *Violence, race, and culture*. Lexington, MA: Heath.

DeLisi, M. (2014). Antisocial traits murdered the Code of the Street in a battle for respect. *Journal of Criminal Justice*, 42: 431–2.

Doucet, J.M., J.M. D'Antonio-Del Rio, and C.D. Chauvin. (2014). G.R.I.T.S.: The southern subculture of violence and homicide offenses by girls raised in the south. *Journal of Interpersonal Violence*, 29: 806–23.

Gabbidon, S.L., and H. Taylor Greene. (2013). *Race and crime, 3rd edition*. Thousand Oaks, CA: SAGE Publications.

Garfinkel, H. (1949). Research note on inter- and intraracial homicides. *Social Forces*, 27: 369–81.

Gastil, R.D. (1971). Homicide and a regional subculture of violence. *American Sociological Review*, 36: 412–27.

Hackney, S. (1969). Southern violence. *American Historical Review*, 74: 906–25.

Hagan, F.E. (2002). *Introduction to criminology: Theories, methods, and criminal behavior*. Belmont, CA: Wadsworth.

Harer, M.D., and D.J. Steffensmeier. (1996). Race and prison violence. *Criminology*, 34: 323–55.

Hawkins, D.F. (1983). Black and white homicide differentials: Alternatives to an inadequate theory. *Criminal Justice and Behavior*, 10: 407–40.

Intravia, J., K.T. Wolff, E.A. Stewart, and R.L. Simons. (2014). Neighborhood-level differences in police discrimination and subcultural violence: A multilevel examination of adopting the code of the street. *Journal of Crime & Justice*, 37: 42–60.

Jessor, R., T.D. Graves, R.C. Hanson, and S.L. Jessor. (1968). *Society, personality, and deviant behavior: A study of a tri-ethnic community*. New York: Holt, Rinehart and Winston.

Johnson, G.B. (1941). The Negro and crime. *Annals of the American Academy of Political and Social Sciences*, 217: 93–104.

Johnson, S.L. (1996). Subcultural backlash: A new variable in the explanation of the over-representation of African Americans in the criminal justice system. Unpublished doctoral dissertation, Pennsylvania State University.

Jones, N. (2004). "It's not where you live, it's how you live": How young women negotiate violence in the inner city. *Annals of the American Academy of Political and Social Sciences*, 595: 49–62.

——. (2008).Working "the code": On girls, gender, and inner-city violence. *Australia and New Zealand Journal of Criminology* 4: 63–83.

——. (2009). *Between good and ghetto: African American girls and inner city violence*. New Brunswick, NJ: Rutgers University Press.

Keil, T.J., and G. Vito. (2009). Lynching and the death penalty in Kentucky, 1866–1934: Substitution or supplement. *Journal of Ethnicity in Criminal Justice*, 7: 53–68.

Kobrin, S. (1951). The conflict of values in delinquency areas. *American Sociological Review*, 15: 653–61.

Kornhauser, R.R. (1978). *Social sources of delinquency: An appraisal of analytic models*. Chicago: University of Chicago Press.

Kubrin, C.E. (2005). Gangstas, thugs, and hustlas: Identity and the code of the streets in rap music. *Social Problems*, 52: 360–78.

Laub, J.H., and M.J. McDermott. (1985). An analysis of serious crime by young black women. *Criminology*, 23: 81–97.

Lee, M.R., T.C. Hayes, and S.A. Thomas. (2008). Regional variation in the effect of structural factors on homicide in rural areas. *The Social Science Journal*, 45: 76–94.

Lichtenstein, M.J. (1984). An empirical test of the subculture of violence and Miller's theory of lower class delinquency. *International Journal of Comparative and Applied Criminal Justice*, 9: 139–49.

Lilly, R.J., F.T. Cullen, and R.A. Ball. (2002). *Criminological theory: Context and consequences*. Thousand Oaks, CA: SAGE.

Loftin, C., and R.H. Hill. (1974). Regional subculture and homicide. *American Sociological Review*, 39, 714–24.

Lopez, R., M.W. Roosa, J.T. Tein, and K.T. Dinh. (2004). Accounting for Anglo-Hispanic differences in school misbehavior. *Journal of Ethnicity in Criminal Justice*, 2: 27–46.

Mann, C.R. (1987). Black women who kill. In *Violence in the black family: Correlates and consequences*, ed. R. Hampton. Lexington, MA: Lexington Books, 157–86.

——. (1990). Black female homicide in the United States. *Journal of Interpersonal Violence*, 5: 176–201.

Martinez, R. (2002). *Latino homicide*. New York: Routledge.

Matsueda, R.L., K. Drakulich, and C.E. Kubrin. (2006). Race and neighborhood codes. In *The many colors of crime: Inequalities of race, ethnicity, and crime in America*, eds. R.D. Peterson, L.P. Krivo, and J. Hagan. New York: New York University Press, 334–56.

McClain, P. (1981). Social and environmental characteristics of black female homicide offenders. *Western Journal of Black Studies*, 5: 224–30.

McGloin, J.M., C.J. Schreck, E.A. Stewart, and G.C. Ousey. (2011). Predicting the violent offender: The discriminant validity of the subculture of violence. *Criminology*, 49: 767–94.

Mears, D.P., E.A. Stewart, S.E. Siennick, and R.L. Simons. (2013). The code of the street and inmate violence: Investigating the salience of imported belief systems. *Criminology*, 51: 695–728.

Messner, S.F. (1983). Regional and racial effects on the urban homicide rate: The subculture of violence revisited. *American Journal of Sociology*, 88: 997–1007.

Miller, J. (2001). Breaking the individual back in: A commentary on Wacquant and Anderson. *Punishment and Society*, 3: 153–60.

Miller, W. (1958). Lower class culture as a generating milieu of gang delinquency. *Journal of Social Issues*, 14: 5–19.

Oliver, W. (1984). Black males and the tough guy image: A dysfunctional compensatory adaptation. *The Western Journal of Black Studies*, 8: 199–203.

———. (1989a). Black males and social problems: Prevention through Afrocentric socialization. *Journal of Black Studies*, 20: 15–39.

———. (1989b). Sexual conquest and patterns of black-on-black violence: A structural-cultural perspective. *Violence and Victims*, 4: 257–73.

———. (1994). *The violent social world of black men*. New York: Lexington Books.

———. (2003). The structural–cultural perspective: A theory of black male violence. In *Violent crime: Assessing race and ethnic differences*, ed. D. F. Hawkins. Cambridge: Cambridge University Press, 280–318.

———. (2006). "The streets": An alternative black male socialization institution. *Journal of Black Studies*, 36: 918–37.

Parker, K. F., and A. Reckdenwald. (2008). Concentrated disadvantage, traditional male role models, and African-American juvenile violence. *Criminology*, 46: 711–36.

Parker, R. N. (1989). Poverty, subculture of violence, and type of homicide. *Social Forces*, 67: 983–1007.

Ray, M. C., and E. Smith. (1991). Black women and homicide: An analysis of the subculture of violence thesis. *The Western Journal of Black Studies*, 15: 144–53.

Rose, M. R., and C. G. Ellison. (2014). Violence as honorable? Racial and ethnic differences in attitudes towards violence. *Crime & Delinquency*, DOI: 10.1177/0 0111 28713496006.

Ross, L. E. (1992). Blacks, self-esteem, and delinquency: It's time for a new approach. *Justice Quarterly*, 9: 609–24.

Sampson, R. J. (1985). Race and criminal violence: A demographically disaggregated analysis of urban homicide. *Crime and Delinquency*, 31: 47–82.

Sellin, T., and M. Wolfgang. (1964). *The measurement of delinquency*. New York: Wiley.

Shoemaker, D. J., and S. J. Williams. (1987). The subculture of violence and ethnicity. *Journal of Criminal Justice*, 15: 461–72.

Short, J. F., and F. L. Strodtbeck. (1965). *Group process and gang delinquency*. Chicago: University of Chicago Press.

Silberman, C. E. (1978). *Criminal violence, criminal justice*. New York: Random House.

Simons, R. L., and P. A. Gray. (1989). Perceived blocked opportunity as an explanation of delinquency among lower-class black males: A research note. *Journal of Research in Crime and Delinquency*, 26: 90–101.

Spirer, J. (1940). *Negro crime*. Baltimore, MD: John Hopkins University Press.

Staff, J., and D. A. Kreager. (2008). Too cool for school? Violence, peer status and high school dropout. *Social Forces*, 87: 445–71.

Stewart, E. A., C. J. Schreck, and R. K. Brunson. (2008). Lessons of the street code: Policy implications for reducing violent victimization among disadvantaged citizens. *Journal of Contemporary Criminal Justice*, 24: 137–47.

Stewart, E. A., C. J. Schreck, and R. L. Simons. (2006). "I ain't gonna let no one disrespect me": Does the code of the street reduce or increase violent victimization among African American adolescents? *Journal of Research in Crime and Delinquency*, 43: 427–58.

Stewart, E. A., R. L. Simons, and R. D. Conger. (2002). Assessing neighborhood and social psychological influences on childhood violence in an African American sample. *Criminology*, 40: 801–29.

Sutherland, E.H. (1925). Murder and the death penalty. *Journal of the American Institute of Criminal Law and Criminology*, 15: 522–9.

Velez-Diaz, A., and E.I. Megargee. (1971). An investigation of differences in value judgments between youthful and nonoffenders in Puerto Rico. *Journal of Criminal Law, Criminology, and Police Science*, 61: 549–53.

von Hentig, H. (1940). The criminality of the Negro. *The Journal of Criminal Law and Criminology*, 30: 662–80.

Voss, H.L., and J.R. Hepburn. (1968). Patterns in criminal homicide in Chicago. *The Journal of Criminal Law, Criminology and Police Science*, 59: 499–508.

Wacquant, L. (2002). Scrutinizing the street: Poverty, morality, and the pitfalls of urban ethnography. *American Journal of Sociology*, 107: 1468–532.

Walker, S., C. Spohn, and M. DeLone. (2011). *The color of justice, 5th edition*. Belmont, CA: Wadsworth/Thomson.

Wendling, A., and D.S. Elliott. (1968). Class and race differentials in parental aspirations and expectations. *Pacific Sociological Review*, 11: 123–33.

Wilson, W.J. (1987). *The truly disadvantaged*. Chicago: University of Chicago Press.

Wilson, W.J., and A. Chaddha. (2009). The role of theory in ethnographic research. *Ethnography*, 10: 549–64.

Wolfgang, M.E. (1958). *Patterns in criminal homicide*. Philadelphia, PA: University of Pennsylvania Press.

Wolfgang, M.E., and F. Ferracuti. (1967). *The subculture of violence: Towards an integrated theory in criminology*. London: Tavistock Publications.

Zimring, F. (2003). *The contradictions of American capital punishment*. New York: Oxford University Press.

5 Labeling Perspectives on Race and Crime

Armour, J.D. (1997). *Negrophobia and reasonable racism: The hidden costs of being black in America*. New York: New York University Press.

Barlow, M.H. (1998). Race and the problem of crime in *Time* and *Newsweek* cover stories, 1946 to 1995. *Social Justice*, 25: 149–83.

Becker, H.S. (1963). *Outsiders: Studies in the sociology of deviance*. London: Free Press of Glencoe.

Blair, I.V., C.M. Judd, and K.M. Chapleau. (2004). The influence of Afrocentric facial features in criminal sentencing. *Psychological Science*, 15: 674–9.

Brown, S.E., F.A. Esbensen, and G. Geis. (2004). *Criminology: Explaining crime and its context, 5th edition*. Cincinnati, OH: Anderson Publishing.

Chambliss, W.J. (1973). The saints and the roughnecks. *Society*, 11: 24–31.

Chavez, J.M., and D.M. Provine. (2009). Race and the response of state legislatures to unauthorized immigrants. *Annals of the American Academy of Political and Social Sciences*, 623: 78–92.

Chavez, L.R. (2013). *The Latino threat: Constructing immigrants, citizens, and the nation, 2nd edition*. Stanford: Stanford University Press.

Chiricos, T., and S. Eschholz. (2002). The racial and ethnic typification of crime and the criminal typification of race and ethnicity in local television news. *Journal of Research in Crime and Delinquency*, 39: 400–20.

Cisneros, J.D. (2008). Contaminated communities: The metaphor of "immigrant as pollutant" in media representations of immigration. *Rhetoric and Public Affairs*, 11: 569–601.

Cooley, C.H. (1902). *Human nature and the social order*. New York: Charles Scribner's Sons.

——. (1922/1967). *Human nature and the social order, revised edition.* New York: Schoken Books.

Cornell, J., B. Park, C.M. Judd, and B. Wittenbrink. (2002). The police officer's dilemma: Using ethnicity to disambiguate potentially threatening individuals. *Journal of Personality and Social Psychology,* 83: 1314–29.

Cornell, J., G.R. Urland, and T.A. Ito. (2006). Event-related potentials and the decision to shoot: The role of threat perception and cognitive control. *Journal of Experimental Social Psychology,* 42: 120–8.

Covington, J. (1995). Racial classification in criminology: The reproduction of racialized crime. *Sociological Forum,* 10: 547–68.

Dixon. T.L. (2005). Skin tone, crime news, and social reality judgments: Priming the stereotype of the dark and dangerous black criminal. *Journal of Applied Social Psychology,* 35: 1555–70.

——. (2007). Black criminals and white officers: The effects of racially misrepresenting law breakers and law defenders on television news. *Media Psychology,* 10: 270–91.

——. (2008a). Who is the victim here? The psychological effects of overrepresenting white victims and black perpetrators on television news. *Journalism: Theory, Practice, and Criticism,* 9: 582–605.

——. (2008b). Network news and racial beliefs: Exploring the connection between national television news exposure and stereotypical perceptions of African Americans. *Journal of Communication,* 58: 530–49.

Du Bois, W.E.B. (1899/1996). *The Philadelphia Negro: A social study.* Philadelphia, PA: University of Pennsylvania Press.

Eberhardt, J.L., P.G. Davies, V.J. Purdie-Vaughns, and S.L. Johnson. (2006). Looking deathworthy: Perceived stereotypicality of Black defendants predicts capital-sentencing outcomes. *Psychological Science,* 17, 383–6.

Eberhardt, J.L., V.J. Purdie, P.A. Goff, and P.G. Davies (2004). Seeing black: Race, crime, and visual processing. *Journal of Personality and Social Psychology,* 87: 876–93.

Entman, R.M. (1990). Modern racism and the images of blacks in local television news. *Critical Studies in Mass Communication,* 7: 332–45.

——. (1992). Blacks in television news: Television, modern racism, and cultural change. *Journalism Quarterly,* 69: 341–61.

Entman, R.M., and A. Rojecki. (2000). *The black image in the white mind: Media and race in America.* Chicago: University of Chicago Press.

Eschholz, S. (2002). Racial composition of television offenders and viewers' fear of crime. *Critical Criminology,* 11: 41–60.

——. (2004). The color of prime-time justice: Racial characteristics of television offenders and victims. In *Racial issues in criminal justice: The case of African Americans,* ed. M.D. Free. Monsey, NY: Criminal Justice Press, 59–76.

Eschholz, S., T. Chiricos, and M. Gertz. (2003). Television and fear of crime: Program types, audience traits, and the mediating effect of perceived neighborhood racial composition. *Social Problems,* 50: 395–415.

Eschholz, S., M. Mallard, and S. Flynn. (2004). Images of prime time justice: A content analysis of NYPD Blue and Law and Order. *Journal of Criminal Justice and Popular Culture,* 10: 161–80.

Fishman, L.T. (2006). The black bogeyman and white self-righteousness. In *Images of color, images of crime: Readings, 3rd edition,* eds. C.R. Mann, M.S. Zatz, and N. Rodriguez. Los Angeles, CA: Roxbury Publishing Company, 197–211.

Franklin, T. (2013). Sentencing Native Americans in US federal courts: An examination of disparity. *Justice Quarterly*, 30: 310–39.

Gabbidon, S. L., and H. Taylor Greene. (2013). *Race and crime, 3rd edition*. Thousand Oaks, CA: SAGE Publications.

Gabbidon, S. L., and K. L. Jordan. (2013). Public opinion on the killing of Trayvon Martin: A test of the racial gradient thesis. *Journal of Crime and Justice*, 36: 283–98.

Goffman, E. (1963/1986). *Stigma: Notes on the management of spoiled identity*. New York: Simon and Schuster.

Graham, S., and B. S. Lowery. (2004). Priming unconscious racial stereotypes about adolescent offenders. *Law and Human Behavior*, 28: 483–504.

Greenwald, A. G., M. A. Oakes, and H. G. Hoffman. (2003). Targets of discrimination: Effects of race on responses to weapons holders. *Journal of Experimental Social Psychology*, 39: 399–405.

Grove, W. R. (1975a). *The labelling of deviance: Evaluating a perspective*. New York: John Wiley & Sons/SAGE Publications.

———. (1975b). The labelling perspective: An overview. In *The labelling of deviance: Evaluating a perspective*. New York: John Wiley & Sons/SAGE Publications, 3–20.

Hagan, J., R. Levi., and R. Dinovitzer. (2008). The symbolic violence of the crime-immigration nexus: Migrant mythologies in the Americas. *Criminology & Public Policy*, 7: 95–112.

Hagan, J., and A. Palloni. (1999). Sociological criminology and the mythology of Hispanic immigration and crime. *Social Problems*, 46: 617–32.

Hirschfield, P. J., and A. R. Piquero. (2010). Normalization and legitimation: Modeling stigmatizing attitudes toward ex-offenders. *Criminology*, 48: 27–55.

Hirschi, T. (1975). Labelling theory and juvenile delinquency: An assessment of the evidence. In *The labelling of deviance: Evaluating a perspective*. New York: John Wiley & Sons/SAGE Publications, 181–203.

Hughes, C. E. (1945). Dilemmas and contradictions of statuses. *American Journal of Sociology*, 50: 353–9.

Jarmon, C. (2003). Sociology at Howard University: From E. Franklin Frazier and beyond. *Teaching Sociology*, 31: 366–74.

Jones, B. A. (1974). The tradition of sociology teaching in black colleges: The unheralded professionals. In *Black sociologists: Historical and contemporary perspectives*, eds. J. E. Blackwell and M. Janowitz. Chicago: University of Chicago Press, 121–63.

Judd, C. M., I. V. Blair, and K. M. Chapleau. (2004). Automatic stereotypes vs. automatic prejudice: Sorting out the possibilities in the Payne (2001) weapon paradigm. *Journal of Experimental Social Psychology*, 40: 75–81.

Lawrence, C. R. (1987). The id, the ego, and equal protection: Reckoning with unconscious racism. *Stanford Law Review*, 39: 317–88.

Lemert, E. (1951). *Social pathology: A systematic approach to the theory of sociopathic behavior*. New York: McGraw-Hill Book Company.

Lundman, R. J., O. M. Douglass, and J. M. Hanson. (2004). News about murder in an African American newspaper: Effects of relative frequency and race and gender typifications. *The Sociological Quarterly*, 45: 249–72.

Mann, C. R., M. S. Zatz, and N. Rodriguez, eds. (2006). *Images of color, images of crime, 3rd edition*. Los Angeles, CA: Roxbury Publishing Company.

Martinez, R. (2000). Immigration and urban violence: The link between immigrant Latinos and types of homicide. *Social Science Quarterly*, 81: 363–74.

———. (2002). *Latino homicide: Immigration, violence, and community*. New York: Routledge.

Martinez, R., M.T. Lee, and A.L. Nielsen. (2001). Revisiting the Scarface legacy: The victim/offender relationship and Mariel homicides in Miami. *Hispanic Journal of Behavioral Sciences*, 23: 37–56.

Martinez, R., J.I. Stowell, and J.M. Cancino. (2008). A tale of two border cities: Community context, ethnicity, and homicide. *Social Science Quarterly*, 89: 1–16.

Mastro, D. E., E. Blecha, A. A. Seate. (2011). Characterizations of criminal athletes: A systematic examination of sports news depictions of race and crime. *Journal of Broadcasting & Electronic Media*, 55: 526–42.

Mata, A.G., and C. Herrerias. (2006). Immigrant bashing and nativist political movements. In *Images of color, images of crime, 3rd edition*, eds. C.R. Mann, M.S. Zatz, and N. Rodriguez. Los Angeles, CA: Roxbury Publishing Company, 151–67.

Merton, R.C. (1967). *Social theory and social structure, revised and enlarged edition*. New York: Free Press.

Miller, K. (1908). *Race adjustment: Essays on the Negro in America*. New York: The Neale Publishing Company.

Moyer, I.L. (2001). *Criminological theories: Traditional and nontraditional voices and themes*. Thousand Oaks, CA: SAGE Publications.

Muniz, E.A., and B.J. McMorris. (2002). Misdemeanor sentencing decisions: The cost of being Native American. *The Justice Professional*, 12: 239–59.

Nobling, T., C. Spohn, and M. DeLone. (1998). A tale of two counties: Unemployment and sentence severity. *Justice Quarterly*, 15: 459–85.

Oliver, M.B. (1994). Portrayals of crime, race, and aggression in "reality-based" police shows: A content analysis. *Journal of Broadcasting and Electronic Media*, 38: 179–92.

———. (1996). Influences of authoritarianism and portrayals of race on Caucasian viewers: Responses to reality-based crime dramas. *Communication Reports*, 9: 141–50.

Oliver, M.B., and G.B. Armstrong. (1995). Predictors of viewing and enjoyment of reality-based and fictional crime shows. *Journalism Quarterly*, 72: 559–70.

———. (1998). The color of crime: Perceptions of Caucasians' and African Americans' involvement in crime. In *Entertaining crime: Television reality programs*, eds. M. Fishman and G. Cavender. New York: Aldine de Gruyter, 19–35.

Oliver, M.B., R.L. Jackson, N.N. Moses, and C.L. Dangerfield. (2004). The face of crime: Viewers' memory of race-related facial features of individuals pictured in the news. *Journal of Communication*, 54: 88–104.

Pager, D.I. (2007a). *Marked: Race, crime, and finding work in an era of mass incarceration*. Chicago: University of Chicago Press.

———. (2007b). Two strikes and you're out: The intensification of racial and criminal stigma. In *Barriers to reentry? The labor market for released prisoners in post-industrial America*, eds. D. Weiman, S. Bushway, and M. Stoll. New York: Russell Sage, 151–73.

Pager, D. I., B. Western, and N. Sugie. (2009). Sentencing disadvantage: Barriers to employment facing young black and white men with criminal records. *Annals of the American Academy of Political and Social Sciences*, 623: 195–213.

Payne, B.K. (2001). Prejudice and perception: The role of automatic and controlled processes in misperceiving a weapon. *Journal of Personality and Social Psychology*, 81: 181–92.

———. (2005). Conceptualizing control in social cognition: How executive functioning modulates the expression of automatic stereotyping. *Journal of Personality and Social Psychology*, 89: 488–503.

Payne, B.K., Y. Shimizu, and L.L. Jacoby. (2005). Mental control and visual illusions: Towards explaining race-biased weapon misidentifications. *Journal of Experimental Social Psychology*, 41: 36–47.

Plant, E.A., and B.M. Peruche. (2005). The consequences of race for police officers' responses to criminal suspects. *Psychological Science*, 16: 180–3.

Plant, E.A., B.M. Peruche, and D.A. Butz. (2005). Eliminating automatic racial bias: Making race nondiagnostic for responses to criminal suspects. *Journal of Experimental Social Psychology*, 41: 141–56.

Podgomy, D.R. (2009). Rethinking the increased focus on penal measures in immigration law as reflected in the expansion of the "aggravated felony" concept. *Journal of Criminal Law & Criminology*, 99: 287–306.

Ramirez, R., J.I. Stowell., and J.M. Cancino. (2008). A tale of two border cities: Community context, ethnicity, and homicide. *Social Science Quarterly*, 89: 1–16.

Robbins, L.N. (1975). Alcoholism and labeling theory. In *The labelling of deviance: Evaluating a perspective*. New York: John Wiley & Sons/SAGE Publications, 21–34.

Rome, D. (2004). *Black demons: The media's depiction of the African American criminal stereotype*. Westport, CT: Praeger.

———. (2006). The social construction of the African American criminal stereotype. In *Images of color, images of crime: Readings, 3rd edition*, eds. C.R. Mann, M.S. Zatz, and N. Rodriguez. Los Angeles, CA: Roxbury Publishing Company, 78–87.

Ruby, C.L., and J.C. Brigham. (1996). A criminal schema: The role of chronicality, race, and socioeconomic status in law enforcement officials' perceptions of others. *Journal of Applied Social Psychology*, 1996: 95–112.

Russell, K.K. (1994). The racial hoax as crime: The law as affirmation. *Indiana Law Journal*, 71: 594–621.

———. (1998). *The color of crime: Racial hoaxes, white fear, black protectionism, police harassment, and other macroaggressions*. New York: New York University Press.

Russell-Brown, K. (2006a). The myth of race and crime. In *Demystifying crime and criminal justice*, eds. R.M. Bohm and J.T. Walker. Los Angeles, CA: Roxbury Publishing Company, pp. 29–36.

———. (2006b). While visions of deviance danced in their heads. In *After the storm: Black intellectuals explore the meaning of hurricane Katrina*, ed. D.D. Trout. New York: New Press, pp. 111–23.

———. (2006c). *Protecting our own: Race, crime, and African Americans*. Lanham, MD: Rowan & Littlefield Publishers.

Schur, E.M. (1973). *Radical nonintervention: Rethinking the delinquency problem*. Englewood Cliffs, NJ: Prentice Hall.

Shoemaker, D.J. (1996). *Theories of delinquency: An examination of explanation of delinquent behavior, 3rd edition*. New York: Oxford University Press.

Skogan, W.G. (1995). Crime and the racial fears of white Americans. *Annals of the American Association of Political and Social Sciences*, 539: 59–71.

Stabile, C.A. (2006). *White victims, black villains: Gender, race, and crime news in US Culture*. New York: Routledge.

Steffensmeier, D., and S. Demuth. (2000). Ethnicity and sentencing outcomes in U.S. federal courts: Who is punished more harshly? *American Sociological Review*, 65: 705–29.

———. (2001). Ethnicity and judges' sentencing decisions: Hispanic–black–white comparisons. *Criminology*, 39: 145–78.

———. (2004). Ethnicity effects on sentence outcomes in large urban courts: Comparisons among white, black, and Hispanic defendants. *Social Science Quarterly*, 85: 994–1012.

Steffensmeier, D., J. Ulmer, and J. Kramer. (1998). The interaction of race, gender, and age in criminal sentencing: The punishment cost of being young, black, and male. *Criminology*, 36: 763–97.

Stupi, E. K., T. Chiricos, and M. Gertz. (2014). Perceived criminal threat from undocumented immigrants: Antecedents and consequences for policy preferences. *Justice Quarterly*, DOI: 10.1080/07418825.2014.902093.

Sutherland, E.H. (1924). *Criminology*. Philadelphia, PA: Lippincott.

Tannenbaum, F. (1938). *Crime and the community*. Boston: Ginn.

Tatum, B.L. (2000). Deconstructing the association of race and crime: The salience of skin color. In *The system in black and white: Exploring the connections between race, crime, and justice*, eds. M.W. Markowitz and D. Jones-Brown. Westport, CT: Praeger, 31–46.

Tittle, C.R. (1975). Labelling theory and crime: An empirical evaluation. In *The labelling of deviance: Evaluating a perspective*. New York: John Wiley & Sons/SAGE Publications, 157–80.

Tonry, M., ed. (1997). *Ethnicity, crime, and immigration: Comparative and cross-national perspectives*. Chicago: University of Chicago Press.

Trawalter, S., A.R. Todd, A.A. Baird, and J.A. Richeson. (2008). Attending to threat: Race-based patterns of selective attention. *Journal of Experimental Social Psychology*, 44: 1322–7.

Walker, S., C. Spohn, and M. DeLone. (2011). *The color of justice: Race, ethnicity and crime in America, 5th edition*. Belmont, CA: Wadsworth/Thomson Learning.

Wacquant, L. (2008). *Urban outcasts: A comparative sociology of advanced marginality*. Cambridge: Polity Press.

Wacquant, L., T. Slater, and V. Borges Pereira. (2014). Territorial stigmatization in action. *Environment and Panning A*, 46: 1270–80.

Wellford, C. (1975). Labelling theory and criminology: An assessment. *Social Problems*, 22: 332–45.

Williams, F.P., and M.D. McShane. (2004). *Criminological theory, 4th edition*. Upper Saddle River, NJ: Pearson/Prentice Hall.

Wilson, D. (2005). *Inventing black-on-black violence: Discourse, space, and representation*. Syracuse, NY: Syracuse University Press.

Winnick, T.A., and M. Bodkin. (2009). Stigma, secrecy and race: An empirical examination of black and white incarcerated men. *American Journal of Criminal Justice*, 34: 131–50.

Young, V.D. (2006). Demythologizing the "criminal Blackman": The carnival mirror. In *The many colors of crime: Inequalities of race, ethnicity, and crime in America*, eds. R.D. Peterson, L.P. Krivo, and J. Hagan. New York: New York University Press, 54–66.

6   Conflict Perspectives on Race and Crime

Abraham, A.A. (1948). Juvenile delinquency in Buffalo and its prevention. *Journal of Negro Education*, 17: 124–33.

Barak, G., P. Leighton, and A. Cotton. (2014). *Class, race, gender, and crime: The social realities of justice in America, 4th edition*. Lanham, MD: Rowman & Littlefield.

Beaver, K.M., M. DeLisi, J.P. Wright, B.B. Boutwell, J.C. Barnes, and M.G. Vaughn. (2013). No evidence of racial discrimination in criminal justice processing: Results from the National Longitudinal Study of Adolescent Health. *Personality and Individual Differences*, 55: 29–34.

Bird, G. (1987). *The "civilizing mission": Race and the construction of crime*. Australia: The Adline Press.

Blalock, H.M. (1967). *Toward a theory of minority group relations*. New York: Wiley.

Blanshard, P. (1942). Negro delinquency in New York. *The Journal of Educational Sociology*, 16: 115–23.

Blau, J. R., and P. M. Blau. (1982). The cost of inequality: Metropolitan structure and violent crime. *American Sociological Review*, 47: 114–29.

Blau, P. M. (1977). *Inequality and heterogeneity: A primitive theory of social structure.* New York: Free Press.

Blauner, R. (1972). *Racial oppression in America.* New York: Harper & Row.

Blumstein, A. (1982). On the racial disproportionality of United States' prison populations. *The Journal of Criminal Law and Criminology*, 73: 1259–81.

Bobo, L. D., and D. Johnson. (2004). A taste of punishment: Black and White Americans' views on the death penalty and the war on drugs. *Du Bois Review*, 1: 151–80.

Bohm, R. M. (1982). Radical criminology: An explication. *Criminology*, 19: 565–89.

———. (2001). *A primer on crime and delinquency theory, 2nd edition.* Belmont, CA: Wadsworth/Thomson Learning.

Bonger, W. A. (1916). *Criminality and economic conditions.* Boston: Little, Brown, and Company.

———. (1943). *Race and crime.* New York: Columbia University Press.

Brown, S. E., F. Esbensen, and G. Geis. (2004). *Criminology: Explaining crime and its context.* Cincinnati, OH: Anderson Publishing.

Brunson, R. K. (2007). "Police don't like Black people": African-American young men's accumulated police experiences. *Criminology & Public Policy*, 6: 71–102.

Buckler, K., and J. D. Unnever. (2008). Racial and ethnic perceptions of injustice: Testing the core hypotheses of comparative conflict theory. *Journal of Criminal Justice*, 36: 270–8.

Buckler, K., J. D. Unnever, and F. T. Cullen. (2008). Perceptions of injustice revisited: A test of Hagan *et al.*'s comparative conflict theory. *Journal of Crime & Justice*, 31: 35–57.

Cantor, N. (1931). Crime and the Negro. *The Journal of Negro History*, 16: 61–6.

Chambliss, W. (1964). A sociological analysis of the law of vagrancy. *Social Problems*, 12: 67–77.

———., ed. (1969). *Crime and the legal process.* New York: McGraw-Hill.

Chambliss, W., and R. T. Seidman. (1971). *Law, order, and power.* Reading, MA: Addison-Wesley.

Chiricos, T., M. McEntire, and M. Gertz. (2001). Perceived racial and ethnic composition of neighborhood and perceived risk of crime. *Social Problems*, 48: 322–40.

Christianson, S. (1981). Our black prisons. *Crime and delinquency*, 27: 364–75.

Clifford, W. (1974). *An introduction to African criminology.* Nairobi: Oxford University Press.

Crenshaw, K., N. Gotanda, G. Peller, and K. Thomas, eds. (1995). *Critical race theory: The key writings that formed the movement.* New York: The New Press.

D'Alessio, S. J., D. Eitle, and L. Stozenberg. (2005). The impact of serious crime, racial threat, and economic inequality on private police size. *Social Science Research*, 34: 267–82.

Delgado, R., and J. Stefancic. (2001). *Critical race theory: An introduction.* New York: New York University Press.

Delisi, M., and R. Regoli. (1999). Race, conventional crime, and criminal justice: The declining importance of skin color. *Journal of Criminal Justice*, 27: 549–57.

DiLulio, J. (1996). My black crime problem, and ours. *City Journal*, 6: 14–28.

Dobbins, D. A., and B. M. Bass. (1958). Effects of unemployment on white and Negro prison admissions in Louisiana. *Journal of Criminal Law, Criminology, and Police Science*, 48: 522–5.

Du Bois, W. E. B. (1899). The Negro and crime. *The Independent*, 51: 1355–7.

———. (1901). The spawn of slavery: The convict-lease system in the south. *The Missionary Review of the World*, 14: 737–45. Reprinted in *African American classics in criminology and criminal justice*, eds. S. L. Gabbidon, H. Taylor Greene, and V. Young, (2002). Thousand Oaks, CA: SAGE Publications, 83–8.

Ducey, K.A. (2008). Using the 1994 Rwanda genocide to integrate critical criminology and liberation sociology. *Critical Criminology*, 16: 293–302.

Eitle, D., and J. Taylor. (2008). Are Hispanics the new "threat"? Minority group threat and fear of crime in Miami-Dade County. *Social Science Research*, 37: 1102–15.

Eitle, D., and S. Monahan. (2009). Revisiting the racial threat thesis: The role of police organizational characteristics in predicting race-specific drug arrest rates. *Justice Quarterly*, 26: 528–61.

Elliot, M.A. (1926). A correlation between rate of juvenile delinquency and racial heterogeneity. *Welfare Magazine*, 17: 5–22.

Fox, V., and J. Volakakis. (1956). The Negro offender in a northern industrial area. *The Journal of Criminal Law, Criminology and Police Science*, 46: 641–7.

Gabbidon, S.L. (1999). W.E.B. DuBois on crime: American conflict theorist. *The Criminologist*, 24: 1, 3, 20.

——. (2003). Racial profiling by store clerks and security personnel in retail establishments: An exploration of "shopping while black." *Journal of Contemporary Criminal Justice*, 19: 345–64.

——. (2007). *W.E.B. Du Bois on crime and justice: Laying the foundations of sociological criminology*. Aldershot, UK: Ashgate Publications.

——. (2009). *Race, ethnicity, crime and justice: An international dilemma*. Thousand Oaks, CA: SAGE Publications.

Gabbidon, S.L., and H. Taylor Greene. (2009). *Race and crime, 2nd edition*. Thousand Oaks, CA: SAGE Publications.

Gabbidon, S. L., and K. L. Jordan. (2013). Public opinion on the killing of Trayvon Martin: A test of the racial gradient thesis. *Journal of Crime and Justice*, 36: 283–98.

Glover, K.S. (2009). *Racial profiling: Research, racism, and resistance*. Lanham, MD: Rowman & Littlefield.

Gordon, P. (1983). *White law: Racism in the police, courts, and prisons*. London: Pluto.

Green, E. (1970). Race, social status, and criminal arrest. *American Sociological Review*, 35: 476–90.

Grimke, A.H. (1915). *The ultimate criminal*. Washington, DC: American Negro Academy.

Haberman, C. (2014). When youth violence spurred 'superpredator' fear. *New York Times*. Retrieved August 10, 2014. www.nytimes.com/2014/04/07/us/politics/killing-on-bus-recalls-superpredator-threat-of-90s.html?_r=0.

Hagan, J., and W. Rymond-Richmond. (2009). *Darfur and the crime of genocide*. Cambridge: Cambridge University Press.

Hagan, J., W. Rymond-Richmond, and P. Parker. (2005). The criminology of genocide: The death and rape of Darfur. *Criminology*, 43: 525–61.

Hagan, J., C. Shedd, and M.R. Payne. (2005). Race, ethnicity, and youth perceptions of criminal injustice. *American Sociological Review* 70: 381–407.

Hallett, M.A. (2006). *Private prisons in America: A critical race perspective*. Urbana, IL: University of Illinois Press.

Hanks, P., and B. Keon-Cohen. (1984). *Aborigines and the law*. Sydney: George Allen & Unwin.

Harris, A. M.G., G.R. Henderson, and J.D. Williams. (2005). Courting customers: Assessing consumer racial profiling and other marketplace discrimination. *Journal of Public Policy and Marketing*, 24: 163–71.

Harris, D.A. (1999). *Driving while black: Racial profiling on our nation's highways*. Washington, DC: American Civil Liberties Union.

Hawkins, D.F. (1987). Beyond anomalies: Rethinking the conflict perspective on race and capital punishment. *Social Forces*, 719–45.

Henderson, M.L., F.T. Cullen, L. Cao, S.L. Browning, and R. Kopache. (1997). The impact of race on perception of criminal injustice. *Journal of Criminal Justice*, 25: 44–62.

Higgins, G.E., and S.L. Gabbidon. (2009). Perceptions of consumer racial profiling and negative emotions: An exploratory study. *Criminal Justice and Behavior*, 36: 77–88.

Hill, J.T. (1936). Report of delinquency situation among Negroes in Richmond. *Virginia Municipal Review*, 13: 276–7, 283.

Hinton, A. L. (2005). *Why did they kill? Cambodia in the shadow of genocide*. Berkeley, CA: University of California Press.

Howard, G.J., G. Newman, and J.D. Freilich. (2002). Population diversity and homicide: A cross-national amplification of Blau's theory of diversity. In *Migration, culture conflict and crime*, eds. J.D. Freilich, G. Newman, S.G. Shoham, and M. Addad. Burlington, VT: Ashgate/Dartmouth, 43–68.

Jackson, A.L., and L.D. Boyd. (2005). Minority-threat hypothesis and the workload-hypothesis: A community-level examination of lenient policing in high crime communities. *Criminal Justice Studies*, 18: 29–50.

Jackson, P.I. (1989). *Minority group threat, crime, and policing: Social context and social control*. New York: Praeger.

Jacobs, D., and D. Tope. (2008). Race, crime, and Republican strength: Minority politics in the post-civil rights era. *Social Science Research*, 37: 1116–29.

Johnson, G.B. (1941). The Negro and crime. *Annals of the American Academy of Political and Social Sciences*, 217: 93–104.

Keen, B., and D. Jacobs. (2009). Racial threat, partisan politics, and racial disparities in prison admissions: A panel analysis. *Criminology*, 47: 209–38.

Kent, S.L., and D. Jacobs. (2005). Minority threat and police strength from 1980 to 2000: A fixed-effects analysis of nonlinear and interative effects in large U.S. cities. *Criminology*, 43: 731–60.

King, R.D., and D. Wheelock. (2007). Group threat and social control: Race, perceptions of minorities and the desire to punish. *Social Forces*, 85: 1255–80.

Krisberg, B. (1975). *Crime and privilege: Toward a new criminology*. Englewood Cliffs, NJ: Prentice Hall.

Lee, N. (1995). Culture conflict and crime in Alaskan native villages. *Journal of Criminal Justice*, 23: 177–89.

Leiber, M.J., J.H. Peck, and N. Rodriguez. (2013). Minority threat and juvenile court outcomes. *Crime & Delinquency*, DOI: 10.1177/0011128713495776.

Lilly, R.J., F.T. Cullen, and R.A. Ball. (2002). *Criminological theory: Context and consequences*. Thousand Oaks, CA: SAGE.

Liska, A.E., and S.F. Messner. (1999). *Perspectives on crime and deviance, 3rd edition*. Upper Saddle River, NJ: Prentice Hall.

Lott, J.R., and J.E. Whitley. (2001). Abortion and crime: Unwanted children and out-of-wedlock births. Yale Law & Economics Research Paper No. 254. Available at SSRN: http://ssrn.com/abstract=270126

Lynch, M.J., R. Michalowski, and W.B. Groves. (2006). *Primer in radical criminology: Critical perspectives on crime, power, and identity, 4th edition*. Monsey, NY: Criminal Justice Press.

Lynch, M.J., E.B. Patterson, and K.K. Childs, eds. (2008). *Racial divide: Racial and ethnic bias in the criminal justice system*. Monsey, NY: Criminal Justice Press.

MacDonald, H. (2003). *Are cops racist? How the war against the police harms black Americans*. Chicago: Ivan R. Dee.

———. (2008). Is the criminal-justice system racist? *City Journal*. Retrieved May 6, 2008. www.city-journal.org/.

Mann, C.R. (1990). Random thoughts on the ongoing Wilbanks–Mann discourse. In *Racism, empiricism, and criminal justice*, eds. B.D. Maclean and D. Milovanovic. Vancouver: Collective Press, 15–19.

McIntosh, P. (2002). White privilege, color, and crime: A personal account. In *Images of color, images of crime, 2nd edition*, eds. C.R. Mann and M.S. Zatz. Los Angeles, CA: Roxbury, 45–53.

McKeown, J.E. (1948–1949). Poverty, race and crime. *Journal of Criminal Law and Criminology*, 39: 480–4.

———. (1993). *Unequal justice: A question of color*. Bloomington: Indiana University Press.

Moon, C. (2011). The crime of crimes and the crime of criminology: Genocide, criminology and Darfur. *British Journal of Sociology*, 62: 49–55.

Moyer, I.L. (2001). *Criminological theories: Traditional and nontraditional voices and themes*. Thousand Oaks, CA: SAGE Publications.

Mullins, C.W., and D.L. Rothe. (2007). The forgotten ones: The Darfur genocide. *Critical Criminology*, 15: 135–58.

Newsom, J.T.C. (1906). Degeneration and crime: The two evils of discrimination and oppression. *The Voice*, November: 495–7.

Ogburn, W.F. (1935). Factors in the variation of crime among cities. *Journal of the American Statistical Association*, 30: 12–34.

Ousey, G.C., and M.R. Lee. (2008). Racial disparity in formal social control: An investigation of alternative explanations of arrest rate inequality. *Journal of Research in Crime and Delinquency*, 45: 322–55.

Parker, K.F., B.J. Stults, and S.K. Rice. (2005). Racial threat, concentrated disadvantage and social control: Considering the macro-level sources of variation in arrests. *Criminology*, 43: 1111–34.

Petersilia, J. (1983). *Racial disparities in the criminal justice system*. Santa Monica, CA: Rand.

Peterson, R.D., and J. Hagan. (1984). Changing conceptions of race: Towards an accounting of anomalous findings of sentencing research. *American Sociological Review*, 49: 56–70.

Platt, T. (1975). Prospects for a radical criminology in the USA," In *Critical criminology*, eds. I. Taylor, P. Walton, and J. Young. Boston: Routledge & Kegan Paul, 95–112.

Quinney, R. (1970). *The social reality of crime*. Boston: Little, Brown.

———. (1977). *Class, state, and crime*. New York: McKay.

Rafter, N. (2008). Criminology's darkest hour: Biocriminology in Nazi Germany. *Australian and New Zealand Journal of Criminology*, 41: 287–306.

Rafter, N., and S. Walklate. (2012). Genocide and the dynamics of victimization: Some observations on Armenia. *European Journal of Criminology*, 9: 514–26.

Reiman, J. (2007). *The rich get richer and the poor get prison: Ideology, class and criminal justice, 8th edition*. Boston, MA: Allyn & Bacon.

Ross, L.E. (2010). A vision of race, crime, and justice through the lens of critical race theory. In *The Sage handbook of criminological theory*, eds. E. McLaurin and T. Newburn. London: SAGE Publication, 391–409.

Russell, K. (1999). Critical race theory and social justice. In *Social justice/criminal justice: The maturation of critical theory in law, crime, and deviance*, ed. B.A. Arrigo. Belmont, CA: West/Wadsworth, 178–88.

Sellin, T. (1928). The Negro criminal: A statistical note. *The American Academy of Political and Social Sciences*, 130: 52–64.

——. (1930). The Negro and the problem of law observance and administration in the light of social research. In *The Negro in American civilization*, ed. C. S. Johnson. New York: Henry Holt and Company, 443–54.

——. (1935). Race prejudice in the administration of justice. *The American Journal of Sociology*, XLI: 212–17.

——. (1938). *Culture conflict and crime*. New York: Social Science Research Council.

Shedd, C., and J. Hagan. (2006). Toward a developmental and comparative conflict theory of race, ethnicity, and perceptions of injustice. In *The many colors of crime: Inequalities of race, ethnicity, and crime in America*, eds. R. D. Peterson, L. P. Krivo, and J. Hagan. New York: New York University Press, 313–33.

Spitzer, S. (1975). Toward a Marxian theory of deviance. *Social Problems*, 22: 638–51.

Taylor, I., P. Walton, and J. Young. (1975). *Critical criminology*. Boston: Routledge and Kegan Paul.

Taylor Greene, H., and S. L. Gabbidon. (2000). *African American criminological thought*. Albany, NY: State University of New York Press.

——., eds. (2009). *Encyclopedia of race and crime*. Thousand Oaks, CA: SAGE Publications.

Tellis, K., N. Rodriguez, and C. Spohn. (2010). Critical race perspectives: Explaining the differential treatment of racial minorities by the criminal justice system. In *Criminology and Public Policy: Putting Theory To Work*, eds. Hugh Barlow and Scott Decker. Philadelphia: Temple University Press.

Thompson, A. J. (1926a). A survey of crime among Negroes in Philadelphia. *Opportunity*, 4: 217–19.

——. (1926b). A survey of crime among Negroes in Philadelphia. *Opportunity*, 4: 251–4.

——. (1926c). A survey of crime among Negroes in Philadelphia. *Opportunity*, 4: 285–6.

Tonry, M. (1995). *Malign neglect*. Oxford: Oxford University Press.

Turk, A. T. (1969a). Introduction. In *Criminality and economic conditions*, W. Bonger (1969/1916). Bloomington: Indiana University Press, 3–20.

——. (1969b). *Criminality and legal order*. Chicago: Rand McNally & Company.

Turner, R. H., and L. M. Killian. (1987). *Collective behavior, 3rd edition*. Englewood Cliffs, NJ: Prentice Hall.

Unnever, J. D., F. T. Cullen, S. A. Mathers, T. E. McClure, and M. C. Allison. (2009). Racial discrimination and Hirschi's criminological classic: A chapter in the sociology of knowledge. *Justice Quarterly*, 26: 377–409.

Vold, G. B. (1958). *Theoretical criminology*. Oxford: Oxford University Press.

Wacquant, L. (2000). The new "peculiar institution": On the prison as surrogate ghetto. *Theoretical Criminology*, 4: 377–89.

——. (2001). Deadly Symbiosis: When ghetto and prison meet and mesh. *Punishment & Society*, 3: 95–134.

——. (2005). Race as a civic felony. *International Social Science Journal*, 181: 127–42.

——. (2007). French "banlieus" and black American ghetto: From conflation to comparison. *Qui Parle*, 16: 5–38

——. (2008a). The place of the prison in the new government of poverty. In *After the war on crime: Race, democracy, and a new reconstruction*, eds. M. L. Frampton, I. H. López, and J. Simon. New York: New York University Press, 23–36.

——. (2008b). The militarization of urban marginality: Lessons from the Brazilian metropolis. *International Political Sociology*, 2: 56–74.

——. (2009a). *Punishing the poor: The neoliberal government of insecurity*. Durham, NC: Duke University Press.

——. (2009b). *Prisons of poverty (expanded edition)*. Minneapolis, MN: University of Minnesota Press.

Walker, S., C. Spohn, and M. DeLone. (2011). *The color of justice: Race, ethnicity, and crime in America, 5th edition*. Belmont, CA: Thomson Learning.

Waring, J.H.N. (1905). Some causes of criminality among colored people. *Charities: A Weekly Review of Local and General Philanthropy*, 15: 45–9.

Webster, C. (2007). *Understanding race and crime*. New York: McGraw-Hill.

Wilbanks, W. (1987). *The myth of a racist criminal justice system*. Pacific Grove, CA: Brooks/Cole.

Wilder, F.S. (1927). Crime in the Superior Courts of North Carolina. *Social Forces*, 5: 423–7.

Williams, F.P., and M.D. McShane. (2014). *Criminological theory, 6th edition*. Upper Saddle, NJ: Prentice Hall.

Wilson, W.J. (1978). *The declining significance of race: Blacks and changing American institutions*. Chicago: University of Chicago Press.

Winterdyk, J. (2009). Genocide: International issues and perspectives worthy of criminal justice attention. *Criminal Justice Review*, 19: 101–14.

Wolfgang, M.E. (1964). *Crime and race*. New York: Institute of Human Relations Press.

Wolfgang, M.E., and B. Cohen. (1970). *Crime and race: Conceptions and misconceptions*. New York: Institute of Human Relations Press.

Wood, A.L. (1947). Minority-group criminality and cultural integration. *Journal of Criminal Law and Criminology*, 37: 498–510.

Work, M. (1900). Crime among the Negroes of Chicago. *American Journal of Sociology*, 6: 204–23.

——. (1913). Negro criminality in the south. *Annals of the American Academy of Political and Social Sciences*, 49: 74–80.

Wright, R.R. (1910). The northern Negro and crime. *Southern Workman*, 39: 137–42.

7   Social Control Perspectives on Race and Crime

Barro, R.J. (1999, September 27). Does abortion lower the crime rate? *Business Week*, p. 30.

Bennett, W.J., J.J. Dilulio, and J.P. Walters. (1996). *Body count: Moral poverty . . . and how to win America's war against crime and drugs*. New York: Simon and Schuster.

Brown, S.E., F. Esbensen, and G. Geis. (2004). *Criminology: explaining crime and its contexts, 5th edition*. Cincinnati, OH: Anderson Publishing.

Burt, C.H., R.L. Simons, and L.G. Simons. (2006). A longitudinal test of the effects of parenting and the stability of self-control: Negative evidence for the general theory of crime. *Criminology*, 44: 353–96.

Cernkovich, S.A., and P.C. Giordano. (1987). Family relationships and delinquency. *Criminology*, 25: 295–321.

——. (1992). School bonding, race, and delinquency. *Criminology*, 30: 261–91.

Chamlin, M.B., A.J. Myer, B.A. Sanders, and J.K. Cocharan. (2008). Abortion as crime control: A cautionary tale. *Criminal Justice Policy Review*, 19: 135–52.

Chang, J., and N.T. Le. (2005). The influence of parents, peer delinquency, and school achievement on academic achievement in Chinese, Cambodian, Laotian or Mien, and Vietnamese youth. *Crime and Delinquency*, 51: 238–64.

Church, W.T., T. Wharton, and J.K. Taylor. (2009). An examination of differential association and social control theory: Family systems and delinquency. *Youth Violence and Juvenile Justice*, 7: 3–15.

Dagan, D., and S. M. Teles. (2014). Locked in? Conservative reform and the future of mass incarceration. *The ANNALS of the American Academy of Political and Social Science,* 651: 266–76.

Delisi, M., and M.G. Vaughn. (2008). The Gottfredson-Hirshi critiques revisited: Reconciling self-control theory, criminal careers, and career criminals. *International Journal of Offender Therapy and Comparative Criminology,* 52: 520–37.

Dilulio, J.J. (1994). The question of black crime. *Public Interest,* 117: 3–32.

——. (1995a). The coming of the super-predators. *The Weekly Standard,* 1: 23.

——. (1995b). White lies about black crime. *Public Interest,* 118: 30–44.

——. (1996). My black crime problem, and ours. *City Journal,* 6: 14–28.

Dinitz, S., B. Kay, and W.C. Reckless. (1957). Delinquent proneness and social achievement. *Educational Research Bulletin,* 36: 131–6.

Dinitz, S., W.C. Reckless, and B. Kay. (1958). A self-gradient among potential delinquents. *The Journal of Criminal Law, Criminology, and Police Science,* 49, 230–3.

Dinitz, S., F.R. Scarpitti, and W.C. Reckless. (1962). Delinquency vulnerability: A cross group and longitudinal analysis. *American Sociological Review,* 27: 515–17.

Donohue, J.J., and S.D. Levitt. (2001). The impact of legalized abortion on crime. *The Quarterly Journal of Economics,* CXVI: 379–420.

——. (2004). Further evidence that legalized abortion lowered crime: A reply to Joyce. *Journal of Human Resources,* 39: 29–49.

——. (2006). Measurement error, legalized abortion and the decline in crime: A response to Foote and Goetz (2005). National Bureau of Economic Research Working Paper no. 11987.

Durkheim, E. (1895/1938). *The rules of sociological method.* New York: Free Press.

——. (1897/1951). *Suicide: A study in sociology.* New York: Free Press.

Elder, G.H. (1985). Perspective on the life course. In *Life course dynamics,* ed. G.H. Elder. Ithaca, NY: Cornell University Press, 23–49.

Elliott, D.S. (1994). Serious violent offenders: Onset, developmental course, and termination—The American Society of Criminology 1993 presidential address. *Criminology,* 32: 1–22.

Elliott, D.S., D. Huizinga, and S.S. Ageton. (1985). *Explaining delinquency and drug abuse.* Newbury Park, CA: SAGE Publications.

Foote, C.L., and C.F. Goetz. (2006). Testing economic hypotheses with state-level data: A comment on Donohue and Levitt (2001). Federal Reserve Bank of Boston Working Paper no. 05–15.

Gerstenfeld, P.B. (2010). *Hate crimes: Causes, controls, and controversies, 2nd edition.* Thousand Oaks, CA: SAGE Publications.

Glueck, S., and E. Glueck. (1950). *Unraveling juvenile delinquency.* New York: The Commonwealth Fund.

Go, C.G., and T.N. Le. (2005). Gender differences in Cambodian delinquency: The role of ethnic identity, parental discipline, and peer delinquency. *Crime and Delinquency,* 51: 220–37.

Gottfredson, M.R., and T. Hirschi. (1990). *A general theory of crime.* Stanford, CA: Stanford University Press.

Greve, F. (2006, March 12). Anticipated wave of teenage crime never materialized: Instead, the U.S. is experiencing the sharpest drop in youth crime in modern history. *Houston Chronicle,* p. 20.

Haberman, C. (2014). When youth violence spurred 'superpredator' fear. *New York Times.* Retrieved August 10, 2014. www.nytimes.com/2014/04/07/us/politics/killing-on-bus-recalls-superpredator-threat-of-90s.html?_r=0.

Hay, C. (2001). Parenting, self-control, and delinquency: A test of self-control theory. *Criminology*, 39: 707–36.

Hay, C., and M.M. Evans. (2006). Has Roe v. Wade reduced U.S. rates? Examining the link between mothers' pregnancy intentions and children's later involvement in law-abiding behavior. *Journal of Research in Crime and Delinquency*, 43: 36–66.

Hayden, T. (2005, December 14). The myth of the super-predator. *Los Angeles Times*, p. B13.

Higgins, G.E., and M.L. Ricketts. (2005). Self-control theory, race, and delinquency. *Journal of Ethnicity in Criminal Justice*, 3: 5–22.

Hirschi, T. (1969). *Causes of delinquency.* Berkeley, CA: University of California Press.

Jang, S.J. (2002). Race, ethnicity, and deviance: A study of Asian and non-Asian adolescents in America. *Sociological Forum*, 17: 647–80.

Junger, M., and I.H. Marshall. (1997). The interethnic generalizability of social control theory: An empirical test. *Journal of Research in Crime and Delinquency*, 34: 79–112.

Kahane, L.H., D. Paton, and R. Simmons. (2008). The abortion-crime link: Evidence from England and Wales. *Economica*, 75: 1–21.

Kirchner, E. E., and G. E. Higgins. (2014). Self-control and racial disparities in delinquency: A structural equation modeling approach. *American Journal of Criminal Justice*, 39: 436–49.

Laub, J.H., and R.J. Sampson. (2003). *Shared beginnings, divergent lives: Delinquent boys to age 70.* Cambridge, MA: Harvard University Press.

Levitt, S.D., and S.J. Dubner. (2005). *Freakonomics: A rogue economist explores the hidden side of everything.* New York: William Morrow.

Lieber, M., K.Y. Mack, and R. A. Featherstone. (2009). Family structure, family processes, economic factors, and delinquency: Similarities and differences by race and ethnicity. *Youth Violence and Juvenile Justice*, 7: 79–99.

Lilly, R.J., F.T. Cullen, and R.A. Ball. (2002). *Criminological theory: Context and consequences, 3rd edition.* Thousand Oaks, CA: SAGE.

Longshore, D. (1998). Self-control and criminal opportunity: A prospective test of the general theory of crime. *Social Problems*, 45: 102–13.

Longshore, D., and S. Turner. (1998). Self-control and criminal opportunity: Cross-sectional test of the general theory of crime. *Criminal Justice and Behavior*, 25: 81–98.

Lott, J. R., and J. E. Whitley. (2001). Abortion and crime: Unwanted children and out-of-wedlock births. Yale Law & Economics Research Paper No. 254. Available at SSRN: http://ssrn.com/abstract=270126 orhttp://dx.doi.org/10.2139/ssrn.270126

Lynam, D.R., P.O.H. Wikstrom, A. Caspi, T.E. Moffitt, R. Loeber, and S. Novak. (2000). The interaction between impulsivity and neighborhood context on offending: The effects of impulsivity are stronger in poorer neighborhoods. *Journal of Abnormal Psychology*, 109: 563–74.

Lynskey, D.P., L.T. Winfree, F. Esbensen, and D.L. Clason. (2000). Linking gender, minority group status and family matters to self-control theory: A multivariate analysis of key self-control concepts in a youth-gang context. *Juvenile and Family Court Journal*, 51: 1–19.

Marenin, O., and M.D. Reisig. (1995). A general theory of crime and patterns of crime in Nigeria: An exploration of methodological assumptions. *Journal of Criminal Justice*, 23: 501–18.

Martin, R., R.J. Mutchnick, and W.T. Austin. (1990). *Criminological thought: Pioneers past and present*. New York: Macmillan Publishing Company.

Matsueda, R.L., and K. Heimer. (1987). Race, family structure, and delinquency: A test of differential association and social control theories. *American Sociological Review*, 52, 826–40.

Moyer, I.L. (2001). *Criminological theories: Traditional and nontraditional voices and themes*. Thousand Oaks, CA: SAGE Publications.

Pabon, E. (1998). Hispanic adolescent delinquency and the family: A discussion of sociocultural influences. *Adolescence*, 33: 941–55.

Piquero, A.R., J.M. MacDonald, and K.F. Parker. (2002). Race, local life circumstances, and criminal activity. *Social Science Quarterly*, 83: 654–70.

Pratt, T.C., and F.T. Cullen. (2000). The empirical status of Gottfredson and Hirschi's general theory of crime: A meta-analysis. *Criminology*, 38: 931–64.

Reckless, W.C. (1961). A new theory of delinquency and crime. *Federal Probation*, 42: 42–6.

Reckless, W.C., S. Dinitz, and B. Kay. (1957). The self-component in potential delinquency and potential nondelinquency. *American Sociological Review*, 22: 566–70.

Reckless, W.C., S. Dinitz, and E. Murray. (1956). Self-concept as an insulator against delinquency. *American Sociological Review*, 21: 744–6.

——. (1957a). Teacher evaluations and evaluations of "good" boys in high-delinquency areas. *The Elementary School Journal*, 57: 221–3.

——. (1957b). The "good" boy in a high-delinquency area. *The Journal of Criminal Law, Criminology, and Police Science*, 48: 18–25.

Rees, C., A. Freng., and L.T. Winfree, Jr. (2014). The Native American adolescent: Social network structure and perceptions of alcohol induced social problems. *Journal of Youth and Adolescence*, 43, 405–25.

Reiss, A.J. (1951). Delinquency as the failure of personal and social controls. *American Sociological Review*, 16: 196–207.

Rodriguez, O., and D. Weisburd. (1991). The integrated social control model and ethnicity: The case of Puerto Rican American delinquency. *Criminal Justice and Behavior*, 18: 464–79.

Ross, E.A. (1901). *Social control: A survey of the foundations of order*. New York: Macmillan.

Sampson, R.J., and J.H. Laub. (1993). *Crime in the making: Pathways and turning points through life*. Cambridge, MA: Harvard University Press.

Shultz, J. (2006, March 14). Society's worst fears about young criminals were wrong. *Knight Ridder Tribune Business News*, p. 1.

Sommers, I., J. Fagan, and D. Baskin. (1993). Sociocultural influences on the explanation of delinquency for Puerto Rican youth. *Hispanic Journal of Behavioral Sciences*, 15: 36–62.

Stewart, E.A., K.W. Elifson, and C.E. Sterk. (2004). Integrating the general theory of crime into an explanation of violent victimization among female offenders. *Justice Quarterly*, 21: 159–81.

Sykes, G.M., and D. Matza. (1957). Techniques of neutralization: A theory of delinquency. *American Sociological Review*, 22: 664–70.

Tapper, J. (2005, September 29). William Bennett defends comments on abortion and crime. *ABC News* online. Retrieved August 3, 2009. http://abcnews.go.com/WNT/Politics/Story?id=1171385&page=1.

Unnever, J.D., F.T. Cullen, S.A. Mathers, T.E. McClure, and M.C. Allison. (2009). Racial discrimination and Hirschi's criminological classic: A chapter in the sociology of knowledge. *Justice Quarterly*, 26: 377–409.

Vazsonyi, A.T., and J.M. Crosswhite. (2004). A test of Gottfredson and Hirschi's general theory of crime in African American adolescents. *Journal of Research in Crime and Delinquency*, 41: 407–32.

Williams, F.P., and M.D. McShane. (2014). *Criminological theory, 6th edition*. Upper Saddle River, NJ: Pearson/Prentice Hall.

8   Colonial Perspectives on Race and Crime

Affor, C. (2008a). My story. In *Colonial systems of control: Criminal justice in Nigeria*, ed. V. Saleh-Hanna. Ottawa: University of Ottawa Press, 131–40.

——. (2008b). A tribute to solidarity: My oasis. In *Colonial systems of control: Criminal justice in Nigeria*, ed. V. Saleh-Hanna. Ottawa: University of Ottawa Press, 141–6.

Agozino, B. (1995). Radical criminology in African literature. *International Sociology*, 19: 315–29.

——. (1997). *Black women and the criminal justice system*. Aldershot, UK: Ashgate.

——. (2003). *Counter-colonial criminology: A critique of imperialist reason*. London: Pluto Press.

——. (2004a). Imperialism, crime and criminology: Towards the decolonization of criminology. *Crime, Law, and Social Change*, 41: 343–58.

——. (2004b). The Iraq war did not take place: Sociological implication of a conflict that was neither just nor just a war. *International Review of Sociology*, 14: 73–88.

——. (2004c). Reparative justice: A pan-African criminology primer. In *Pan-African issues in crime and justice*, eds. A. Kalunta-Crumpton and B. Agozino. Aldershot, UK: Ashgate Publishing Company, 228–48.

——. (2005). Crime, criminology and post-colonial theory: Criminological reflections on West Africa. In *Traditional and comparative criminology*, eds. J. Sheptycki and A. Wardak. London: Glass House Press, 117–34.

Akporherhe, C. (2008). My Nigerian prison experience. In *Colonial systems of control: Criminal justice in Nigeria*, ed. V. Saleh-Hanna. Ottawa: University of Ottawa Press, 127–30.

Alfredo, M. (1987). *Gringo justice*. Notre Dame, IN: University of Notre Dame Press.

Austin, R.L. (1983). The colonial model, subcultural theory and intragroup violence. *Journal of Criminal Justice*, 11: 93–104.

——. (1987). Progress toward racial equality and reduction of black criminal violence. *Journal of Criminal Justice*, 15: 437–59.

Bachman, R. (1992). *Death and violence on the reservation: Homicide, family violence, and suicide in American Indian populations*. New York: Auburn House.

Banks, C. (2007). Ordering the other: Reading Alaskan Native culture past and present. In *Race, gender and punishment: From colonialism to the war on terror*, eds. M. Bosworth and J. Flavin. New Brunswick, NJ: Rutgers University Press, 32–48.

Barrera, M. (1979). *Race and class in the southwest*. Notre Dame, IN: University of Notre Dame Press.

Beirne, P. (1993). *Inventing criminology: Essays on the rise of homo criminalis*. Albany, NY: State University of New York Press.

Blackwell, J.E. (1971). Race and crime in Tanzania. *Phylon*, 32: 207–14.

Blauner, R. (1969). Internal colonialism and ghetto revolt. *Social Problems*, 16: 393–408.

——. (1972). *Racial oppression in America*. New York: Harper & Row.

Brown, M. (2014). *Penal power and colonial rule*. New York: Routledge.

Capeheart, L.J. (2006). A review of *Counter-colonial criminology: A critique of imperialist reason. Journal of Criminal Justice and Popular Culture*, 13: 50–5.

Carmichael, S., and C.V. Hamilton. (1967). *Black power: The politics of liberation in America.* New York: Vintage.

Christian, M. (2006). Book review of *Counter-colonial criminology: A critique of imperialist reason. African Studies Quarterly*, 8: 56–7.

Clark, K.B. (1965). *Dark ghetto: Dilemmas of social power.* New York: Harper & Row.

Cox, O.C. (1976). *Race Relations: Elements and social dynamics.* Detroit, MI: Wayne State University Press.

Flood, D. R. (2007). Deviance gendered, criminology exposed. *Journal of Women's History*, 19: 214–23.

Fanon, F. (1963). *The wretched of the earth.* New York: Grove Press.

——. (1967a). *Black skin, white masks.* New York: Grove Press.

——. (1967b). *A dying colonialism.* New York: Grove Press.

Godfrey, B. S., and G. Dunstall, eds. (2013). *Crime and empire, 1840–1940: Criminal justice in local and global context.* London: Routledge.

Greenburg, D., B. Agozino. (2012). Execution, imprisonment, and crime in Trinidad and Tobago. *British Journal of Criminology*, 52: 113–140.

Grier, W.H., and P. M. Cobb. (1968). *Black rage.* New York: Basic Books.

Hawkins, D. F. (2011). Things fall apart: Revisiting race and ethnic differences in criminal violence amidst a crime drop. *Race and Justice*, 1: 3–48.

Igbinovia, P.E. (1989). Criminology in Africa. *International Journal of Offender Therapy and Comparative Criminology*, 33: v–x.

Jeff, M. F.X. (1981). Why black-on-black homicide? *The Urban League Review*, 6: 25–34.

Killingray, D. (1986). The maintenance of law and order in British colonial Africa. *African Affairs*, 85: 411–37.

Kitossa, T. (2012). Criminology and colonialism: Counter colonial criminology and the Canadian context. *The Journal of Pan African Studies*, 4: 204–26.

Mars, J. R. (2002). *Deadly force, colonialism, and the rule of law: Police violence in Guyana.* Westport, CT: Greenwood Press.

McIntosh, K. (2005). Book review of *Counter-colonial criminology: A critique of imperialist reason. African Journal of Criminology and Justice Studies*, 1: 82–3.

Moore, J.W. (1970). Colonialism: The case of the Mexican Americans. *Social Problems*, 17: 463–72.

Mosley, T.S. (2005). Book review of *Counter-colonial criminology: A critique of imperialist reason. African Journal of Criminology and Justice Studies*, 1: 77–9.

Nakajima, Y. (2004). Book review of *Counter-colonial criminology: A critique of imperialist reason. African American Review*, 38: 740–2.

Odo, J.C. (2005). Book review of *Counter-colonial criminology: A critique of imperialist reason. African Journal of Criminology and Justice Studies*, 1: 74–6.

Olutola, A. A. (2014). Crime rate in Africa: Time for African criminological theory. *Journal of Public Administration*, 49: 314–29.

Onyeozili, E.C. (2004). Gunboat criminology and the colonization of Africa. In *Pan-African issues in crime and justice*, eds. A. Kalunta-Crumpton and B. Agozino. Aldershot, UK: Ashgate Publishing Company, 205–27.

——. (2005). Book review of *Counter-colonial criminology: A critique of imperialist reason. African Journal of Criminology and Justice Studies*, 1: 80–1.

Oriola, T.B. (2006). Biko Agozino and the rise of post-colonial criminology. *African Journal of Criminology and Justice Studies*, 2: 104–31.

Pavlich, G. (2014). Occupied cape judges and colonial knowledge of crime, criminals, and punishment. *SAGE Open*, January-March: 1–11.

Pouissant, A.F. (1972). *Why blacks kill blacks*. New York: Emerson Hall Publishers.

——. (1983). Black-on-black homicide: A psychological-political perspective. *Victimology*, 8: 161–9.

Saleh-Hanna, V. (2008). Penal coloniality. In *Colonial systems of control: Criminal justice in Nigeria*, ed. V. Saleh-Hanna. Ottawa: University of Ottawa Press, 17–54.

Saleh-Hanna, V., and C. Ume. (2008). An evolution of the penal system: Criminal justice in Nigeria. In *Colonial systems of control: Criminal justice in Nigeria*, ed. V. Saleh-Hanna. Ottawa: University of Ottawa Press, 55–68.

Sen, S. (2004). Book review of *Counter-colonial criminology: A critique of imperialist reason*. *Journal of Colonialism and Colonial History*, 5. Retrieved June 5, 2006. http://muse.jhu.edu.ezaccess.libraries.psu.edu /journals/journal _of_ colonialism_and_colonial_history/v005/5.1sen2.html.

Shalhoub-Kevorkian, N. (2014). Criminality in spaces of death: The Palestinian case study. *British Journal of Criminology*, 54: 38–52.

Staples, R. (1974). Internal colonialism and black violence. *Black World*, 23: 16–34.

——. (1975). White racism, black crime and American justice: An application of the colonial model to explain crime and race. *Phylon*, 36: 14–22.

——. (1976a). *Introduction to black sociology*. New York: McGraw-Hill Book Company.

——. (1976b). Race and family violence: The internal colonialism perspective. In *Crime and its impact on the black community*, eds. L.E. Gary and L.P. Brown. Washington, DC: Howard University's Institute for Urban Affairs and Research, 85–96.

Tatum, B.L. (1994). The colonial model as a theoretical explanation of crime and delinquency. In *African American perspectives on crime causation, criminal justice administration and prevention*, eds. A.T. Sulton. Engelwood, CO: Sulton Books, 33–52.

——. (2000a). Toward a neocolonial model of adolescent crime and violence. *Journal of Contemporary Criminal Justice*, 16: 157–70.

——. (2000b). *Crime, violence and minority youths*. Aldershot, UK: Ashgate.

Taylor, I., P. Walton, and J. Young. (1973). *The new criminology*. London: Routledge, Kegan and Paul.

Urbina, M.G., and L. Smith. (2007). Colonialism and its impact on Mexicans' experiences of punishment in the United States. In *Race, gender and punishment: From colonialism to the war on terror*, eds. M. Bosworth and J. Flavin. New Brunswick, NJ: Rutgers University Press, 49–61.

Vold, G.B., and T.J. Bernard. (1986). *Theoretical criminology, 3rd edition*. Oxford: Oxford University Press.

Wilson, A.N. (1990). *Black-on-black violence: The psychodynamics of black self-annihilation in service of white domination*. New York: Afrikan World Infosystems.

Wilson, D.B., R.B. Parks, and S.D. Mastrofski. (2011). The impact of police reform on communities of Trinidad and Tobago. *Journal of Experimental Criminology*, 7: 375–405.

Zoller, C., and I. Onwudiwe. (2005). Book review of *Counter-colonial criminology: A critique of imperialist reason*. *African Journal of Criminology and Justice Studies*, 1: 71–3.

9   Gender and Race-Centered Perspectives on Race and Crime

Adams, T. M., and D. B. Fuller. (2006). The words have changed but the ideology remains the same: Misogynistic lyrics in rap music. *Journal of Black Studies*, 36: 938–57.

Adler, F. (1975). *Sisters in crime: The rise of the new female criminal*. New York: McGraw-Hill Book Company.

Agozino, B. (1997). *Black women and the criminal justice system: Towards the decolonisation of victimization*. Aldershot, UK: Ashgate.

Arnold, T. K. (2014). Review of *A theory of African American offending: Race, racism, and crime*. *International Criminal Justice Review*, 24: 107–9.

Beirne, P., and J. W. Messerschmidt. (2006). *Criminology, 4th edition*. Los Angeles, CA: Roxbury.

Bonnet, F. (2012). Review of *A theory of African American offending: Race, racism, and crime*. *Contemporary Sociology*, 41: 242–3.

Bui, H. N., and M. Morash. (1999). Domestic violence in the Vietnamese immigrant community: An exploratory study. *Violence against Women*, 5: 769–95.

Burns, S. (2012). The Central Park Five: The untold story behind one of New York city's most infamous crimes. New York: Vintage.

Burt, C. H., R. L. Simons, and F. X. Gibbons. (2012). Racial discrimination, ethnic-racial socialization, and crime: A micro-social model of risk and resilience. *American sociological Review*, 77: 648–677.

Bush-Baskette, S. R. (1998). The war on drugs as a war against black women. In *Crime control and women: Feminist implications of criminal justice policy*, ed. S. L. Miller. Thousand Oaks: SAGE Publications, 113–29.

Castro, D. O. (2006). "Hot blood and easy virtue": Mass media and the making of racist Latino/a stereotypes. In *Images of color, images of crime, 3rd edition*, eds. C. R. Mann, M. S. Zatz, and N. Rodriguez. Los Angeles, CA: Roxbury Publishing Company, 88–101.

Chigwada, R. (1989). The criminalization and imprisonment of black women. *Probation Journal*, 36: 100–5.

Chigwada-Bailey, R. (1997). *Black women's experiences of criminal justice: Discourse on disadvantage*. Winchester: Waterside Press.

——. (2003). *Black women's experiences of criminal justice: Discourse on disadvantage, 2nd edition*. Winchester: Waterside Press.

Chilton, R., and S. K. Datesman. (1987). Gender, race, and crime: An analysis of urban arrest trends, 1960–80. *Gender and Society*, 1: 152–71.

Cohen, S. (2003). *The wrong man: America's epidemic of wrongful death row convictions*. New York: Carrol and Graf.

Collins, C. F. (1997). *The imprisonment of African American women*. Jefferson, NC: McFarland & Company.

Collins, P. H. (1986). Learning from the outsider within: The sociological significance of black feminist thought. *Social Problems*, 33: 514–32.

——. (1989). The social construction of black feminist thought. *Signs: Journal of Women in Culture and Society*, 14: 745–73.

——. (1990). *Black feminist thought: Knowledge, consciousness, and the politics of empowerment*. London: HarperCollins Academic.

Covington, J. (1988). Crime and heroin: The effects of race and gender. *Journal of Black Studies*, 18: 486–506.

Daly, K., and M. Chesney-Lind. (1988). Feminism and criminology. *Justice Quarterly*, 5: 497–538.

Daly, K., and D.J. Stephens. (1995). The "dark figure" of criminology: Towards a black and multi-ethnic feminist agenda for theory and research. In *International feminist perspectives in criminology: Engendering a discipline*, eds. N.H. Rafter and F. Heidensohn. Philadelphia, PA: Open University Press, 189–215.

Daly, K., and M. Tonry. (1997). Gender, race, and sentencing. *Crime and Justice: A Review of Research*, 22: 201–52.

Davis, A.Y. (1983). *Women, race and class*. New York: Vintage Books.

Farrant, F. (2009). Gender "race," and the criminal justice process. In *Race and criminal justice*, ed. H. Singh Bhui. London: SAGE Publications, 122–36.

Fischer, K. (2002). *Suspect relations: Sex, race, and resistance in colonial North Carolina*. Ithaca, NY: Cornell University Press.

Fishman, L.T. (1995a). Slave woman, resistance and criminality: A prelude to future accommodation. *Women and Criminal Justice*, 7: 35–65.

——. (1995b). The vice queens. In *The modern gang reader*, eds. M.W. Klein, C.L. Maxson, and J. Miller. Los Angeles, CA: Roxbury Publishing Company, 83–92.

——. (1999). Black female gang behavior: An historical and ethnographic perspective. In *Female gangs in America: Essays on girls, gangs and gender*, eds. M. Chesney-Lind and J.H. Hagedorn. Chicago: Lake View Press, 64–84.

Freedman, E.B. (1996). The prison lesbian: Race, class, and the construction of the aggressive female homosexual, 1915–65. *Feminist Studies*, 22: 1–17.

Gabbidon, S.L. (2001). Biography of Frances A. Kellor (1873–952). In *Criminological theories: Traditional and nontraditional voices and themes*, ed. I.L. Moyer. Thousand Oaks, CA: SAGE Publications, 41.

Greene, H.T. (1981). Black women in the criminal justice system. *The Urban League Review*, 6: 55–61.

——. (1994). Black female delinquency. In *African American perspectives on crime causation, criminal justice administration, and crime prevention*, ed. A.T. Sulton. Englewood, CO: Sulton Books, 109–21.

Hagan, J. (1985). Toward a structural theory of crime, race, and gender: The Canadian case. *Crime and Delinquency*, 31: 129–46.

Hawkins, D.F. (2014). Review of *A theory of African American offending: Race, racism, and crime. Race and Justice*, 4: 175–180.

Hazen, A.L., and F.I. Soriano. (2007). Experiences with intimate partner violence among Latina women. *Violence Against Women*, 13: 562–82.

Hill, G.D., and E.M. Crawford. (1990). Women, race, and crime. *Criminology*, 28: 601–26.

hooks, b. (1981). *Ain't I a woman: Black women and feminism*. Boston, MA: South End Press.

——. (1984). *Feminist theory: From margin to center*. Boston, MA: South End Press.

——. (1989). *Talking back: Thinking feminist, thinking black*. Boston, MA: South End Press.

——. (1990). *Yearning: Race, gender, and cultural politics*. Boston, MA: South End Press.

——. (1993). *Sisters of the yam: Black women and self-recovery*. Boston, MA: South End Press.

——. (2004). *We real cool: Black men and masculinity*. New York: Routledge.

Hooton, E.A. (1939). *Crime and the man*. Cambridge, MA: Harvard University Press.

Huey, J., and M. Lynch. (1996). The image of black women in criminology: Historical stereotypes as theoretical foundation. In *Justice with prejudice*, eds. M.J. Lynch and E. Britt Patterson. Albany, NY: Harrow and Heston, 72–88.

Huisman, K.A. (1996). Wife battering in Asian American communities. *Violence against Women*, 2: 260–83.

Joe, K.A., and M. Chesney-Lind. (1995). "Just every mother's angel": An analysis of gender and ethnic variations in youth gang membership. *Gender and Society*, 9: 408–31.

Kellor, F.A. (1901a). The criminal Negro: I. A sociological study. *The Arena*, 25: 59–68.

——. (1901b). The criminal Negro: II. Southern conditions that influence Negro criminality, *The Arena*, 25: 190–7.

——. (1901c). The criminal Negro: III. Some of his characteristics. *The Arena*, 25: 308–16.

——. (1901d). The criminal Negro: IV. Advantages and abuse of southern penal institutions. *The Arena*, 25: 419–28.

——. (1901e). The criminal Negro: V. Physical measurements of females. *The Arena*, 25: 510–20.

——. (1901f). The criminal Negro: VII. Childhood influences. *The Arena*, 25: 304–10.

——. (1901g). The criminal Negro: VIII. Environmental influences. *The Arena*, 25: 521–7.

Kindle, P.A. (2012). Review of *A theory of African American offending: Race, racism, and crime. Journal of Forensic Social Work*, 2: 186–8.

Klein, D. (1973). The etiology of female crime: A review of the literature. *Issues in Criminology*, 8: 3–30.

Laub, J.H., and M.J. McDermott. (1985). An analysis of serious crime by young black women. *Criminology*, 23: 81–98.

Lee, J. (2012). Review of *A theory of African American offending: Race, racism, and crime. Criminal Justice Review*, 37: 408–410.

Lesane-Brown, C. L. (2006). A review of race socialization within black families. *Developmental Review*, 26: 400–26.

Lewis, D.K. (1981). Black women offenders and criminal justice: Some theoretical considerations. In *Comparing female and male offenders*, ed. M.Q. Warren. Beverly Hills, CA: SAGE Publications, 89–105.

Lorde, A. (1984). *Sister outsider: Essay and speeches*. Trumansburg, NY: Crossing Press.

——. (1985). *Sister outsider*. Trumansburg, NY: Crossing Press.

Mann, C.R. (1984a). *Female crime and delinquency*. Tuscaloosa, AL: Alabama University Press.

——. (1984b). Race and sentencing of female felons: A field study. *International Journal of Women's Studies*, 7: 160–72.

——. (1988). Getting even? Women who kill in domestic encounters. *Justice Quarterly*, 5: 33–51.

——. (1991). Black women who kill their loved ones. In *Black family violence: Current research and theory*, ed. R.L. Hampton. Lexington, MA: D.C. Heath, 129–46.

——. (1993). Sister against sister: Female intrasexual homicide. In *Female criminality: The state of the art*, ed. C. Culliver. New York: Garland Publishing, 195–223.

McCann, C.R., and S.K. Kim, eds. (2003). *Feminist theory reader: Local and global perspectives*. New York: Routledge.

Messerschmidt, J.W. (1993). *Masculinities and crime: Critique and reconceptualization of theory*. Lanham, MD: Rowman & Littlefield Publishers.

——. (1997). *Crime as structured action: Gender, race, class, and crime in the making*. Thousand Oaks, CA: SAGE Publications.

——. (2013). *Crime as structured action. Gender, race, class, and crime in the making, 2nd edition*. Lanham, MD: Rowman & Littlefield Publishers.

Meyers, M. (2004). African American women and violence: Gender, race, and class in the news. *Critical Studies in Media Communication*, 21: 95–118.

Miller, E.M. (1986). *Street woman*. Philadelphia: Temple University Press.

Miller, J. (1998). Up it up: Gender and the accomplishment of street robbery. *Criminology*, 36: 37–65.

———. (2008). *Getting played: African American girls, urban inequality, and gendered violence.* New York: New York University Press.

Moyer, I. L. (2001). *Criminological theories: Traditional and nontraditional voices and themes.* Thousand Oaks, CA: SAGE Publications.

Nakayama, T. K. (2006). Framing Asian Americans. In *Images of color, images of crime, 3rd edition*, eds. C. R. Mann, M. S. Zatz, and N. Rodriguez. Los Angeles, CA: Roxbury Publishing Company, 102–10.

Polizzi, D. (2013). Review of *A theory of African American offending: Race, racism, and crime. Journal of Theoretical and Philosophical Criminology*, 5: 96–8.

Pollak, O. (1950). *The criminality of women.* New York: A. S. Barnes & Company.

Portillos, E., N. Jurik, and M. Zatz. (1996). Machismo and Chicano/a gangs: Symbolic resistance or oppression. *Free Inquiry in Creative Sociology*, 24: 175–84.

Potter, H. (2006). An argument for black feminist criminology: Understanding African American women's experiences with intimate partner abuse using an integrated approach. *Feminist Criminology*, 1: 106–24.

———. (2008). *Battle cries: Black women and intimate partner abuse.* New York: New York University Press.

Rice, M. (1990). Challenging orthodoxies in feminist theory: A black feminist critique. In *Feminist perspectives in criminology*, eds. L. Gelsthorpe and A. Morris. Philadelphia: Open University Press, 57–69.

Richie, B. E. (1996). *Compelled to crime: The gender entrapment of battered black women.* New York: Routledge.

Schaffner, L. (2008). Latinas in US juvenile detention: Turning adversity to advantage. *Latino Studies*, 6: 116–36.

Schiller, N. (2000). A short history of black feminist scholars. *The Journal of Blacks in Higher Education*, 29: 119–25.

Simon, R. J. (1975). *Women and crime.* Lexington, MA: Lexington Books.

Simpson, S. S. (1989). Feminist theory, crime, and justice. *Criminology*, 27: 607–31.

———. (1991). Caste, class, and violent crime: Explaining difference in female offending. *Criminology*, 29: 115–35.

Stanko, E. (1985). *Intimate intrusions: Women's experience of male violence.* London: Unwin Hyman.

Staples, R. (1982). *Black masculinity: The black male's role in American society.* San Francisco, CA: The Black Scholar Press.

Stewart, R. (1996). Kemba's nightmare. *Emerge*, May: 28–53.

Sule, D. D. (2005). Correlates of Hispanic female gang membership. *Journal of Gang Research*, 12: 1–23.

Thomas, W. I. (1907). *Sex and society: Studies in the social psychology of sex.* Chicago: University of Chicago Press.

———. (1923). *The unadjusted girl: Cases and standpoint for behavior analysis.* Boston: Little, Brown, and Company.

Unnever, J. D. (2014). A theory of African American offending: A test of core propositions. *Race and Justice: An International Journal*, 4: 98–123.

Unnever, J. D., and S. L. Gabbidon. (2011). *A theory of African American offending: Race, racism, and crime.* New York: Routledge.

———. (2014). Do blacks speak with one voice? Immigrants, public opinions, and perceptions of criminal injustices. *Justice Quarterly*, DOI: 10.1080/07418825.2013.791714.

Valdez, A., and R. Flores. (2005). A situational analysis of dating violence among Mexican American females associated with street gangs. *Sociological Focus*, 38: 95–114.

von Hentig, H. (1942). *The criminality of the colored woman*. University of Colorado *Study Series*, 1: 231–60.

West, C.M., G.K. Kaufman, and J.L. Jasinski. (1998). Sociodemographic predictors and cultural barriers to help-seeking behavior by Latina and Anglo American battered women. *Violence and Victims*, 13: 361–75.

White, A. M., M.J. Strube, and S. Fisher. (1998). A black feminist model of rape myth acceptance: Implications for research and antirape advocacy in black communities. *Psychology of Women Quarterly*, 22: 157–75.

Williams, F.P., and M.D. McShane. (2010). *Criminological theory, 5th edition*. Upper Saddle River, NJ: Pearson/Prentice Hall.

Wolfgang, M.E. (1958). *Patterns in criminal homicide*. Philadelphia, PA: University of Pennsylvania Press.

Wright, J. P., and D. Boisvert. (2009). What biosocial criminology offers criminology. *Criminal Justice and Behavior*, 36: 1228–40.

Young, V.D. (1980). Women, race, and crime. *Criminology*, 18: 26–34.

———. (1986). Gender expectations and their impact on black female offenders and victims. *Justice Quarterly*, 3: 305–27.

Young, V.D., and T. Adams-Fuller. (2006). Women, race/ethnicity and criminal justice processing. In *Rethinking gender, crime, and justice: Feminist readings*, eds. C.M. Renzetti, L. Goodstein, and S. Miller. Los Angeles, CA: Roxbury Publishing, 185–99.

Zara, M.J., and R.H. Adler. (2008). Latina immigrant victims of interpersonal violence in New Jersey: A needs assessment study. *Journal of Aggression, Maltreatment, and Trauma*, 16: 22–39.

10   Conclusion

Bachman, R. (1992). *Death and violence on the reservation: Homicide, family violence, and suicide in American Indian populations*. New York: Auburn House.

Bucerius, S.M., and M. Tonry, eds. (2014). *The Oxford handbook of ethnicity, crime, and immigration*. Oxford: Oxford University Press.

Gabbidon, S.L. (2009). *Race, ethnicity, crime and justice: An international dilemma*. Thousand Oaks, CA: SAGE Publications.

Godfrey, B. S., and G. Dunstall, eds. (2013). *Crime and empire, 1840–1940: Criminal justice in local and global context*. London: Routledge.

Kalunta-Crumpton, A., ed. (2010). *Race, crime and criminal justice: International perspectives*. New York: Palgrave, Macmillan.

Oliver, W. (2006). "The streets": An alternative black male socialization institution. *Journal of Black Studies*, 36: 918–37.

Phillips, C., and C. Webster, eds. (2014). New directions in race, ethnicity and crime. London: Routledge.

Wilson, W.J. (1987). *The truly disadvantaged*. Chicago: University of Chicago Press.

Wright, J. P., and D. Boisvert. (2009). What biosocial criminology offers criminology. *Criminal Justice and Behavior*, 36: 1228–40.

Index

Note: Page numbers in italics indicate figures and tables.